# MINIMUM COMPETENCE
# IN SCIENTIFIC ENGLISH

## *Grenoble Sciences*

Grenoble Sciences poursuit un triple objectif :

- réaliser des ouvrages correspondant à un projet clairement défini, sans contrainte de mode ou de programme,
- garantir les qualités scientifique et pédagogique des ouvrages retenus,
- proposer des ouvrages à un prix accessible au public le plus large possible.

Chaque projet est sélectionné au niveau de Grenoble Sciences avec le concours de referees anonymes. Puis les auteurs travaillent pendant une année (en moyenne) avec les membres d'un comité de lecture interactif, dont les noms apparaissent au début de l'ouvrage. Celui-ci est ensuite publié chez l'éditeur le plus adapté.
(Contact : Tél. : (33)4 76 51 46 95 - E-mail : Grenoble.Sciences@ujf-grenoble.fr)

Deux collections existent chez EDP Sciences :

- la ***Collection Grenoble Sciences***, connue pour son originalité de projets et sa qualité
- ***Grenoble Sciences - Rencontres Scientifiques***, collection présentant des thèmes de recherche d'actualité, traités par des scientifiques de premier plan issus de disciplines différentes.

### *Directeur scientifique de Grenoble Sciences*

Jean BORNAREL, Professeur à l'Université Joseph Fourier, Grenoble 1

### *Comité de lecture pour "Minimum Competence in Scientific English"*

- M. BARRALI, Responsable du département d'anglais à l'IUT 1 de Grenoble
- J. DE LEIRIS, Professeur à l'Université Joseph Fourier, Grenoble 1
- L. DELORME, Maître de conférences à l'Université de Bordeaux 2
- J. HAY, Directrice du Pool de langues de l'Université Joseph Fourier, Grenoble 1
- K. HENDERSON, Professeur d'anglais, EREA, Berck-sur-Mer
- E. JOLIVET, Maître de conférences à l'Université d'Orléans
- N. POTEAUX, Equipe SESAM, Université Louis Pasteur de Strasbourg

Grenoble Sciences reçoit le soutien
du **Ministère de l'enseignement supérieur et de la Recherche**
et de la **Région Rhône-Alpes**.

Réalisation et mise en pages : **Centre technique Grenoble Sciences**
Illustration de couverture : **Alice GIRAUD**

**ISBN 978-2-7598-0808-3**

# MINIMUM COMPETENCE IN SCIENTIFIC ENGLISH

*nouvelle édition - pap-ebook*

**Sue Blattes - Véronique Jans - Jonathan Upjohn**
Pool de langues de l'Université Joseph Fourier de Grenoble

edp sciences
17, avenue du Hoggar
Parc d'Activité de Courtabœuf, BP 112
91944 Les Ulis Cedex A, France

## Minimum Competence in Scientific English (MCSE) est un *pap-ebook*

### Qu'est-ce qu'un *pap-ebook®* ?

Le *pap-ebook* se compose de deux éléments : le livre papier et un site web en accès libre :

- Le livre est l'objet central totalement autonome. Il a bénéficié de toute la démarche d'expertise et, une fois sélectionné, d'une optimisation propres au label de Grenoble Sciences.
- Le site web compagnon peut, suivant les cas, proposer :
  - des prérequis permettant de combler certaines lacunes,
  - des exercices pour s'entraîner,
  - des compléments pour approfondir un thème, trouver des liens sur internet, etc.

Pour accéder à la liste des pap-ebooks de Grenoble Sciences :

*http://grenoble-sciences.ujf-grenoble.fr/pap-ebooks/*

### Le site web en libre accès de *MCSE*

Le site web de ***MCSE*** comprend une part notable d'exercices qui renforcent l'action du livre, notamment par des apports audio. Ce site s'enrichit à chaque réédition du livre ***MCSE*** et constitue une véritable porte d'entrée sur un environnement d'apprentissage en développement permanent. Pour accéder au site web :

*http://grenoble-sciences.ujf-grenoble.fr/pap-ebooks/upjohn*

# AVANT-PROPOS

**MCSE NOUVELLE ÉDITION –** Depuis sa première édition en 1991, *Minimum Competence in Scientific English* a joué un rôle important dans l'enseignement de l'anglais scientifique en France. Plus de 200 000 scientifiques l'ont utilisé et il a semblé opportun de l'améliorer pour mieux répondre à l'attente des nouvelles générations d'étudiants. La structure de base ayant fait ses preuves, nous l'avons gardée comme telle. En revanche, les textes ont été renouvelés et furent affinés les *key points* et le *lexis*, élargie la gamme des activités linguistiques et communicatives et intégrée l'utilisation du *web*.

- **Public visé –** MCSE a été conçu d'abord pour les étudiants des universités scientifiques et technologiques, des IUT et des écoles d'ingénieurs ayant une base d'au moins trois années d'anglais, mais il est également adapté à tous les scientifiques francophones.
- **Contenu linguistique –** L'ouvrage est fondé sur une analyse du discours scientifique, notamment sur un recensement de la fréquence du lexique scientifique, et des fonctions qui sous-tendent le discours scientifique. C'est cette analyse préalable qui a permis d'établir un contenu particulièrement pertinent.
- **Contenu pédagogique –** Pédagogiquement, l'utilisateur se voit doté des armes nécessaires à un apprentissage efficace. D'abord il dispose d'un système d'auto-évaluation combiné avec une check list et peut établir avec clarté ce qu'il doit apprendre. Ensuite l'utilisation répétée des éléments permet d'optimiser l'apprentissage.

MCSE regroupe donc pour l'étudiant un inventaire de ce qu'il doit savoir, avec les outils pour l'apprendre. Il permet un parcours d'apprentissage rapide, efficace et, par conséquent, un parcours qui apporte beaucoup de satisfaction.

**MODE D'EMPLOI –** MCSE peut être utilisé de plusieurs façons : dans le cadre d'un cours traditionnel, en semi-autonomie ou en autonomie. Les quelques suggestions qui suivent sont loin d'être exhaustives.

L'ouvrage est divisé essentiellement en 2 sections : les 12 *units*, suivies d'*annexes* et d'un *lexis*. Chaque ***unit*** correspond à une fonction de base de l'anglais scientifique, *measurement*, *frequency*, *hypothesis*, etc. et comprend :

- ***Entry test* –** Ce test permet de faire d'emblée une évaluation réaliste de son niveau ; trop fréquemment, l'apprentissage est entravé par l'ignorance de l'étudiant quant à ses propres lacunes.
- ***Key points* –** Les *key points* doivent être considérés comme une check list, indiquant tous les éléments qui doivent être sus. Ainsi, et après avoir fait l'*entry test*, l'étudiant est en situation, dès le départ de l'*unit*, de déterminer avec précision ce qu'il doit faire, c'est-à-dire son "contrat d'apprentissage".

***Exercises*** – Ce sont les exercices qui permettent de mettre la langue en pratique, de la manipuler et donc de l'assimiler. Ceux-ci se caractérisent par une répétition et une réutilisation continuelle des fonctions et du vocabulaire, pour qu'en fin de parcours tout étudiant "ne puisse pas ne pas avoir appris".

Notons, dans cette nouvelle édition, les ***starters***, dont le but est d'amorcer un travail d'imagination de l'étudiant et de l'impliquer avant d'aborder le texte. Nouveaux également, les ***talking points***, qui ouvrent la voie vers une interaction orale en petit groupe.

Les ***checkpoints*** constituent une autre innovation conçue pour permettre une révision et un approfondissement de trois domaines cruciaux pour l'apprentissage :

- *In other words* – Savoir reformuler est une compétence essentielle pour l'apprenant qui, par définition, a des difficultés à se faire comprendre. Il est donc de première importance qu'il puisse maîtriser les outils lui permettant de clarifier, de reformuler, et de "dire autrement".
- *Back to basics* – Trop souvent, hélas, les apprenants, même avancés, traînent d'année en année comme des boulets certaines erreurs de débutant, déjà corrigées 100 fois mais sans résultats. Cet exercice donne à l'étudiant la possibilité de faire le point sur son propre savoir et, ensuite, lui donne les outils pour se débarrasser de ses erreurs.
- *The word web* – Un mot n'existe pas seul, mais seulement en relation avec les autres. Cet exercice donne l'occasion de revenir sur les familles lexicales, les homonymes et les synonymes, la formation et la structure et de les approfondir.

Nouveaux aussi sont ***web search*** et ***word search***. Le premier prolonge le travail sur les textes en exploitant les richesses du web, le second, technique originale, amène l'étudiant à utiliser le web comme corpus pour personnaliser son propre apprentissage.

***Exit test*** – Comme dans les éditions précédentes, chaque *unit* se termine par un *exit test* où l'étudiant peut faire un constat objectif de ses progrès et en tirer les conclusions.

Le lecteur trouvera ensuite des ***annexes*** : *OHP* (utilisation du rétroprojecteur), ***answers*** (corrigés des exercices) et ***grammar notes*** (notes grammaticales).

Enfin, le ***lexis*** joue un rôle primordial dans MCSE. A ce stade, et contrairement à ce que tant de personnes pensent, ce n'est pas la structure mais bien le lexique qui est le maillon faible des apprenants. Cette liste de vocabulaire de haute fréquence, organisée en rubriques, est construite à partir d'un pré-acquis du vocabulaire de base de quelques 1 200 mots et des homographes communs à l'anglais et au français. Elle constitue un outil puissant, permettant à un étudiant de "couvrir" 85% des mots de tout texte dans sa spécialité.

MCSE s'adresse à des apprenants volontaristes et motivés qui ont fait le choix de passer au stade d'utilisateur professionnel. Il permet à celui qui s'investit et qui travaille de façon intelligente d'atteindre, après une année ou dix-huit mois, un niveau de langue où il pourra utiliser indifféremment des documents en anglais ou dans sa langue maternelle, où il pourra parler de sa spécialité, sinon dans un anglais parfait, du moins avec clarté et aisance.

Le **site web** comprend des éléments associés à chaque *unit* du livre et des apports plus transversaux.

Ainsi, l'apprenant pourra s'exercer sur les *entry tests* et *exit tests* de chaque *unit* en proposant des mots dans leur contexte scientifique. Il entendra ensuite la phrase qu'il vient de compléter ou, en cas d'erreur, une invitation à donner d'autres réponses.

Dans le même esprit lui sont proposés des *reading texts* qui permettent, tout en travaillant au livre, d'entendre des parties de textes pour chaque *unit*.

Enfin, des exercices plus transversaux sont proposés : applications ***Word coach***, ***Enigma*** et ***Diktator***.

Le livre MCSE est l'entrée incontournable de toute une méthode d'apprentissage. Le **pap-ebook** en accès libre est un des éléments de l'ensemble.

Pour accéder au site web :

*http://grenoble-sciences.ujf-grenoble.fr/pap-ebooks/upjohn*

# ACKNOWLEDGEMENTS

The authors would like to express their gratitude to all those colleagues and students at the Pool de langues – Université Joseph Fourier – Grenoble and elsewhere who have helped in the development of this book. Particular thanks are due to *Elizabeth Anne, Marcel Barrali, André Deblock, Marie-Hélène Fries, Josiane Hay, Karen Henderson, Elisabeth Jolivet,* and *Grace Wilson* whose comments and suggestions have contributed in improving the final text.

Their thanks also to *Michel Terrasse* for permission to adapt the text on vultures (p. 63) and to the following for permission to reproduce photographs: le comité régional du sport universitaire de Lyon et Grenoble (p. 28), *Pascal Dubois* (p. 64), CargoLifter GmbH (p. 39), *Claire Gemonet* (p. 76), le CNRS – laboratoire de Cristallographie (p. 83), Oregon University (p. 109), Dr *Kakuichi Shiomi* (p. 120), Professor *Stephen Salter* (p. 143) and *Isabelle Girault*, Senior Lecturer, Chemistry Department – Université Joseph Fourier – Grenoble (p. 130).

Finally, the authors would like to thank *Julie Ridard, Christiane Guiraudie* and *Thierry Morturier* of Grenoble Sciences for their assistance and patience in designing the layout of the book.

■■■

# TABLE OF CONTENTS

# *Introduction*

Some years ago, Jean Bornarel, professor of Physics at Grenoble University, remarked: "We scientists are fast learners – what we want to know most of all about languages is just what we need to learn". ***Minimum Competence in Scientific English*** and the other books in the series[1], are attempts to provide answers to that question. In writing the book our essential preoccupation has been to take into account what students **do know**, what they **don't know** and what, if they are to function in the real world, they **must know**. We have targeted the essential and all that is of secondary importance has been left to one side. In this way, we believe that learning can become faster, more effective and far more satisfying.

The present volume is a completely revised edition of the successful *Minimum Competence in Scientific English*, first published in 1991. The texts have been renewed and many new features, including communicative, web and group activities have been added.

The book has been written for students working in the fields of science, technology and engineering who have a basic knowledge of general English and wish to make that fundamental change – to move from the status of learner to the status of user. ***Minimum Competence in Scientific English*** has been designed specifically for learners whose ambition it is to master English as a worktool within the next 12 months.

## *MCSE – How does it function?*

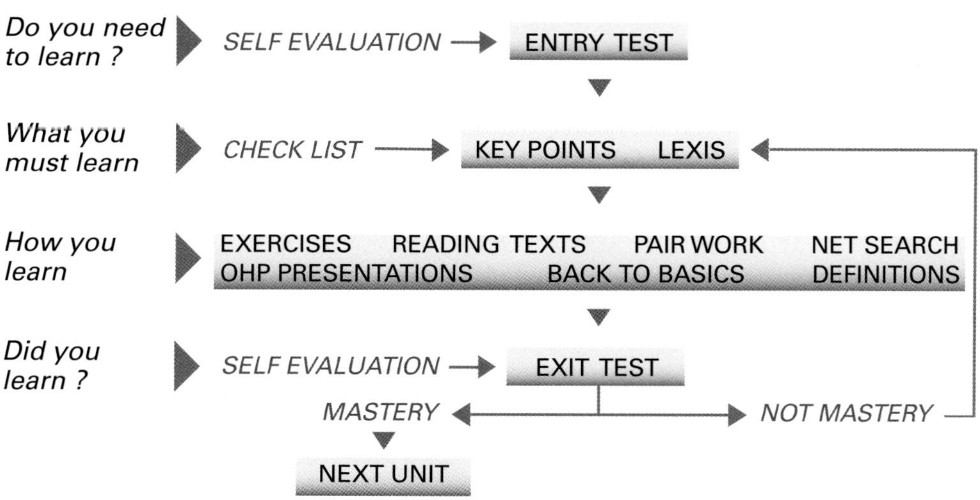


1 *Listening Comprehension for Scientific English* – J. Upjohn. PUG, Grenoble, 1993.
*Speaking Skills in Scientific English* – J. Upjohn, M-H. Fries, D. Amadis. PUG, Grenoble, 1997.

# 1. MEASUREMENT

*In this first unit, we look at some of the different ways of expressing the function of* ***measurement****. Why start with measurement? As Lord Kelvin*[1] *wrote in 1890, "without quantification there is no scientific subject", and it is true to say that the history of scientific progress has run parallel to, and been dependent on, the ever-increasing precision in measurement.*

## Self evaluation – entry test

▮ *Fill in the gaps in the sentences according to the definitions. The first two letters are given.*

*Example:*
*How* ***de*** *........... is the Pacific ocean?* (distance from the surface to the bottom)
→ *How* ***deep*** *is the Pacific ocean?*

1. In 1841, Sir George Everest, a colonial official, recorded the location and the **he** .................... of the most famous mountain in the world. *(altitude)*
2. GIS (geographic information systems) are designed to process massive **am** ...................... of data. *(quantities)*
3. The hearing **ra** ............ of bats is enormous; it goes from 50 to 100,000 cycles. *(from the lowest to the highest limit, extent)*
4. It is said that Galileo dropped objects from the leaning tower of Pisa to prove that the speed of fall is not proportional to **we** ......... . *(a force measured in kg)*
5. Colonial power depended on navigation. In 1714, the British Parliament offered a prize of £20,000 to the first man to develop an **ac** ..................... marine chronometer. *(exact, precise)*
6. A six-year-old, male alligator has a **le** ........... of approximately 190 centimetres. *(longitudinal dimension)*
7. Xavier LePichon, a French seismologist, was able to **wo** ....................... the basic geometry of plate tectonics from seismic evidence. *(calculate – 2 words)*
8. As a meteorite enters the atmosphere, it **sl** .......................... . *(decelerates – 2 words)*
9. The **av** ........................... brain temperature of animals hibernating in the Arctic may drop to 6°C. *(statistically normal, mean)*
10. The notion of square **ro** ...... was invented in the 9$^{th}$ century by Arabian mathematicians. *(a factor of a number that when multiplied by itself gives the number)*

---

1 Lord Kelvin: 1824-1907, British physicist who introduced the absolute scale of temperature.

# *Functions & Grammar*

## KEY POINTS – MEASUREMENT

### *1. Adjectives*

deep ≠ shallow · far ≠ near · fast ≠ slow · heavy ≠ light · high ≠ low · long ≠ short · odd ≠ even · thick ≠ thin · wide / broad ≠ narrow

➤ *All prime numbers are **odd** numbers.*

accurate ≠ inaccurate · average / mean · standard ≠ sub-standard

➤ *The **mean** density of Mercury is similar to that of the Earth.*

### *2. Nouns*

amount · extent · measurement · range · size · span · speed

accuracy · average · level · mean · rate · scale · stage · step

➤ *The **rate** of acceleration is expressed in metres per second per second.*

check · study · survey

area · circumference · cross-section · diameter · radius

➤ *The **cross-section** of the wire is 0.22 mm². (nought point two two square millimetres)*

▌ *Rules for noun formation – suffixes*

*ADJ/VERB + **-th/-t** (+ VOWEL CHANGE)*

dep**th** · heig**ht** · long / leng**th** · weig**ht** · wid**th**

*ADJ + **-ness***

hard**ness** · heavy / heavi**ness** · near**ness** · thick**ness**

*VERB + **-ment***

to develop / develop**ment** · measure**ment** · move**ment**

## 3. Verbs

### *Rules for forming verbs*

*NOUN/ADJ + **Ø***
*(NO CHANGE)*

to narrow ≠ to thin · to range / to span / to extend[G. Notes 1] / to reach · to rate / to check / to monitor · to record / to plot

➤ *The trajectory of the missile was **plotted** on a graph.*

*NOUN/ADJ + **-en***

to deep**en** · to length**en** · to short**en** · to thick**en** · to wid**en**

➤ *The river **widens** when it leaves the canyon.*

*NOUN/ADJ + **adv particle***

to check **up** · to level **off** · to slow **down** ≠ to speed **up** · to step **up** · to work **out**

➤ *The speed of the neutrons is **slowed down** by the beryllium moderator.*

## 4. Structures

Dimensions can be expressed by 4 different structures.

It **is** 56 m | **high** / wide / long / thick

It **is** 56 m | **in height** / in width / in depth / in diameter

**Its** | radius **is** 5 m / length / cross-section / circumference

**It has** | **a** diameter **of** 10 m / a length of / a weight of

### *5. Other measurements*

▮ *Area*

To obtain the area, you **multiply** the length **by** the width.
It measures 10 cm **by** 10 cm. The area is 100 $cm^2$ (a hundred **square** cm).
$\pi r^2$ (**pi r squared**)*G. Notes 2* · $\sqrt{x}$ (the **square root** of x)

▮ *Volume*

The volume is 1,000 $cm^3$ (a thousand **cubic centimetres**).
$x^3$ (x **cubed**) · $\sqrt[3]{y}$ (the **cube root** of y)

▮ *Power*

$x^9$ (x **to the power** nine / x **to the** ninth)
$x^{-9}$ (x to the **power minus** nine / x to the **minus ninth**)

### *6. Approximate measurements*

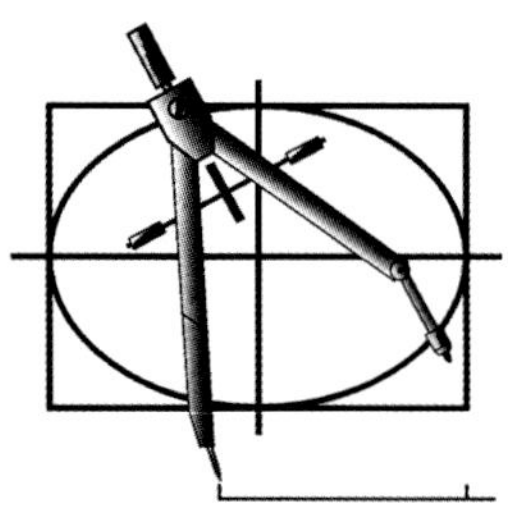

These can be expressed by means of **adverbial modifiers**.

| | |
|---|---|
| It is | **approximately** 5 cm long |
| | about / roughly / more or less |
| | almost / nearly |
| ◀ | a little over / slightly under |

### *7. Questions*

Note the question forms.

It weighs 10 kg → **How heavy** is it? / **How much** does it **weigh**?
**What** does it **weigh**?

It is 5 km away → **How far** (away) is it? / **How many** kilometres **away** is it?
**What** is the **distance**?

## *Examples in context*

### *DEAD DUCKS FROM DOWN UNDER*[2]

*Words mentioned in the Key points are written in **bold**.*

▮ *Replace the words which are in **bold** and <u>underlined</u> by synonyms, antonyms or by an explanation.*

*Dromornis stirtoni*, an extinct flightless bird, lived in Australia **<u>roughly</u>** 8 million years ago. It was probably the heaviest bird in the history of evolution, with a **<u>weight</u>** of **<u>slightly more</u>** than 500 kg although its **<u>wing span</u>** was very small. A considerable

2 Down Under: a name for Australia and New Zealand, the Antipodes.

**amount** of information has been obtained from recent fossil finds in Queensland, enabling scientists to **work out** basic **measurements**. From a morphological point of view, *Dromornis stirtoni* appears to be similar to an emu or an ostrich, however, scientists now believe that it is related to the duck species, as the massive dimensions of the head show. The bird **attained** a **height** of over 3 meters. The large head and formidable beak[3] suggest that the bird was carnivorous. The **cross-section** of fossils of the leg bones reveals that the bird had **short, thick** legs indicating that it could not have run as fast as the ostrich. The **width** of the body was about the same as the **length** of the neck and legs.

*DROMORNIS STIRTONI*

*Estimated dimensions*
*Height: 3 m*
*Weight: > 500 kg*
*Egg length: 26 cm*
*Egg width: 21 cm*

**TALKING POINT** ***Tell your partner to close his book and then ask him these questions.***

- Why couldn't dromornis stirtoni fly?
- Why do we know so much about the bird?
- How do we know it is not the same species as an ostrich?
- What makes it possible for an ostrich to run so fast?

## *Exercises*

### *1.1. Exercise*

*The Normandy bridge was opened on January 20th, 1995. It is one of the largest bridges in the world and holds the record for the height of its two towers and for the length of its central span.*

**starter**

**Bridges have played a key role in cultural development; the oldest known stone bridge being built in Dabylon in about 1000 DC.**

- **What can you say about bridges? With your partner make a list of three facts / questions (WHY – WHEN – WHERE – HOW – CONSEQUENCES…).**

*A. Look at the photograph and guess the dimensions of the bridge by selecting one of the three options offered. Write out your answer in full. Check in the answer section when you have finished.*

1. What would you guess is the total length of the bridge? (900 m - 2.2 km - 3.9 km) → It probably has a total ............... of approximately ........... .
2. How long is the central span? (550 m / 856 m / 1655 m ) → The central span ................ in ............... .

3 Beak: hard, bony mouth of a bird.

3. How wide is the roadway? (10.5 m / 16.6 m / 23.6 m) → The ................ is .................. .
4. What is the approximate height of each tower? (60 m / 130 m / 210 m) → Each tower ...... roughly ............... in .............. .
5. What is the height of the bridge above sea level? (25 m / 52 m / 93 m) → The .................. about .......... .
6. Give a rough estimation of the weight of each concrete tower. (2,000 t / 8,000 t / 20,000 t) → Each tower .................. at least ................ tonnes.

*B. Underline the 11 words listed in the **Key points** which express **measurement**.*

The Normandy bridge is built across the river Seine just below Le Havre, where the river widens before flowing into the sea. It is considered to be one of the most elegant examples of modern bridge construction with its two narrow concrete towers extending high up over the ships as they pass in the river below. It is a "cable-stayed bridge"; that is to say, the weight is supported by 184 thin steel cables which spread out on each side of the towers. The bridge was built to withstand wind speeds of up to 300 km an hour. The amount of lorry traffic using the bridge is rising each year and the average annual rate has now reached 300,000.

## 1.2. Fetal development

***7th week***
*the hand begins to form*

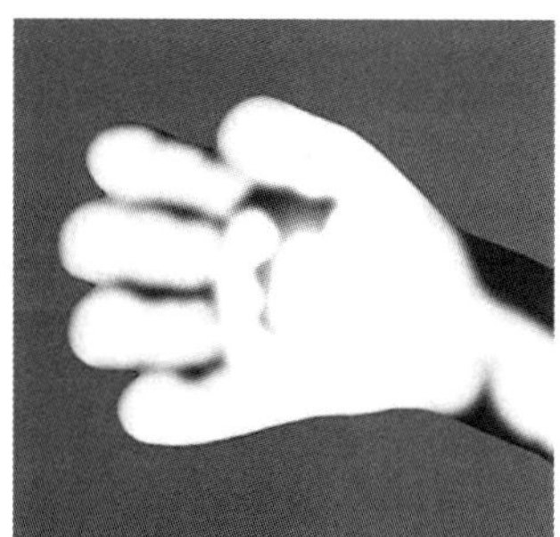

***8th week***
*the fingers separate*

***The fetus – 11th week***
***Mean measurements***

*Length: ≈ 6.9 cm*
*Weight: ≈ 28-35 gm*
*Head circumference: ≈ 8.1 cm*
*Volume amniotic fluid: ≈ 60 ml*

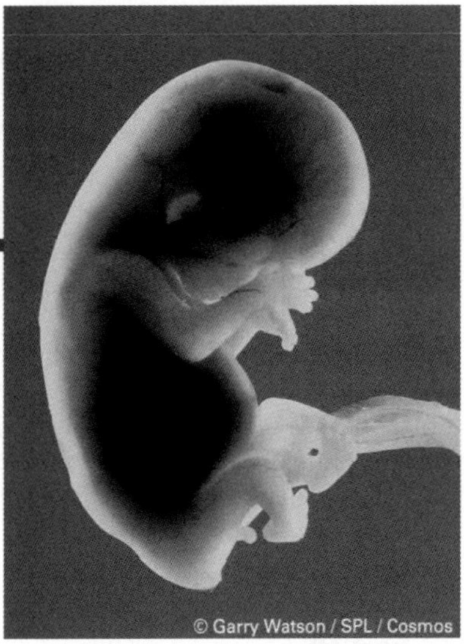


The fetus is now becoming more human. The head is still disproportionately big, but the vital organs – liver, intestines and brain – function and the genitalia are visible. The heartbeat can be heard with a stethoscope and the legs are beginning to move. The fetus floats in the amniotic fluid and nutrients are supplied via the arteries in the umbilical cord. Tiny blood vessels can be seen through the translucent skin.

***A. Describe the pictures using the following words.***

1. average *(+ almost)*

   ..........................................................................................

2. to range *(+ weight)*

   ..........................................................................................

3. circumference *(+ slightly over)*

   ..........................................................................................

4. volume *(+ roughly)*

   ..........................................................................................

5. odd *(+ each hand)*

   ..........................................................................................

6. width *(+ what?)*

   ..........................................................................................

7. narrow *(+ arteries)*

   ..........................................................................................

8. monitor *(+ heartbeat)*

   ..........................................................................................

9. thin *(+ skin)*

   ..........................................................................................

*B. Here are some answers to FAQs (Frequently Asked Questions) concerning the fetus. Write the corresponding questions.*

1. It usually begins to beat in week 5-7. → At what stage ..........................................................................
2. The fetus monitors its own temperature from 30 weeks onwards. → When .............................................................................
3. No they don't. The fetus of the male weighs more than that of the female. → Do ...............................................................................
4. This happens at about 30 weeks (it can be checked by moving a light across the skin of the mother's abdomen. The fetus moves its head towards the light). → In which week ......................................................................

*C. Make sentences using the following words.*

1. **harden** / bones / begin / 13$^{th}$ week ..........................................................................................................................
2. **lengthen** / femur / 4$^{th}$ week / considerably ..........................................................................................................................
3. **thicken** / the wall / uterus / fertilisation ..........................................................................................................................

## *1.3. The Tambora eruption and the battle of Waterloo*

*Is there any link between the climate and world history? According to geologist, Kenneth Spink, the destiny of Europe may well have been changed by a geological phenomenon; the eruption of Mount Tambora in 1815.*

**starter**

**• With your partner, find examples of ways that the climate has affected history.**

- *Fill in the missing words. The first two letters and a definition have been given.*

The most powerful volcanic eruption in **re** .................. *(officially registered)* history occurred on Sumbawa Island in southern Indonesia, in April, 1815, with the cataclysmic eruption of Mount Tambora.

As a result of the eruption, the peak of the mountain completely disappeared, reducing the **he** ............... *(altitude, vertical measurement)* from about 4,300 m to 2,851 m and leaving a crater 1,000 m in **de** ................ *(measurement downwards)* with a **cr** .............. .................. *(transversal measurement)* of 7 km. It has been estimated that 50 **cu** ............. *(measurement of volume)* km of magma and sulphur dioxide were injected into the stratosphere, while a **th** ....................... *(opposite of thin)* layer of volcanic ash, extending over a **ra** ............ *(half the diameter)* of 1,000 km, was deposited on the surrounding islands.

It is difficult to evaluate the **sc** ............... *(extent, relative size)* of the damage with **ac** ................ *(precision, reliability)*. Estimations for deaths caused directly by the eruption **ra** ............ *(vary, extend)* from 10,000-15,000. However, a far larger number of people died from various secondary effects. The heated lava flowing into the sea caused giant tsunamis, more than 30 m high and there was widespread famine due to agricultural losses and harvest failure. It is believed that the total number of deaths may have **at** .................... *(reached)* **al** ................... *(nearly)* 150,000.

*Caldera – St Helens*

It was not only the southern hemisphere that was affected. Aerosols of dust and sulphur dioxide injected into the stratosphere have a relatively long life as they are situated above rain clouds and so are not washed back to Earth by precipitation. The aerosol scatters and reduces incoming solar radiation which can lead to significant atmospheric cooling. In 1816, the weather patterns were chaotic; it was called "the year without a summer". The temperature in Europe and North America dropped 3°C below the annual **me** ............ *(average)*. In July, snow fell, the crops froze in the fields and in Switzerland, France and the United Kingdom food riots[4] were reported.

Recently, Kenneth Spink, a geologist, has suggested that the Tambora eruption may have had political consequences that perhaps changed the course of history. He points out that in the summer of 1815, the weather conditions were already beginning to deteriorate. There was much talk at the time of the extraordinarily vivid red sunsets and the enormous **am** ................ *(quantity, total)* of rain that fell. This was particularly true in the **ar** ....................... *(zone, region)* around the Charleroi-Brussels road in Belgium. As Napoleon prepared for the battle of Waterloo, he found that the wet conditions and soft ground **sl** ............................. *(delayed, held back)* his army since the number of feasible routes for his **he** ............. *(which weighs a lot)* equipment was restricted. This prevented him using his artillery till late in the day. This lack of manoeuvrability could well have been a crucial factor in deciding the outcome of the battle of Waterloo.

**TALKING POINT**

***Explain to your partner:***

- Why there was a famine in Europe.
- Why dust aerosols have a long life.
- What exactly Napoleon's problems were.

4 Riot: public disorder, violent political protest.

### *1.4. Checkpoints*

IN OTHER WORDS

**Simple definitions:** the simplest way of defining a word is by using the verb **"to be"**.

*Example:* a woman
*"A woman **is** an adult, female human being."*

- *The following words are used in Exercise 1.3. Define them:*
  *magma ▪ island ▪ famine ▪ stratosphere*
- *Compare with the examples in the answers.*

BACK TO BASICS

**Asking questions**: are you sure you **never** make a mistake?

- *Write a question about the words in **bold**.*

1. It became extinct about **8 million years ago**.
2. An emu weighs slightly more than **50 kg**.
3. Specialists examined **the bones**.
4. **An ostrich** runs very fast.

- *Check your answers.*
- *If you have made mistakes, how do you intend to deal with the problem?* *G. Notes 3*

THE WORD WEB – SUFFIXES

- *As we have seen in the Key points, suffixes can be used to transform adjectives into nouns and verbs. Complete the columns using the suffixes: -ment ▪ -th ▪ -ness ▪ -en ▪ Ø.*

| ***Adjectives*** | ***Nouns*** | ***Verbs*** |
|---|---|---|
| 1. The road is not **wide** enough. | The main problem is the ................ of the road. | Why don't they ................ the road? |
| 2. We need better **measuring** techniques. | All the .......................... were wrong. | We require techniques to ................ more accurately. |
| 3. A lack of vitamins can have wide-**ranging** effects. | The ............... of potential diseases is considerable. | Lack of vitamins causes illnesses which ................ from goitre to anaemia. |

| ***Adjectives*** | ***Nouns*** | ***Verbs*** |
|---|---|---|
| 4. Cotton is a textile with **short** fibres. | It is cheap because of the .................... of the fibres. | Genetically modified cotton can ............... the growing season. |
| 5. There is a **weak** attractive force between the molecules. | Because of the ............... of attraction, the molecules can be separated. | Raising the temperature .................. the molecular attraction. |
| 6. The deluxe model is well-**equipped**. | The car has got first class ............................... . | It has been ................... with the latest gadgets. |
| 7. When the eye becomes **red**, it is a symptom of bacterial infection. | ................ of the eye is a symptom of conjunctivitis. | The eye .................... as the bacteria spread. |
| 8. How ................... is a horse? | The ................. of a horse can attain roughly 1,000 kg. | A horse can **weigh** almost 1,000 kg. |

### *1.5. Web search*

- Search the web for an image illustrating a famous or unusual bridge. Make a 3 minute presentation (with dimensions) on the overhead projector.
- Find a site dealing with pregnancy and fetal development and make a report on the fetus in week 30. You could try the following for a simple description:

  ➤ http://www.babycentre.co.uk**/refcap/785.html** *G. Notes 31*

  or this site for a more complex discussion of fetal perception and fetal dreaming:

  ➤ http://www.birthpsychology.com**/lifebefore/fetalsense.html** *G. Notes 31*

### *Word search*

- Choose 5 important words from the *Key points*. Search the web for examples in context. Prepare a 5 sentence test (cf. *Entry test*) for your partner *G. Notes 32*.

## *Self evaluation – exit test*

- *Complete the sentences by filling in the blanks with an appropriate word.*

1. Between 2005 and 2025, the average world death rate is expected to decline only **sl** .................. . *(a little, by a small amount)*
2. The biosphere refers to the **th** ........... layer surrounding the Earth where living organisms are found. *(small transversal dimension, ≠ thick)*
3. The original estimation of the cost of building the Three Gorges Dam in China was extremely **in** ........................ . *(imprecise)*

4. A chain reaction is a series of reactions in which the result of each **st** .................. causes the next. *(step, part of the process)*
5. If you add two odd numbers together, you get an **ev** .......... number. *(the opposite of odd)*
6. The Arctic Ocean is joined to the Pacific Ocean by the Bering Strait, a narrow and **sh** ..................... channel with a depth of no more than 55 m. *(≠ deep)*
7. Satellite photographs provide valuable information about the **ex** ............... of desertification. *(degree)*
8. All over the world, research centres are closely **mo** ........................ pollution levels. *(following the evolution)*
9. In Greenland and Iceland there are a variety of small-**sc** ........... manufacturing industries. *(size, dimension)*
10. Bacteria can acquire resistance to antibiotics by mutations which may **st** ........................ their resistance. *(make stronger)*

# 2. FREQUENCY

***Frequency** is the expression of repetition. It refers to events that occur more often than once and less often than always. Frequency is, of course, related to measurement and consequently you will meet certain expressions already seen in Unit 1 for a second time. This function can be expressed by:*

- *lexical items (particularly adverbs),*
- *grammatical structures (particularly word formation),*
- *certain fixed adverbial phrases.*

## Self evaluation – entry test

▮ *Fill in the blanks using appropriate expressions. The first two letters of the answer are printed.*
*Example:*
*The batteries must be recharged* ***tw*** ...................... *a month.* (two times)
→ *The batteries must be recharged* ***twice*** *a month.*

1. Under stress, the heart **be** ...................... faster. *(pulsates)*
2. Over the past 100,000 years, the polar ice sheets have advanced or retreated depending on periodic **sw** .................. in the climate. *(variations, oscillations)*
3. The famous 19th century millionaire, Carnegie, emigrated to the US from Scotland and began work in a factory for $1.20 **pe** .................. week. *(each)*
4. There will be a **re** ..................... of epidemics as soon as natural immunisation dies out. *(they will happen again, repeated incidence)*
5. The Ebola virus produces a mortality **ra** ............. which can be as high as 88% in human beings. *(a measure of frequency)*
6. Over the past 300 years, the average height of Europeans has increased **st** ....................... . *(regularly)*
7. The world population is growing fast. A new child is born **ev** ........................ 60 seconds. *(each minute)*
8. The **se** .............. of earthquakes that struck Missouri in 1811 were among the most powerful ever experienced in the United States. *(succession, repeated incidents)*
9. It is estimated that the **ho** ..................... flow of water of the Amazon river is between 12,000 and 44,000 million litres. *(every 60 minutes)*
10. The strength of a steel alloy depends on the **ra** ................ of iron to carbon. *(mathematical relationship of proportion)*

# Functions & Grammar

## KEY POINTS – FREQUENCY

### 1. Adverbs

always ← constantly, steadily, non-stop — often, frequently, usually — sometimes, occasionally, periodically, from time to time, now and then — rarely, seldom, hardly ever → never

➤ *Politicians **seldom** admit their mistakes.*
➤ ***From time to time**, there are violent cyclones in the Gulf of Mexico.*

### 2. Adjectives

- regular · steady · even · constant · non-stop
- irregular · random · unpredictable
- periodic · intermittent · recurrent · repeated · cyclic
- oscillating · alternating · fluctuating

➤ *There were **recurrent** interruptions throughout the whole meeting.*
➤ *There is a relatively **even** distribution of the population in Holland.*

### 3. Nouns

- an oscillation · wave · wave-length · pulse · beat
- a group · set · cluster · range · array · pattern

➤ *A **series** of remarkable events occurred.*
➤ *The Galápagos consist of a **cluster** of islands in the Pacific.*

### 4. Verbs

- to recur · repeat · reduplicate · echo
- to oscillate · fluctuate · vibrate · alternate · beat · swing

➤ *In politics, public opinion periodically **swings** from left to right.*
➤ *If the symptoms **recur**, you should consult a doctor at once.*

### 5. Word formation

NOUN (TIME UNIT) + ***-ly***

hour**ly** · dai**ly**
week**ly** · year**ly**

➤ *A **weekly** newspaper.*

***re-*** + VERB

to **re**new · **re**build
**re**place · **re**arrange
**re**organise · **re**produce

➤ *They **rearranged** the furniture in the office.*

### 6. Fixed expressions are also used to indicate:

- *Recurrence*

| | | | | |
|---|---|---|---|---|
| **every** | month<br>two weeks / three weeks<br>other / second / third day | once<br>twice<br>three times | **a / per** | minute<br>day<br>week |

> ➤ *They are producing cars at a rate of 100* ***a / per day****.*
> ➤ *He goes to the hospital for a check-up* ***every other month****.*

- *Ratio*

> ➤ ***Two out of three*** *road accidents are caused by alcohol.*
> ➤ *In Denmark,* **three in ten** *people speak two foreign languages.*
> ➤ *The normal ratio of girls to boys is* ***100:106****.* (a hundred **to a** hundred and six)

## Examples in context

### COMPETITION RUNNING: 800 METRES

- *Replace the* *<u>underlined</u>* *words by synonyms, antonyms or by explanation.*
- *Find out what AT running is.*

**starter**

**• Before reading the text, answer the following questions.**

**1. What are aerobic exercises? • 2. What is lactate acid – when is it produced? • 3. Is it advisable for athletes to train without running shoes?**

**PRE-SEASON TRAINING SCHEDULE**

*The following schedule was designed by Australian trainers to prepare athletes for the 1st week of the final month before the season begins.*

| | ***Aerobic running*** | | | | ***Gym*** |
|---|---|---|---|---|---|
| ***Day 1*** | 30 min | 2 × 100 m<br>3 × 400 m<br>2 × 200 m | Time 11.0 s<br>Time 54.0<br>Time 25.0 | Rest 5 min<br>Rest 6 min<br>Rest 5 min | |
| ***Day 2*** | 45 min | | | | 45 min |
| ***Day 3*** | 30 min | 1 × 3,000 m at AT pace<br>6 × 60 m | <br>Time 8.0 | <br>Rest 3 min | |
| ***Day 4*** | 45 min | 10 × 200 m | Time 25.0 | Rest 3 min | 45 min |
| ***Day 5*** | 30 min | Hill sessions<br>2 × 10 × 100 m | <br>Time 18.0 | <br>Rest 2 min | |
| ***Day 6*** | 45 min | 3 × 3 × 400 m | | Rest 5 min | 45 min |

### *Notes*

- The importance of aerobic running is crucial to 800 m training. Aerobic running involves continued, **non-stop** activity at a steady and relatively slow speed. The necessary oxygen is provided by the respiratory and cardiovascular system and virtually no lactate acid should build up in the muscles. The heart rate should be approximately 60-75% of maximum, seldom exceeding 130-145 **beats** per minute. As aerobic capacity improves, running speeds will be gradually increased. Training should be carried out **daily**.

© CRSU / Lyon et Grenoble

- To avoid monotony, the pattern of track training must be varied. A set of runs over different distances, followed by short recuperation periods, enables the body to **rebuild** its forces.
- Aerobic threshold training (AT) should be carried out no more than **once a week** at the beginning of the period, and **twice a week** when the season begins.
- Hill sessions are exercises designed to develop power. They consist of short, low speed, up-hill runs on slopes with gradients of no more than 1 in 6.
- Work in the gymnasium is scheduled every second day. Exercises will range from weight-lifting to exercises designed to improve body posture, arm swing and to strengthen muscles in the back and abdomen. Relaxation of foot muscles can be obtained by walking barefoot in sand or on grass.

# *Exercises*

## *2.1. Exercise*

*ADVERBS – Answer the questions and give a reason why.*

*Example: **Periodically**, I go to see the doctor – in order to have a check up.*

1. What is **steadily** decreasing? ..........................................................

   ..........................................................

2. Give an example of an event that happens **from time to time**. ..........................................................

   ..........................................................

3. In what sort of situation do people work **non-stop**? ..........................................................

   ..........................................................

4. What sort of accident **seldom** occurs? ..........................................................

   ..........................................................

5. Where do you **hardly ever** go? ..........................................................

   ..........................................................

## *ADJECTIVES – Supply the missing words.*

6. Gases consist of molecules that are in fast .................. motion.
7. Glaciers are formed by a ......................... process of sublimation and recrystalisation.
8. The .................... climate during the Pleistocene period was responsible for the extinction of many species.
9. The "Spirit of St Louis" made the first .................. transatlantic flight in 1927.
10. Pulsars emit short ............................ bursts of radiation about once per second.

a. recurrent
b. fluctuating
c. periodic
d. random
e. non-stop

## *NOUNS*

11. The depth of the sea can be measured by echo-sounding techniques consisting of acoustic .................. .
12. Coconuts grow on trees in .................... of 10 or 20.
13. Its high strength-to-weight ............... makes aluminium useful in the construction of aircraft.
14. The fermented liquid which contains between 7 and 12% ethanol is concentrated to 95% by a ...................... of distillations.
15. Antibiotics came into use in the 1950s and have totally changed the ........................ of disease and death.

f. pattern
g. series
h. clusters
i. pulses
j. ratio

## *VERBS*

16. The electric current from standard generators .............................. in direction.
17. The radio beam ..................... more strongly in this part of the moon which suggests that there may be underground ice.
18. The speed at which the pendulum ..................... depends on its length.
19. At this stage, the organism ........................ itself and combines several genes producing immunoglobulins.
20. Yellow fever is a disease that never ................. ; one attack provides immunity for life.

k. echoes
l. swings
m. recurs
n. reorganises
o. alternates

## *2.2. Bats versus butterflies*

*The "arms race" does not apply just to human beings. According to Darwin, evolution is a non-stop struggle between the species, with survival depending on genetic improvement. The text gives one illustration of this process.*

**starter**

- **Before reading the text ask your partner 4 questions about bats. Use the words: WHEN ▪ WHY ▪ HOW ▪ WHAT ...**
- **Find 3 ecological advantages for bats for being nocturnal.**

▮ *Insert the following words in the gaps:*

*RATE ▪ ECHOES ▪ PERIODICALLY ▪ WAVES ▪ RANGE ▪ PER ▪ SERIES (1-7)*

*RANDOM ▪ FREQUENCIES ▪ USUALLY ▪ WAVELENGTH ▪ DAILY ▪ PROPORTION ▪ PULSES ▪ PATTERN (8-15)*

It is well known that bats use a sonar system to navigate, that is to say, that they emit sound *(1)* .................... which are reflected back as ........................ . It is this that enables them to locate objects and food. These waves are emitted ......................... and are in the 20-50 kilohertz .................... . As the bat gets nearer to its target, the .................. increases, finally reaching several hundred emissions .............. second.

The ability to navigate acoustically has several advantages for bats. It means that they can fly by night when the temperature is lower which reduces the danger of dehydration. This is critical for bats because of their enormous skin area. It also means that they are free from attack from predators and above all, it means that there is less competition for food.

However, faced with such a predator some lepidoptera have undergone a ................... of genetic mutations, developing more sensitive hearing organs which enable them to detect the acoustic *(8)* ............................ used by bats. They can consequently take evasive action and survive.

But nature, as Darwin pointed out, is not static and the race between the predators and their victims does not stop there. Jens Rydell of the University of Aberdeen and Raphael Arlettaz of the University of Lausanne have shown that a certain European bat, "Tadarida teniotis" searches for its prey using much lower ...................... than those ........................... used by other bats. They are so low (between 11 and 12 kHz) that insects are incapable of detecting them. This development in echolocation has, however, an evolutionary cost. The 12 kHz frequency corresponds to a .......................... of 3 cm; consequently, objects which are smaller than the wavelength are not detected.

Rydell and Arlettaz concluded that the feeding ......................... of "Tadarida teniotis" would therefore be different from that of other bats and their diet would not include insects with a wing span smaller than 3 cm, except for ...................... catches, as these would be too small to detect.

Rydell and Arlettaz carried out an experimental study to check this hypothesis. Over a period of 3 weeks, they made a .................... examination of samples of bat droppings[1] found in caves in Sisteron in south-eastern France. The findings confirmed the hypothesis. Rydell and Arlettaz found the ......................... of large insects was significantly higher, ranging from 68.3 to 86.8% of the total diet.

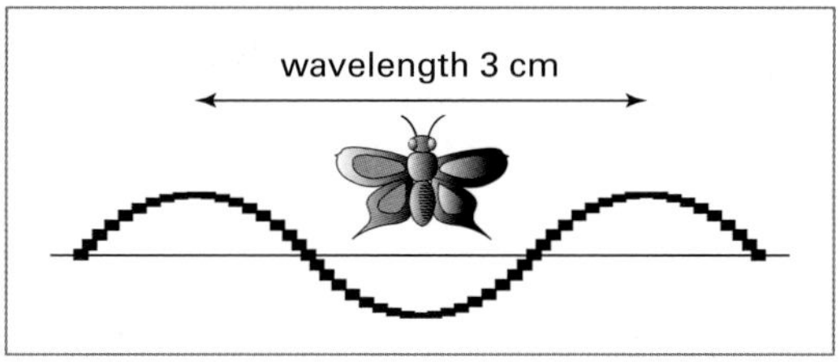


TALKING POINT

- Explain in detail to your partner exactly why "Tadarida teniotis" rarely eats small insects.
- What is the difference between Darwinism and Lamarckism?
- Give an example of Darwinian selection.

### 2.3. A space gymnasium

*A major issue facing space medicine is the potentially harmful effects of residence in a microgravity environment. Future long-term space missions depend on finding solutions to these problems.*

▌ *Supply the missing words.*

**starter**

- **Do you think these statements are true or false?**

**1. Astronauts can spend up to two and a half hours a day on exercises. - T/F.**
**2. There have been "rebellions" during missions when astronauts have refused to obey ground control. - T/F.**
**3. Approximately 50% of cosmonauts can walk unaided when they arrive back on Earth. - T/F.**
**4. Physical exercises are intensified just before returning to Earth. - T/F.**

Past experience has shown that prolonged conditions of weightlessness during space missions can lead to **re** ......................... *(repeated)* problems of cardio-vascular and muscle atrophy, to bone calcium loss, to sleep disturbance, to fluid redistribution and to psychological asthenia, stress and depression. Psychological disorders, though **se** ............... *(rarely)* serious, can in fact be crucial and, in one case (Skylab 4), led to a 24-hour "rebellion" when the crew refused to co-operate with ground control.

In so far as muscular atrophy is concerned, a **se** .................... *(succession, set)* of remedial exercises to minimise physical de-conditioning was introduced from the start (Gemini 1965). Little by little however, it became plain that they were

1 Droppings: excreta.

insufficient or applied too **ra** .................... *(without method)* as they failed to maintain pre-flight musculoskeletal mass. Approximately **one** .............. ten *(1 : 10)* cosmonauts was unable to walk unaided on re-entry.

Valeri Polyakov spent more than 1 year in space on the MIR mission which has provided the largest amount of data concerning extended space flight. The remedial exercises used during this mission were divided into 3 phases. The first phase lasted only 5 days and was designed to allow the astronauts to adapt to the space environment. Then, the exercises **st** ................. *(at a constant rate)* increased in length and load until they reached 2 hr 30 minutes per day. Finally, there was a slight reduction during the 2 month pre-entry phase.

*Shanon Lucid walking on the treadmill in Mir Space Station – 1996*

***TRAINING SCHEDULE***

- *Phase 1*
  Voluntary isometric exercises involving neck, back and leg muscles.
- *Phase 2*
  **Al** ..................................... *(one after the other)* bicycle ergometer and treadmill exercises **tw** ......... *(2 times)* a day, the length of the exercises **gr** ..................... *(little by little)* increasing to 2 × 1 hour a day.
- *Phase 3*
  Additional walking exercises using bungee[2] cords for upper body musculation for 30 minutes per day.

The International Space Station programme involves **no** ...................... *(continual)* residence in space. Consequently, it will be necessary to reorganise protocols in a more systematic way. This will be facilitated by the more sophisticated instrumentation that will be available, allowing **pe** .................. *(from time to time)* check-ups to monitor the heart **be** ............. *(pulsation)*, **fl** ............................ *(changes)* in cardiac rhythm and weekly verification of osteoporosis by ultra-sound probes.

**TALKING POINT**

- Although you have probably never met the word before try and explain to your partner what "treadmill" means (see photo).
- With your partner, exchange questions on the text using: WHO? – WHY? – WHEN? – WHERE?

2 Bungee: elastic cords.

## 2.4. Checkpoints

IN OTHER WORDS

**Definitions – relative clauses: "which / that"**

*Make a definition using the pattern:*
"An X is a Y **which** does Z."

*Example: "A bat is a mammal which flies by night."*

▮ *Define these words used in Exercise 2.2:*

*predator ▪ sonar system ▪ skin ▪ food*

BACK TO BASICS

**"Actually"**: do you use this word correctly?

▮ *Is the following sentence correct or not?*

"Actually, the number of illiterate people in the world is increasing steadily."

▮ *Check in the answer section.*

THE WORD WEB – MULTI-WORD VERBS

*The meaning of many verbs depends on the preposition or adverb that follows. These are called multi-word (or phrasal) verbs.*

▮ *Match the meaning of the verb with the definition and then write in the correct particle for each verb: IN ▪ OF ▪ UP ▪ OUT ▪ FOR ▪ ON.*

1. When visibility is reduced, airports **rely** ........ radar control.
2. In 1830, Babbage designed a machine to **carry** ....... complex arithmetical calculations.
3. A protein may **consist** ....... several polypeptide chains held together by weak molecular bonds.
4. In 1937, four Soviet scientists **set** ....... temporary scientific stations on drifting icebergs in the Arctic.
5. Chemists can **work** ....... the number of carbon atoms from the weight of the object.
6. Testosterone is **involved** ....... the development of secondary sex characteristics such as the growth of body hair, and changes in the larynx.
7. It is the ability to use the Sun and the stars to navigate which **accounts** ....... the migration of birds.
8. The level of pH **depends** ......... the strength of the acid.

a. to do / to perform
b. to be made of / formed from
c. to be determined by
d. to calculate / find the solution
e. to create / establish
f. to use because you have confidence
g. to be linked / a necessary part of
h. to provide an explanation

### 2.5. Web search

- Find out more about space travel. Consult the FAQs at the NASA Life science site:
  ➤ http://weboflife.ksc.nasa.gov**/faq.htm/**

- Who was Babbage? (see *The word web*, question n°2)
  Use the search string:
  < Charles Babbage analytical machine >

#### Word search

- If you are not sure of how to use "actually" (see *Back to basics*), make a Web search and find 6 examples in context. Which of the following expressions matches your examples best?

  IN PRACTICE ▪ REALLY ▪ IT IS SURPRISING, BUT TRUE

## Self evaluation – exit test

- *Fill in the gaps according to the definitions given in brackets.*

1. Six days after fertilisation, the embryo consists of a **cl** .......................... of 100-300 cells. *(agglomeration, concentrated group)*
2. Because of the high altitude, climatic conditions in Afghanistan exhibit great **da** .................... and seasonal variations. *(over a period of 24 hours)*
3. The skeleton of reptiles fits the general bone **pa** .................... of the other vertebrates. *(schema, model)*
4. Mid-ocean earthquakes are fairly frequent, but **se** .................... have any harmful effect. *(not often, rarely)*
5. The hepatitis B virus is present throughout the world and the cause of **re** .................... epidemics. *(repeated, again and again)*
6. There was an **ar** ........................ of solar panels on the roof of the building. *(a series, display)*
7. A major health problem is that medical facilities are not **ev** .................... distributed across the country. *(regularly, equally)*
8. The figures for those employed in agriculture **ra** .................... from 64% in Africa to less than 4% in Canada. *(extend, vary)*
9. Evolutionary artificial intelligence copies biology. Its programs make **ra** ...................... changes to its own rules and select the best results. *(unpredictable)*
10. It **ha** ......................... ever rains in the Gibson desert in Australia. *(rarely)*

# 3. COMPARISON

***Comparison** is one of the ways of relating ideas and objects to each other. The comparison can either be one of **difference** or one of **similarity**. Of course, comparison is frequently expressed by means of grammatical forms such as the comparative and the superlative. However, there is also a large store of lexical items which express similar meanings. For example:*

- *"**to accelerate**" means "to go faster",*
- *"the two samples are **similar**" means that they have been compared.*

## Self evaluation – entry test

▮ *Fill in the blanks, using comparatives, superlatives or other lexical forms.*
*Example:*
*Before building the prototype,* **fu** ......... *research will be necessary.* (more)
→ *Before building the prototype,* **further** *research will be necessary.*

1. In the early 1970s, **bo** ........ the American and Russian space agencies began exploring the possibility of long-term habitation in space. *(the two of them)*
2. The upper salinity limit for irrigation is **le** ........ than 15% of the salt content of seawater. *(≠ more)*
3. Fever has a useful medical function; it not only increases the metabolic rate, but the **ho** ............ environment facilitates the destruction of pathogens. *(higher temperature)*
4. **Un** ............... true organisms, viruses are unable to synthesise proteins because they lack ribosome. *(as opposed to)*
5. Many of the drugs prescribed for human therapy are the **sa** ...................... those used for farm animals. *(identical – 2 words)*
6. Chemicals can be added to vary the properties of the glass. For example, the addition of lead oxide **en** ................. the refractive index. *(makes better)*
7. Fleming noticed that a penicillin solution prevented the **sp** ................. of bacteria. *(growth, proliferation)*
8. The smallest blood cells (averaging 2-4 micrometers in diameter) grow **ha** ......-.......... filaments from their membranes. *(similar to hair)*
9. **Im** ................. production techniques have enabled industrialists to reduce the risk of fire. *(better)*
10. Wegener was able to demonstrate the movement of tectonic plates by **ma** ................ the shapes of the five continents. *(comparing, fitting together)*

# Functions & Grammar

## KEY POINTS – COMPARISON

### 1. Irregular forms

- good / better / the best ≠ bad / worse / the worst
- many / more / the most ≠ few / fewer / the fewest
- much / more / the most ≠ little / less / the least
- far / farther / the farthest · far / further / the furthest

**Note**

– **Farther** is used to indicate greater distance.
– **Further** often means "supplementary, additional".

➢ *I can go no* ***farther****.*
➢ ***Further*** *details can be obtained at the information office.*

### 2. Difference

**Comparative (superiority)**

*TO BECOME / MAKE SOMETHING (+) BIG*

to increase · grow · expand · lengthen · widen · enlarge · extend · spread

*(+) HIGH*

to raise · lift · heighten

*(+) GOOD*

to improve · boost · enhance

➢ *Blood transfusion is used by athletes to* ***enhance*** *performance.*

**Comparative (inferiority)**

*TO BECOME / MAKE SOMETHING (–) BIG*

to decrease · reduce · lessen · shorten · lower

*(–) GOOD*

to worsen · weaken · deteriorate

➢ *Little by little the patient's condition* ***worsened****.*

### *Superlative meaning*

*(++) IMPORTANT*
the chief · main · leading · foremost

*(++) HIGH*
the top · peak · tip

➤ *The **foremost** concern of the government is unemployment.*

## ***3. Similar or equal things can be contrasted***

*SIMILARITY / DISSIMILARITY*
it is like / unlike · similar to · the same as · equal to · in comparison · by contrast

*COMPATIBILITY*
to match · fit · suit · correspond

*DUALITY*
both · either / or · neither / nor

➤ *Before transfusion the blood groups must be **matched**.*

## ***4. As + as***

| | | | | | |
|---|---|---|---|---|---|
| twice<br>3 times<br>half<br>nearly<br>almost | + | **AS** | + | large<br>fast<br>expensive<br>much/many<br>likely | + **AS** |

➤ *Meteorite craters are roughly **20 times as large as** the objects that caused them.*
➤ *Electrons can travel **almost as fast as** light.*

## ***5. Other comparative patterns***

➤ *The situation is getting **worse and worse**. (COMP + AND + COMP)*
➤ ***The richer** people become, **the less happy** they are.*
*(COMP + S + V) + (COMP + S + V)*

### *6. Word formation*

*Adjectives of comparison expressing similarity.*

- *NOUN + like* ➤ *An* ***earth-like*** *atmosphere* (similar to the Earth)
- *NOUN + shaped* ➤ *A* ***bell-shaped*** *curve* (with the shape of)

### *7. Prefixes*

*Comparison can also be expressed by prefixes.*

▮ *Over (more than required)*

to **overload** a circuit · to **overestimate** the results · to **overheat** an engine · to **overeat**

▮ *Under (less than required)*

the meat is **undercooked** · an **underdeveloped** country · **underpaid** workers · an **understaffed** research project

▮ *Out (better or greater than)*

to **outdo** the competitors · women **outnumber** men · the advantages **outweigh** the disadvantages

## *Examples in context*

### *THE CL 160 – BACK TO THE FUTURE*

*Is it possible for old, outdated technologies to find a place in the modern world? This report seems to suggest that they can.*

**starter**

**1. When and where did the Hindenburg Zeppelin crash? • 2. Where was it coming from? • 3. Why did it crash? • 4. What did the Zeppelins carry?**

▮ *Replace the underlined words by antonyms.*

- CARGOLIFTER NETWORK GMBH: This Berlin-based company plans to build a new generation of airships, the CL 160, for heavy transport. One survey suggests that there is a potential world market for **at least** 200 airships. *CargoLifter* believes that this is a considerable underestimation.
- HELIUM: The new generation of airships will be helium-filled. Although helium is heavier than hydrogen and has 7% **less** lifting power, it is not flammable which considerably lessens fire risks.

- POLYESTER MEMBRANES: Recent breakthroughs in materials science will be exploited to enhance performance. The craft's skin will be made of a multi-layered polyester membrane which, **unlike** the cotton used in pre-war models, is waterproof. This will minimise **both** weight **increases** due to rain and gas leaks. The structure will be strengthened by an aluminium frame.

© Cargolifter WG

- DIMENSIONS: The CL 160 is 260 m long with a diameter of 65 m and a gas volume of 550,000 $m^3$. Power is provided by eight gas-turbine engines driving six-meter propellers **boosted** by 12 thrust units for manoeuvring. The cruising speed is 90 kph at an altitude of 2,000 m. The CL 160 is designed to carry payloads weighing **as much as** 160 tonnes, with volumes up to 3,200 $m^3$. The potential range is 3,000-10,000 kilometres.
- ADVANTAGES: The foremost advantage of the CL 160 is that it does not need to land to unload. Cargo is lowered by cable from an altitude of 100 m. This reduces the need for large-scale ground infrastructures such as roads, major airfields and ports. Economically, this is crucial, as the fewer infrastructures there are, the cheaper transport costs become. A **further** advantage is that delivery times to remote destinations can be considerably shortened.
- USES: The airship is **best-suited** for transporting heavy and voluminous cargoes such as turbines. It will be especially useful for construction industries and for inshore and offshore oil exploration firms. It could also play a leading role in the humanitarian aid sector.

***HINDENBURG LZ 194***

→ ***Specifications***
*Length:* 245 m
*Diameter:* 41.2 m
*Empty weight:* 118 tonnes
*Service weight:* 220 tonnes
*Engines:* 4 propellers powered by 1100 HP 16 cylinder diesel engines
*Gas volume:* 200,000 $m^3$
*Maximum range:* 10,000 km
*Cruising speed:* 120 kph

***The Hindenburg crash***
*One of the **worst** crashes in pre-war air history*

TALKING POINT

- Compare the CL 160 and the Hindenburg LZ 194.

# Exercises

## 3.1. Exercise

*A. Work in pairs. First, give a definition of the word to your partner, then explain the different rules for making the comparative and superlative.*

1. Warm
2. Easy
3. Expensive (+)
4. Expensive (–) (i.e. the comparative of inferiority – the opposite of n°3)
5. Thin
6. The phrase: "+ expensive car = + good car"
7. Why is the superlative form (nearly) always preceded by "the"?

*B. Use the adjectives to ask 6 different* ***superlative*** *questions about the nouns in the box. When possible, use qualifying expressions like "the biggest* ***in the world*** *– the biggest* ***in Europe*** *– the biggest* ***I have ever seen****".*
*Example: What is the most dangerous snake* ***in India****?*
→ *The cobra is* ***the most dangerous*** *snake* ***in India****.*

*IRREGULAR*
bad ▪ good ▪ little

*1 SYLLABLE*
near ▪ large ▪ fast ▪ hot

*2 SYLLABLES + Y*
early ▪ healthy ▪ easy ▪ heavy

*2 + SYLLABLES*
dangerous ▪ serious ▪ influential ▪ recent ▪ common ▪ important ▪ widespread

city ▪ galaxy ▪ hospital ▪ language learning method ▪ desert ▪ written documents ▪ profession ▪ climate ▪ star ▪ layer ▪ temperature ▪ scientist ▪ animal ▪ plane crash ▪ means of transport ▪ food ▪ threat ▪ metal ▪ molecule

*C. Ask, and then answer questions from the box below using the form: (COMP + S + V) + (COMP + S + V). Pay special attention to the word order.*
*Example: What will happen if the population increases?*
→ ***The more*** *it increases,* ***the*** *less there will be to eat.*

standard of living ▪ number of cars ▪ temperature ▪ wind strength ▪ road accidents ▪ the price of petrol ▪ electronic fraud

## 3.2. A Mars analog – Haughton crater

*Space research cannot ignore the safety factor. This means that new technologies must be tested in exceptionally severe conditions. As such conditions rarely exist in everyday life, it is therefore necessary to find some way in which they can be simulated. Here is one example.*

**starter**

**• Exchange with your partner information about Mars.**

▌ ***Find acceptable synonyms or replacement expressions for the words in bold and for the gaps.***

*Example: The upper Arctic – the most northern regions.*

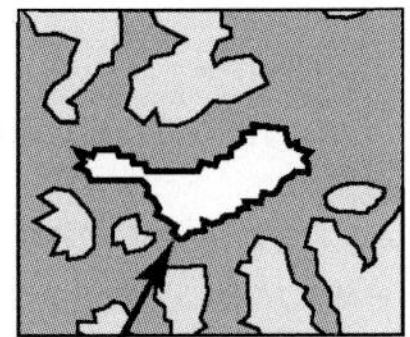

Haughton crater was formed by a meteorite impact 23 million years ago. It is located on Devon Island which is in the upper Arctic regions and the **largest** uninhabited island on Earth. The area is classified as a polar desert, i.e. it experiences extreme sub-zero temperatures, the top soil is thin and rocky and precipitation averages ........................ (**> little**) 8 cm per year. This means that in summer it is virtually snow-free. As features of the climatic and geological conditions **closely match** those that can be found on Mars, Haughton crater has been selected by NASA as being **well-suited** for space training programmes.

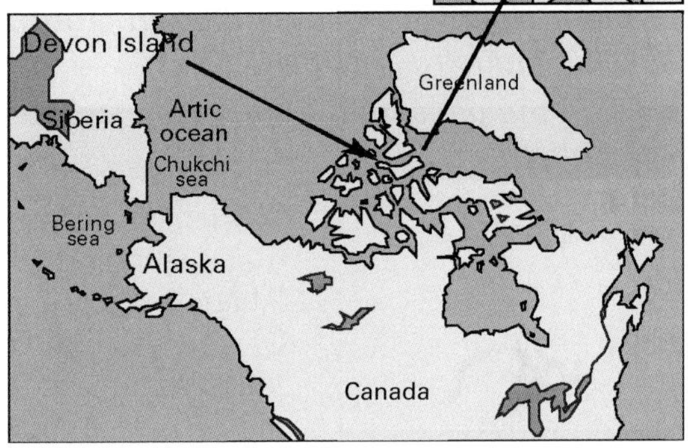


Clearly, no site on the Earth can offer identical conditions to those on Mars. **Unlike** Mars, the Earth has an atmosphere and ground level pressure is ................................................................ (**100 x > great**) than on Mars. The atmosphere provides protection from high level radiation while the intensity of the sunlight is relatively strong. Nevertheless, although winter temperatures on Mars may fall to –90°C, summer temperatures can be compared to those on Devon Island and scientists believe that present conditions on Devon Island are similar to those that were found on Mars 1 million years ago when the climate was **warmer and more humid**.

These **Mars-like conditions** therefore, provide an ideal testing ground for the NASA space programme and are being exploited to develop **improved** technology and human exploration procedures. The **major** projects include the development of more sophisticated information sharing systems, **enhanced** permafrost drills, more efficient robotic vehicles and a DNA reader for examining potential microbial remains.

*Haughton-crater: testing space suits*

The Haughton-Mars project will also be used **to further** fundamental research. In particular, the comparable morphology will provide insights into the evolution of Mars and offer a testing ground to study climate models and other geological phenomena such as the enigmatic Martian ............................ (**similar in shape to a U**) glacial melt-water channels.

**TALKING POINT**

- In what ways, not mentioned in the text, is Haughton crater similar or dissimilar to Mars?
- Can you think of other "analogs" for testing, training or developing models?

### *3.3. Mnemotechnology – SMPs versus SMAs*

*Synthetic polymers are macromolecules, manufactured from low molecular-weight compounds called monomers and consist of long chains of molecules. Modern chemistry allows the structure of these chains to be designed to fit specific industrial needs.*

- *Fill in the gaps with appropriate comparative and superlative forms or with synonyms.*

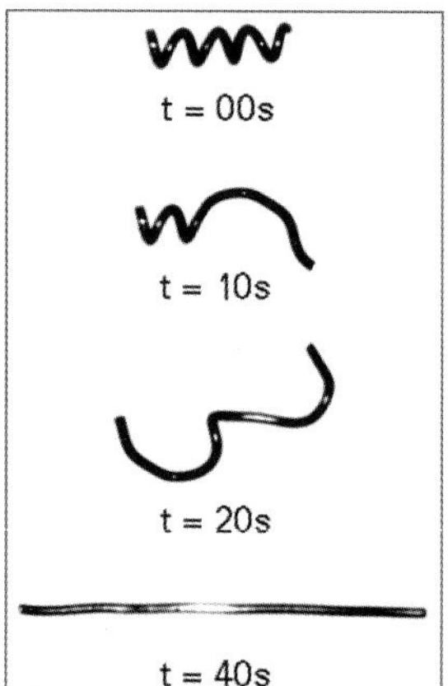

*SMP transformation*

MNEMOSCIENCE, a German company specialising in polymer technology, has announced its intention to market "shape-memory polymers" (SMPs) in the near future. Dr Andreas Lendlein, of the *"German Wool Research Institute"* at Aachen, in collaboration with Prof. R. Langer of *MIT*, are currently developing a new family of **en** ................. *(improved)* SMPs providing ................. *(+ good)* performance and ................................... *(+ versatility)*. The new process is based on polymers containing *oligo (e-caprolactone) dimethacrylate* which provides a "switching" segment, determining the temporary and the permanent shape of the polymer. The material is programmed by forming it into the required parent shape and then **ra** ...................... *(increasing)* the temperature so that crystallisation of the "switching" segment occurs and cross links are formed. The material can then be bent into any other configuration and will switch back to the former parent form at the transient temperature.

Shape-memory substances are, in fact, not new. The .............. *(≠ worst)* known is "Nitinol", a nickel-titanium alloy that has been widely used for actuators in robotic applications and medical devices for a considerable time. However, SMPs have a considerable number of advantages over shape-memory alloys (SMAs) and offer a far wider range of applications. Their **fo** .................. *(main)* advantage is that they are much ............... *(+ easy)* to make and consequently .................................. *(– expensive)*. This is because, **un** ............. *(in contrast to)* alloys, the programming of polymers can be carried out rapidly and at ...................... *(+ low)* temperatures, about 70°C instead of several hundred degrees. Other advantages include:

- The reaction time after the transient temperature has been reached is much faster.
- By varying the proportions of the two monomers, the specification of deformations can be adjusted with ................................. *(+ accuracy)*. This means that SMPs with predetermined mechanical strength and transient temperatures can be designed to **su** ............ (*match, correspond to*) specific functions.
- The deformation capability is ......................................... *(20 x > great)* SMAs.

- Finally, there are considerably ............... *(≠ more)* problems in producing bio-compatible and bio-degradable SMBs. This **wi** ............... *(extends, enlarges)* the potential range of uses and has considerable importance for medical applications. It will be possible, for example, to insert bio-degradable implants which do not require ..................... *(+ far)* intervention in order to be removed and thus **le** .............. *(reduce)* the need for invasive follow-up surgery.

*TALKING POINT*

- With your partner, complete the following flow chart showing the programming and function of SMPs.

1. First of all, ........................................... programmed by ............................................... into the parent shape.
2. Next, the ......................................
3. (Result?) ..................................
4. After that, ......................... ...................................... ......... another configuration.
5. When it is reheated
6. ................................... ........... to the parent form.
7. (When?) ..............................................

### 3.4. Checkpoints

In other words

**Definitions – defining by comparison**

*Use the following pattern:*
"X is **similar to** Y **but much ... + er**."

*Example:* a tiger
*"A tiger is **similar to** a cat **but much** larg**er**."*

- *Define the following words:*
  *a rat • diamond • a village • Mars*
- *Choose a word of your own that can be defined in this way and ask your neighbour to define it.*

Back to basics

**"To agree"**: do you agree or disagree with these statements? Write a full answer, using the word "agree". "I ........... that ..........."

We can learn things from astrology.
As science develops, it is becoming more dangerous.
Happiness has got nothing to do with the standard of living.
The major problems for the future are ethical not technological.

- *Check in the answer section.*

## THE WORD WEB – SUFFIXES

- *You can use suffixes to form nouns or verbs: -(at)ion ▪ -sion ▪ -ise* G. Notes 1.
  *Examples: to vary → variation; to divide → division; character → to characterise.*

| ***Verbs*** | ***Nouns*** |
|---|---|
| 1. It is cheaper to **regulate** the temperature automatically. | Automatic temperature ..................... is more economical. |
| 2. If gases ....................... very rapidly, cryogenic temperatures are attained. | Rapid **expansion** of the gases produces temperatures of below 120 Kelvin. |
| 3. The committee was set up to **standardise** civil aviation procedures. | His job involves the ......................... of aviation safety procedures. |
| 4. People get old because the body ............................ genetic damage. | Ageing is a result of the **accumulation** of genetic damage. |
| 5. The first atomic bomb **exploded** on August 6, 1945. | 80,000 people were killed in the Hiroshima ...................... . |
| 6. The astronauts are provided with a 14-day supply of **pressurised** oxygen. | The oxygen supply is stored under .................... . |
| 7. Solar energy is ............................... from hydrogen. | The **generation** of solar energy involves the conversion of hydrogen. |
| 8. Heat losses can be ......................... by thermal protection. | Efficient insulation reduces heat losses to a **minimum**. |
| 9. It was necessary to **extend** the research facilities. | Because of the increase in staff, an .............................. had to be built. |

### *3.5. Web search*

- Make a web search for images / graphs illustrating comparative data. Make a 3 minute OHP presentation.

  Choose "images" on the tool bar of the research motor and write strings like:

  < graph data > or < graph statistics >

  To focus the search, you could add words of your own e.g. "arctic", "cinema", etc. *G. Notes 33*

- Go to the following address to find out more about civil applications of airships:

  ➢ http://aerosml.com/civil.asp

### *Word search*

- Choose two important words from each of the *Key points* of Units 1-3 and prepare a revision test for your partner (cf. *Entry test*).

## *Self evaluation – exit test*

- *Supply the missing words.*

1. As a result of the dust cloud raised by the impact of a large asteroid **ne** ............... heat ............ light would penetrate the Earth's atmosphere. *(not one, not the other)*
2. Optical fibres will produce **en** .......................... performances for computers. *(better)*
3. The government would like to **bo** ................ imports. *(help to improve)*
4. The two colours do not **ma** ............... . *(go together)*
5. The disease is **sp** .......................... rapidly. *(advancing)*
6. The constant stress and vibration **we** ................. the metal. *(≠ make stronger)*
7. Chameleons, **un** ........................ human beings, can survive a drop of 46% of the body fluid. *(in contrast to)*
8. The reason why NASA is interested in nuclear propulsion is that space travel would be .............................. fast. *(x 2)*
9. ........................................................................................................ . *(+ people poor / – they eat)*
10. If you drive up the hill too fast, the engine will **ov** ..................... . *(get too hot)*

# 4. MODIFICATION

*This unit reviews **modification**, a function which is much more important than is commonly realised. It is easy enough to say that something is "good" or "bad", "hot" or "cold". But the problem when learning a language is to go beyond the expression of simplistic ideas so that nuances and subtle differences can be expressed with ease.*

*Modification is expressed typically by adjectives to modify the meaning of nouns and by adverbs to modify the meaning of other adverbs, adjectives, verbs or phrases.*

## Self evaluation – entry test

▮ *Supply suitable modifiers.*

*Example:*

*Epidemics in the third world are **ma** .......... due to malnutrition.* (above all)

→ *Epidemics in the third world are **mainly** due to malnutrition.*

1. **Al** .............. 15,000 people have been killed in traffic accidents over the last 10 years. *(nearly, slightly fewer than)*
2. There has been a **st** .................. increase in viruses which are resistant to antibiotics. *(constant)*
3. The Roman calendar was **ba** .................. a lunar calendar and contained only 355 days. *(essentially, fundamentally)*
4. It has been said that in science, the major problem is not finding answers, but asking the **re** .................. questions. *(appropriate, pertinent)*
5. Since World War II, there has been a **wi** .................. Americanisation of Japanese society. *(extensive, throughout the country)*
6. The dimensions of dwarf stars are **ro** .................. comparable to those of the Sun. *(approximately)*
7. Light is emitted and absorbed in **mi** .................. units or corpuscles called photons or quanta. *(exceedingly small, tiny)*
8. Enzymes have an **ou** ...................... ability to biodegrade natural products. *(exceptional)*
9. Statistics must always be used with care; their interpretation is often not **re** ............... . *(sure, dependable)*
10. **St** ........... hillsides are inevitably under threat of erosion. (*with a big gradient, inclination*)

# *Functions & Grammar*

## KEY POINTS – MODIFICATION

### *1. Adjectives*

▌ *Importance*

important · significant · crucial · meaningful · relevant

➤ *What Bachelard wrote in 1934 is still* ***relevant*** *to contemporary scientific problems.*

▌ *Dimension*

enormous · tremendous · huge · widespread ≠ small-scale · tiny · minute

➤ *Blood plasma contains* ***minute*** *quantities of creatinine.*

▌ *Hierarchy*

major · main · chief · leading · primary · foremost · outstanding ≠

- secondary · minor · common
- average · typical · standard

➤ *Little by little the patient's condition* ***worsened****.*

▌ *Intensity*

dramatic · striking · acute · steep · sharp

➤ *There has been a* ***sharp*** *decline in the quality of river water.*

▌ *Aptitude and utility*

- appropriate · suitable
- useful · reliable · efficient

➤ *If electromagnetic radiation of* ***suitable*** *wavelength falls upon the metal, electrons are ejected.*

### 2. Adverbs

▮ *Essence*

essentially · fundamentally · basically · on the whole

➤ ***Basically**, there is little difference between the two processes.*

▮ *Manner*

carefully · steadily · thoroughly · accurately · properly

➤ *The $1^{st}$ law of thermodynamics was not **properly** formulated until the middle of the $19^{th}$ century.*

▮ *Negation*

hardly (any) · scarcely (any) · barely (any)

➤ *After processing, **hardly any** of the nutrients remain.*

▮ *Degree*

a little · a bit · slightly

relatively · quite [G. Notes 5] · rather · fairly

very · extremely · exceedingly

➤ *The results were **slightly** better than last year.*

▮ *Approximation*

nearly · almost · roughly · more or less · virtually · to a certain extent · partly

totally · quite [G. Notes 5] · entirely · utterly · thoroughly

➤ *For most people, living without a motor car would be **utterly** unacceptable.*

## Examples in context

**starter**

**• Why do women live longer than men?**

### LIFE EXPECTANCY AND SEXUAL INEQUALITY

*Philosophers say that we are all born equal. It appears, however, that things are a little bit more complicated than that. The text discusses the difference in death rates for men and women.*

▮ *Select important words in **bold** and ask your partner for definitions.*

▮ *Draw the graph.*

The line graph in the figure below gives comparative data for the evolution of **average** death rates for males and females between birth and the age of 90.

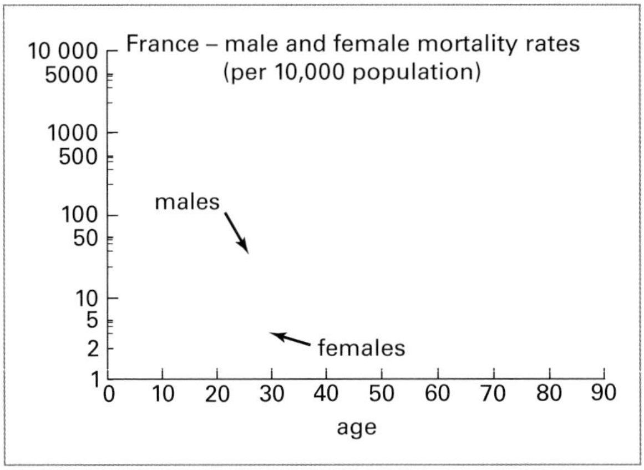


The period immediately after birth is naturally a high risk period, with figures standing at **slightly** over 60‱. Over the next five years, however, there is a **sharp** drop to **roughly** 3‱ for males and 2‱ for females. The rate for males continues to fall, but more slowly, attaining 2‱ at the age of 13. In early adolescence the pattern changes. There is a **steep** rise to 14‱ by the age of 19. For the next 14 years, despite minor fluctuations, the rate of increase slows down and attains 20‱. From then on, the curve continues to rise **steadily**, reaching 200‱ at the age of 64 and just over 2000‱ at the age of 90.

By contrast, the curve for young females is significantly different. The lowest point of approximately 1.5‱ occurs at the age of 13. This is followed by a rapid rise until it levels off at just over 4‱ between the ages of 18 to 24. It then starts to rise again, **more or less** parallel to the male curve, reaching 80‱ at the age of 65. From the age of 65 onwards, the gap between the two sexes begins to narrow and finally, at the age of 90, the probability of death for females is in the vicinity of just over 1000‱.

The data raises a number of interesting points. It is striking that the difference in life expectancy lasts **virtually** throughout the **entire** life span. At all stages, except from birth to the age of 3, males are more vulnerable. This difference may be accounted for **to a certain extent** by sociological factors. It is true to say that, **on the whole**, male adolescent life styles are more risk oriented, involving activities including dangerous sports and a greater consumption of alcohol. It is traffic accidents that are the **foremost** cause of death for young adults and, in the 15-35 year old range, 80% of the deaths are males.

Similarly, the higher levels for adult males can be partially related to traditional working roles. **Basically**, there is a tendency for more males to be employed in manual work or in jobs involving high stress, inducing work-related mortality such as industrial accidents and cardio-vascular diseases.

However, the overall lower mortality rates for females, particularly in the 5-12 period which is common to most cultures (it is also **widespread** among higher animals) would seem to indicate that there is some genetic factor involved which makes females the more resistant sex.

# Exercises

## 4.1. Exercise

### *A. Match the modifiers on the left with the crossword puzzle definitions on the right.*

1. Typical
2. Efficient
3. Huge
4. Reliable
5. Virtually
6. To a certain extent
7. Thoroughly
8. Roughly
9. Outstanding
10. Widespread
11. Basically
12. Hardly any

a. Quite exceptional – you just can't class it with the others
b. Almost
c. A little more than nothing – but not much
d. Could be more, could be less – not much precision here
e. Within limits
f. Completely, carefully and conscientiously
g. Conforms totally to expectations – zero surprise
h. The capitalist's dream – maximum work, minimum waste
i. All over the place – ubiquitous in fact
j. Not just big – a macro-dimension
k. You can count on this – it will never let you down
l. To start at the beginning or, more accurately, to go right down to the foundations

### *B. Insert the above modifiers into one of the phrases below.*

1. Farms are most ............................ when they comprise a thousand hectares or more.
2. Although it has a ........................ population, China has successfully reduced both fertility and mortality.
3. ............................ , there are four types of language in Europe.
4. Historical records of earthquakes before the middle of the $18^{th}$ century are not ......................... .
5. There is still ................................ fear that genetically modified viruses might escape from the laboratory.
6. A human being requires ........................... 3,000 calories a day.
7. Intra-species fighting can be observed in ........................... all vertebrates.
8. Osteoporosis (thinning of the bones) is a ........................... example of an age-related disease.
9. Military trainee pilots are very .............................. prepared.
10. From a technological point of view, Concorde has been an ........................ success.
11. There are ............................... tigers left – they'll soon be extinct.
12. ............................... , I agree with you.

## *4.2. Maps, medicine and cholera*

*The statistics for third world infant mortality show only too well the close connection that there is between medicine and geography. The text below describes one of the first and most famous examples of spatial geography.*

**starter**

**• The table below gives comparative figures for life expectancy in different places and at different times. Before reading the text try to suggest potential explanations for the English figures.**

▌ *Replace the words in **bold** with modifiers from the list:* *ALMOST • MINUTE • LEADING • RELIABLE • REAL • HUGE • EXCEEDINGLY • ENTIRELY • BARELY • ACUTE • HARDLY • CAREFUL • APPROPRIATE • PRACTICALLY.*

From the moment that coal became the main raw material for power supplies, the industrial revolution was characterised by the massive expansion of the new towns as hundreds and thousands of unskilled workers left the countryside, drawn by the promise of work in the new industrial centres. Towns sprang up from **virtually** nothing and within a span of 30 or 40 years **tiny** villages had grown to become **major** industrial centres.

***LIFE EXPECTANCY AND INFANT MORTALITY COMPARATIVE DATA***

| | *Period* | *Life expectancy* | *Infant mortality* |
|---|---|---|---|
| France | 1990s | 78.5 | 6‰ |
| India | " | 60 | 60 |
| Papua | " | 57 | 60 |
| Yemen | " | 49 | 130 |
| **England** | **1600** | **42** | **–** |
| **Liverpool** | **1841** | **–** | **259** |
| **Manchester** | **1843** | **24** | **–** |

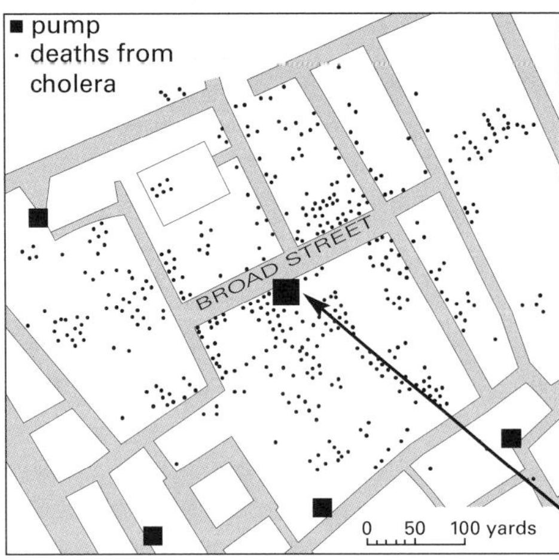


*The famous map by Dr John Snow shows the connection between the London cholera infection and a single polluted water **pump** in Broad street.*

However, in the 19th century, Britain was neither socially, politically, technologically nor scientifically prepared for such a **massive** change. It must be remembered that the new populations flooded into the towns at a time when there was **practically** no public transport. The direct outcome of this was that workers were obliged to dwell near their work places resulting in **extremely** high population densities around the mines and factories. To make matters worse, centralised government and the notion of town planning **hardly** yet existed in Europe which meant that there were no laws setting minimum standards for housing, space and sanitation. The new overcrowded slums[1] were built without any **proper** means of disposing of the vast volume of sewage and waste, as the relevant technology had not yet

1 Slum: poor, dirty, overcrowded urban area.

been developed. **Efficient** steam pumping engines capable of evacuating the sewage only came into use in the 1840s and the metallurgists lacked the **relevant** know-how which would have permitted the mass production of iron pipes with joints that could withstand the high pressures.

Urban society has also a **crucial** need for great quantities of drinking water, but here again, little had changed since the Romans. It was thus inevitable that the traditional underground wells should become contaminated. But, once more, there was a deficit in knowledge. In those days, medicine was **scarcely** more than a folk art. Doctors had little understanding of disease and were **utterly** ignorant of how infections were transmitted. In 1854, there was an outbreak of cholera in London. John Snow, a London doctor, carried out a **thorough** spatial analysis and, by plotting the cases on a map, was able to demonstrate how the epidemic in central London was linked to the Broad street water pump. Only then, was it understood that cholera must be a water borne disease. The solution was extremely simple; the handle was removed from the pump and the epidemic died out.

TALKING POINT

- What other examples can you find of historical events being dependent on, or influenced by social, technological or scientific knowledge?

### *4.3. The disposal of high level radioactive waste*

*It appears to be a law of nature that the richer countries become, the more waste they produce. The UK currently produces 500 million tonnes annually, much of it polluting, toxic or hazardous. Developing techniques for coping with different types of waste, and particularly nuclear waste, will be one of the major problems of this century.*

**starter**

- **What are the main risks, and what solutions have been proposed for disposing of nuclear waste?**

*Read the text and complete the blanks with the following words:*

*CRUCIAL • FOREMOST • QUITE • RELIABLE • ROUGHLY • STEADILY • WIDESPREAD • THOROUGH (1-8)*

*ALMOST • BASICALLY • FAIRLY • HUGE • MINUTE • SUITABLE • VIRTUALLY (9-15)*

As a result of the present *(1)* ..................... *(extensive)* concern for ecological problems, one of the ........................ *(key)* issues facing the nuclear industry today is the disposal of High Level Waste (HLW). HLW is primarily a by-product of nuclear power facilities and weapons programmes and although, in fact it is ........................ *(relatively, fairly)* small in volume, it accounts for 95% of radioactive waste. Accumulated world stocks stand currently, at ............................... *(approximately)* 110,000 tonnes, but this figure is ................. *(constantly)* growing at an estimated 10,500 tonnes a year. It should also be mentioned that present storage facilities have not proved to be totally .......................... *(dependable)*; there have been several reports of cracks developing in the concrete cooling tanks, leading to incidents of leaking.

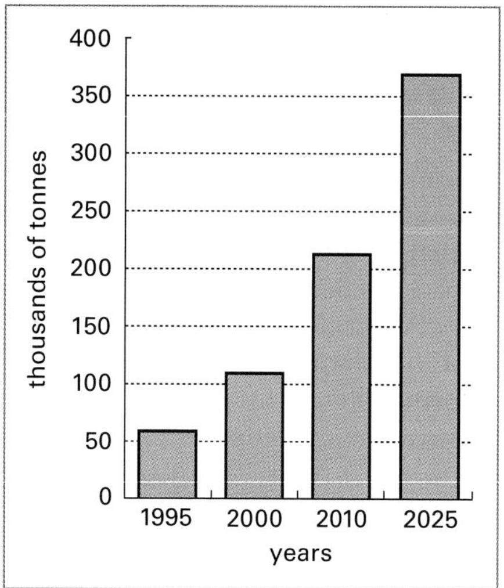


*HLW – world stocks*

A large array of different HLW disposal procedures have been proposed, including disposal of the waste in space, in glaciated areas and destruction by nuclear transmutation. At present, the .......................... *(leading)* candidate is disposal in deep geological formations and recently, there have been a series of .......................... *(careful)* feasibility studies carried out to this end. A lesser known variant of this technique is disposal of HLW under the sea bed which some researchers claim has certain very worthwhile advantages.

*(9)* .......................... *(essentially)*, the process works as follows. Standard, well-tried petroleum drilling technology would be used to drill a hole to a depth of several hundred meters through the upper layer of sediments on the ocean bed. A cylindrical steel pipe would then be inserted and containers of vitrified nuclear waste lowered into the pipes by cable. Each container would be packed vertically and separated from the next by 20 m of sediment. As the ocean floor covers ......................... *(nearly)* 70% of the Earth's surface, it would be .......... *(relatively)* easy to locate sites remote from populated areas. Furthermore, the danger of seismic activity would be ................. *(on a very small scale, tiny)*, as there is a wide range of sites in the Atlantic or Pacific oceans that are far from the boundaries of tectonic plates and which have remained geologically inert for tens of millions of years. The natural plasticity and low permeability of the ocean sediment provides ..................... *(satisfactory)* packing material to stop any cracks which may appear and, at a depth of one meter below the ocean bed, there are ............ *(practically)* no living organisms capable of transporting radio active material. This means that even after the inevitable corrosion of the steel pipe and the container, radioactive migration would not exceed one meter in 24,000 years. Finally, the ocean provides a ............... *(tremendous, enormous)* dilution capacity if the safety system fails.

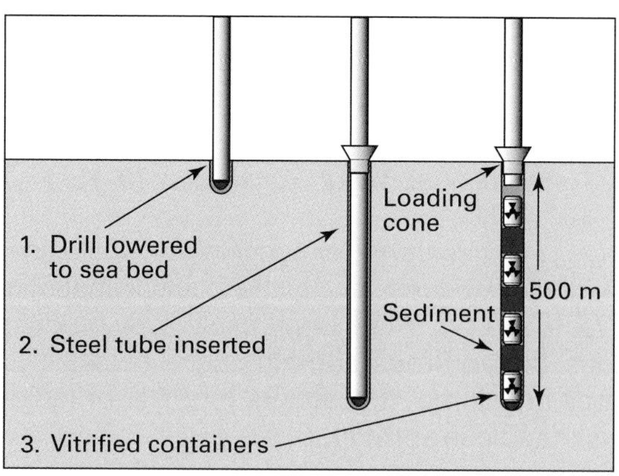


**TALKING POINT**

- People are concerned with HLW because of the enormous time it takes to decay. But what other sorts of pollution do you find worrying? What can you say about their time span?

## *4.4. Checkpoints*

**IN OTHER WORDS**

**Definitions – reformulation: "that is to say"**

*Use the following pattern:*
"X is Y, **that is to say** it is Z."

*Example:* a cataract
*"A cataract is when the eye becomes opaque, **that is to say**, no longer transparent."*

- *Define these words:*
  *an adolescent • a bus • cancer • an antibiotic*
- *Look at Exercise 4.3 and find a word that you can define in the same way. Compare with your neighbour.*

**BACK TO BASICS**

**"Important"**: are you sure you know what this word means?

- *In which sentences can you use the word "important"?*

1. Cambridge is a small but .................... university.
2. The graph shows that production is getting more and more ........... year by year.
3. They have got a very ........... number of research laboratories at NASA.
4. Because of the .............. population the country is obliged to import food.

- *Check in the answer section.*

**THE WORD WEB – ADJECTIVES + PREPOSITIONS**

- *Insert the correct preposition:* AT • IN • FOR • TO • OF • WITH.

1. Although they have normal motor activities, people suffering from somnambulism are not aware .......... their surroundings.
2. Contrary to what most people think, musicians are not particularly good .......... languages.
3. The virus responsible .......... Ebola fever comes from animal sources.
4. What he told the police is incompatible .......... the facts.
5. Satellite images are capable .......... detecting objects less than 15 cm across.
6. One of the effects of aspirin is to make patients less liable .......... heart attack and thrombosis.
7. They want to recruit a doctor who is qualified .......... tropical diseases.
8. Five research students were involved .......... industrial espionage.

### *4.5. Web search*

- Go to the World Health Organisation site and look at the FAQs on cholera. Make a 3 minute report using the OHP.

  ➢ http://www.who.int**/csr/disease/cholera/en/**

- Find the main causes of mortality in the 15-30 year range.

#### *Word search*

- If you made a mistake with "important" (see *Back to basics*), search the web and note down 6 examples in context. Use advanced search strings such as:

  < important microgravity >   < HLW risk important >

## *Self evaluation – exit test*

- ***The following examples refer to air transport in Papua New Guinea. Complete the sentences using suitable synonyms.***

1. No **ma** ................. or even small town in Papua New Guinea is complete without its airstrip. *(large and important)*
2. The aeroplane has, for **ro** ..................... 40 years, formed the only link across Papua New Guinea's mountainous terrain. *(approximately)*
3. Prior to the development of airstrips, it was **vi** ........................ impossible to get from one side of the country to the other. *(almost, nearly)*
4. Half a century ago, **sl** ........................ more than two million inhabitants of Papua lived cut off from the rest of the world. *(a little)*
5. To a certain **ex** .......... , it was the gold rush of the late 1920s that precipitated the development of the air industry in New Guinea. *(up to a point)*
6. In 1933, an airstrip was built at Mount Hagen and it was at this stage that flying became the inhabitants' **ch** ................... form of transport. *(leading)*
7. As the aircraft became more **re** .................. , air traffic expanded rapidly. *(sure)*
8. Experience has shown that the most **su** ...................... type of plane in such mountainous terrain is light, single-engined aircraft. *(appropriate)*
9. On the **wh** ................ , the natives living in the highlands of New Guinea are afraid of the sea and prefer to travel by air. *(generally speaking)*
10. As there was **sc** ................... any aviation fuel available, there was a decline in air transport during World War II. *(hardly)*

# 5. LINK WORDS

*The structures and functions that we have seen up to now have been concerned mainly with single ideas. However, relating one idea to another is also one of the essential roles of language. One way of doing this is by means of **link words**. These are conjunctions and adverbs that can be used, for example, to indicate that:*

- *the information is supplementary to something already said (**and** ...),*
- *the information stands in contrast to what has been said before (**but** ...),*
- *the information is a cause, a consequence or an illustration (**because, for example** ...).*

## Self evaluation – entry test

▌ *Choose the correct answer.*

1. The device enables temperatures to be monitored, .................. improving the safety margin.
   **a.** thereby **b.** neverthless **c.** namely **d.** e.g.
2. A new technique, .................. the infra-red camera, means that dust surrounding new stars can be penetrated.
   **a.** whereas **b.** namely **c.** besides **d.** for instance
3. Superconducting, ...................................... when materials lose all resistance, will boost computer performances.
   **a.** thus **b.** obviously **c.** besides **d.** that is to say
4. Programmable electronic systems are more reliable. .................... , they can be used to handle radio-active material.
   **a.** whereas **b.** such as **c.** moreover **d.** in other words
5. Computers can process data extremely fast. ........................ this, they have several serious drawbacks.
   **a.** in spite of **b.** whereas **c.** however **d.** moreover
6. The new engine is far more efficient. ........................... more work is required to reduce noise levels.
   **a.** nevertheless **b.** whereas **c.** i.e. **d.** besides
7. The presence of high concentrations of elements that are rarely found on Earth, ........................ iridium, suggests there was a meteorite impact at that spot.
   **a.** on the whole **b.** moreover **c.** such as **d.** that is to say
8. The data is stored on hard disk, ........................ it is easily accessible.
   **a.** actually **b.** whereas **c.** e.g. **d.** hence
9. Applicants for the job should speak at least one other European language .................. French.
   **a.** obviously **b.** besides **c.** moreover **d.** actually
10. .................. , in the initial stages there were minor problems to be overcome, but from then on, the prototypes were perfectly reliable.
    **a.** besides **b.** as a rule **c.** namely **d.** despite

# *Functions & Grammar*

## KEY POINTS – LINK WORDS

### *1. Giving additional information*

and · not only / but · as well as · in addition · furthermore · moreover · besides · apart from

➢ *The flat is too small and **furthermore**, it is not in the town centre.*

### *2. Contrast*

but · however · nevertheless · yet [G. Notes 7] · although · (even) though · in spite of / despite · whereas · on (the) one hand / on (the) other hand

➢ *Geologists are using radio-active analysis of rocks more and more, **nevertheless** it is not suitable in every case.*

### *3. Contrast to what people think*

actually [G. Notes 8] · in fact · in actual fact · in reality

➢ *Most people think that Fleming was the father of penicillin, but **actually** most of the work was done by Florey.*

### *4. Introducing a cause / consequence*

- because · as · since
- consequently · therefore · thus · hence · as a result · thereby [G. Notes 11]

➢ *The arteries become gradually blocked, **thereby** reduc**ing** the oxygen supply to the brain.*

### *5. Introducing something obvious / generally accepted*

obviously · naturally · of course · clearly · doubtless [G. Notes 9]

➢ ***Obviously**, unless the birth rate decreases, there will be a major food crisis.*

### *6. Making a general statement*

in general · generally speaking · on the whole · as a rule

➢ ***As a rule**, metals are inflammable.*

### 7. Clarification

for example • for instance • e.g. G. Notes 10 • that is to say • in other words • i.e. G. Notes 10 • such as • namely

➢ *The quantity of heat is expressed in the same units as energy and work,* ***namely*** *joules.*

## Examples in context

### PROFESSOR STEPHEN HAWKING

▮ *Replace the words in* ***bold*** *by synonyms, antonyms or by explanation.*

**starter**

**• Who is Stephen Hawking? – what do you know about him?**

Stephen Hawking is **doubtless** the most well-known theoretical physicist and cosmologist of our time.

At the age of 21, while he was still a young student, Stephen Hawking was diagnosed as having amyotrophic lateral sclerosis, **that is to say**, a degenerative motor neurone disease that prevents voluntary control of the muscles. He was informed that he had not long to live.

**Despite** the disease, or as he himself says, perhaps **as a result of** it, he continued with his studies and was awarded his PhD in 1977 and so started a brilliant scientific career. He has made important contributions to the theory of black holes and the origin of the universe.

**Besides** losing the ability to control his arm and leg muscles, he gradually lost the ability to speak clearly. This meant that, **as a rule**, at scientific conferences or seminars he was obliged to speak via an interpreter.

In 1985, he caught pneumonia and was obliged to undergo a tracheotomy, **i.e.** an incision of the oesophagus.

The tracheotomy operation, **however**, removed his ability to speak altogether. For a time, the only way he could communicate was by signalling with his eye muscles.

A computer expert in California designed him a program linked to a voice synthesiser that could be activated with one finger, **thereby** enabling Hawking to move the cursor. At present he can produce 15 words a minute.

Hawking is **nevertheless**, very active. He travels a great deal and recently has given conferences in the US, India, South Korea and the UK.

© Reuters NewMedia Inc / CORBIS

# Exercises

## 5.1. Exercise

*A. Link the two halves of the sentences together.*

1. It must be six o'clock. No, **actually** ...
2. If you heat copper to 400°C, it becomes viscous, **in other words** ...
3. The current was too high, **as a result** ...
4. Mercury is a metal, **nevertheless** ...
5. Amphetamines are dangerous, **therefore** ...
6. **As a rule**, water freezes at 0°C, but ...
7. Glass is fragile, **thus** ...
8. The motor was out of date, **besides** ...
9. Hydrocarbons are relatively light, **in fact** ...
10. Water usually boils at 100°C, **however** ...

a. it begins to melt.
b. they float on water.
c. it should be handled with care.
d. they should be kept away from children.
e. it does not do so if you add salt.
f. the wires began to overheat.
g. it consumed too much fuel.
h. it is a fluid.
i. at higher altitudes, the temperature is lower.
j. it is five past six.

*B. Use the following words to join the phrases: DESPITE THE FACT • NAMELY • OBVIOUSLY • ACTUALLY • YET • HENCE • THEREBY.*

1. Symptoms such as pain, fever, and vomiting are not diseases. ...................... they are defence mechanisms.
2. "Psychotic" means that a patient has lost touch with reality, ..................... "neurotic" refers to a less serious state.
3. People have always recognised the waste, brutality, and inhumanity of war, ................ it goes on.
4. The mesosphere is important .............................. that it contains only about 0.1 per cent of the total mass of the atmosphere.
5. As a rule, aquatic reptiles use the same means of propulsion as fish and whales, ......................... they use powerful beats of the tail.
6. The heat increases, ......................... the entropy increases.
7. Cells and antibodies may co-operate, ................... destroying invading bacteria.
8. For a person who weighs less, the concentration of alcohol will ...................... be proportionally higher.

*C. LINK WORDS – Study the example below of a chain of linked sentences.*

*Example:*

More women are getting executive jobs in high finance.

**1. Clearly**, this means that they are under greater stress.

↳ **2.** The number of women drinking alcohol is **therefore** rising.

↳ **3. In addition**, many of the women suffer from depression.

▌ *Write 2 similar chains, using different link words, each time based on **one** of following the sentences.*

1. Gold is a very expensive metal.
2. Death rates from infectious diseases will be reduced by 20% over the next 30 years.
3. The first atomic bomb was dropped in 1945.
4. Oil reserves will run out by the middle of the next century.
5. Girls are now getting better results than boys at school.
6. There is more and more congestion in the town centre.

- in addition, furthermore, besides
- however, nevertheless, yet, in spite of, on the other hand
- but actually, but in reality, in fact
- obviously, clearly, doubtless
- in general, on the whole, as a rule
- in other words, that is to say, namely
- consequently, therefore, thus

1. ........................................................................................................................
↪ 2. ........................................................................................................................
↪ 3. ........................................................................................................................

1. ........................................................................................................................
↪ 2. ........................................................................................................................
↪ 3. ........................................................................................................................

### *5.2. Solar flares*

*Solar activity is cyclic, fluctuating from periods of low activity to periods of high activity every 11 years. Solar flares are most frequent during periods of maximum sun spot activity when occurrences can attain as many as 25 daily.*

**starter**

**• Before looking at the text, what information can you provide about solar flares?**

▌ *Read the passage on solar flares and then complete the outline below.*

The exact nature of solar flares, which constitute the most powerful releases of energy within the solar system, is still not fully understood. They consist of rapid and intense variation of brightness, resulting from the liberation of magnetic energy. The quantities of energy involved are enormous, with temperatures attaining typically 10 to 20 million degrees K, but temperatures as high as 100 million K have been recorded. The energy released consists essentially of ultraviolet radiation, accompanied by X-ray emissions. These are converted in the chromosphere into solar plasma heat, releasing accelerated particles, including electrons, protons and heavy nuclei into the solar system. The duration of the flares is variable, lasting sometimes several hours. Light emitted from the flares reaches Earth within 8 minutes – particles travel more slowly, taking 36 to 48 hours to arrive.

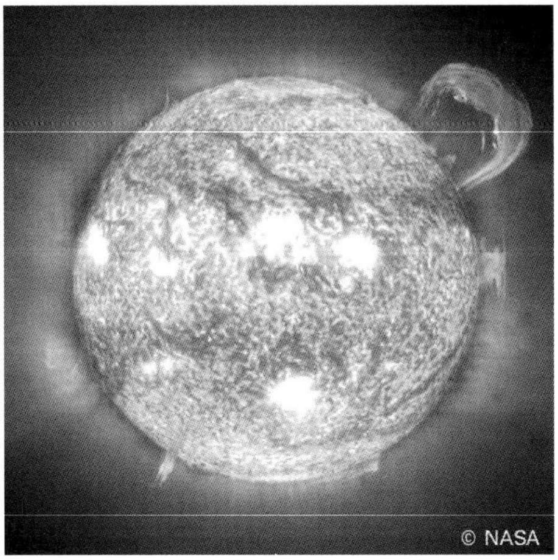


The distance involved means that only a small part of the energy reaches Earth, but the effect it has on the magnetosphere and ionosphere directly influences the terrestrial environment in several different ways:

- the atmosphere of the Earth facing the sun undergoes increased ionisation from the X-ray radiation, thus disrupting radio communications;
- the material released causes magnetic storms and auroras in polar regions.

The flares are also potentially hazardous to space projects:

- the intense heat generated increases the temperature of the Earth's upper atmosphere, causing it to expand and become denser. This means that the velocity of low orbiting satellites is slowed down. It was because of this phenomenon that the re-entry of the MIR satellite in February 2001 had to be delayed;
- the particles themselves are a potential hazard, as they can damage electronic instrumentation and endanger space-walking astronauts.

▌ *Reconstruct the text (it may be necessary to reformulate the phrases).*

1. Solar flares ................................................................................................ ................................................, **yet** they are still not totally understood.
2. **As a rule**, temperatures attain ........................................................................ .
3. Temperatures are usually in the vicinity of 20 million K. Sometimes, **however**, ................................................................................................................ .
4. **Basically**, the energy released .......................................................................... .
5. ................................................................................................................, **thereby** releasing accelerated particles.
6. ..........................................., **such as** ............................................................ ...................................................... are released.
7. ................................................................................................................, **whereas** light arrives within 8 minutes.
8. The distance Sun-Earth is considerable, **hence** ..................................................... ................................................................................................................ .
9. The distance is considerable, **nevertheless**, ......................................................... ................................................................................................................ .
10. **Since** the atmosphere is ionised, ....................................................................... ................................................................................................................ .
11. **Besides** disrupting radio communications, ............................................................. ................................................................................................................ .
12. ................................................................................................................, **therefore** it becomes denser.
13. ................................................................................................................ **furthermore**, they can endanger space-walking astronauts.

## *5.3. Introducing the Griffon vulture into the Massif Central*

*Griffon Vultures disappeared from the southern Massif Central around 1945. In 1981, a reintroduction project began and ten years later, the new colony consisted of about a hundred individuals. This report describes the different stages of the process.*

**starter**

**• The text describes a reintroduction programme for vultures.**
**1. What do you know about vultures? • 2. Why do you think they became extinct? • 3. Where did the new vultures come from? • 4. What do you imagine were the main problems after release?**

▌ *Insert the words into the text: WHEREAS • NAMELY • FURTHERMORE • SINCE • AS A RESULT • AS • HOWEVER (1-7)*
*NATURALLY • ALTHOUGH • THEREFORE • SUCH AS • BESIDES • THEREBY • IN FACT • HENCE (8-15)*

INTRODUCTION

Griffon vultures were gradually eliminated from south central France during the first part of the 20th century, victims of direct destruction by gun and poison *(1)* ................. the local population wrongly considered them as pests. ...................... , by 1945, they were totally extinct. ..................... , in 1968 a reintroduction project was started. The locality chosen was the last known breeding site in the Causses region in the Massif Central. This is an excellent habitat for vultures for two major reasons, .................. farming is still focussed on sheep breeding and it is also an area of high cliffs and canyons. This study analyses the implementation of the project and the precautions that were taken to ensure a successful settlement.

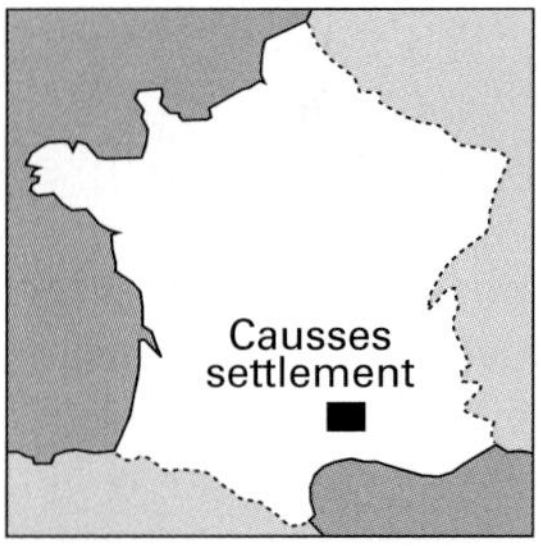


PROJECT DESIGN

The project was carried out in three successive stages:

- 1968-1981: preparation of public opinion, education of hunters, obtaining strychnine prohibition and gathering 50 captive Griffon vultures;
- 1981-1986: release phase;
- post 1986: free evolution of the population.

© Keith Regan

VULTURES USED

Between 1970 and 1987, 86 Griffon vultures were obtained from different origins:

- 47 came from the wild or rehabilitation centres (31 from Spain and 16 from France);
- 24 were given or exchanged by zoos;
- 6 were seized from dealers (unknown origin);
- 9 were born in the project aviary[1].

1 Aviary: a large cage for keeping or breeding birds.

More than one third of these vultures had lived in captivity for a considerable length of time, (5-10 years) .................. , of those held in captivity for shorter periods, some were already accustomed to man.

RELEASE CONDITIONS

During the Causses project, only adult pairs were released, ................ in previous raptor introduction programmes immature birds had often been used. This policy was adopted to maximise the chances of settlement and to facilitate the fixing of breeding groups. The first vultures (1981-1982) were all paired adults, the majority of which had been bred in an aviary. They were released in December, at the time of display and sexual pairing.

MONITORING

All individuals were monitored daily. In the initial stages, released vultures were marked with leg bands displaying a plastic letter, but this technique proved to be unsatisfactory ........... identification at distances over 300 m was often difficult, if not impossible. Today, *(8)* .................. , young vultures are marked in the nest with a system of coloured rings which are more easily identifiable. From 1981-1983, all released birds wore radio transmitters (weight 17 gm) fixed to the two central tail feathers[2]. Radio-tracking made it possible to recapture vultures who had landed during their first flights in anomalous sites .................. dense vegetation or steep slopes. After 1983, however, radio tracking was abandoned, for .................... the maximal theoretical range of the transmitters was 20 km, ................. transmission distances proved to be less than 1 km and, ................. , the life span of the transmitters never exceeded 6 months.

ADAPTATION OF RELEASED VULTURES

......................... , during the first few weeks after release, birds presented poor flight abilities. They had considerable difficulty landing and they did not make proper use of the thermal currents rising from the cliffs, ............. wasting a great deal of energy beating their wings to little effect. This high energy cost, combined with the fact they had difficulty feeding, resulted in a certain number of losses; one vulture died after 40 days without food. A further problem was that the birds

| | ***Released birds*** | ***Wild born birds*** | ***Dead birds*** | ***Recaptured birds*** |
|---|---|---|---|---|
| **1980** | 1* | – | – | – |
| **1981** | 10 | – | – | – |
| **1982** | 8 | 1 | 3 | 2 |
| **1983** | 17 | 1 | 1 | 1 |
| **1984** | 11 | 1 | – | 2 |
| **1985** | 12** | 5 | 4 | – |
| **1986** | 2 | 6 | – | – |
| **1987** | – | 12 | 1 | 1 |
| **1988** | – | 10 | 3 | – |
| **1989** | – | 9 | 2 | 1 |
| **1990** | – | 15 | 5 | 1 |
| **1991** | – | 17 | 1 | 1 |
| **total** | 61 | 77 | 20 | 9 |

** This bird escaped from the aviary but returned 3 years later. ** Non-marked birds escaped.*

2 Feather: natural coating, plumage covering birds.

scattered and adults of the same pair sometimes found themselves several kilometres apart.

From 1983 onwards, 2-4 year old birds were released. These birds had been in captivity for less than one year and .................... , they managed to fly much more quickly. Of the 59 birds released, 10 were found dead and 4 were removed from the wild. The main cause of mortality was electrocution.

Migration

There is a tendency among juvenile birds for seasonal migrations in search of areas with high food availability. One 1-year-old bird disappeared in 1985 to return in 1988, while another was found poisoned in North Senegal in 1991. Since 1983, the colony has been enlarged by 9 immigrants coming from Spain and the Pyrenees.

*TALKING POINT*

- There are a growing number of reintroduction programmes for different species. Give examples. What are the main problems involved?

## *5.4. Checkpoints*

In other words

**Definitions – consists of**

Another way of explaining a word is to enumerate the different parts of which it is made:
"X **consists of** Y and Z."

*Example:* a bicycle
*"**Basically**, a bicycle **consists of** a frame and two wheels."*

- *Define two of these words:*
  *the solar system • a zoo • a telescope • water*

Back to basics

**"According to"**

- *Which, if any, of the following sentences are correct?*

**According to** Peter, it will rain tomorrow.
**According to** the first law of thermodynamics, heat and work are inter-convertible.
**According to** me, public transport is underdeveloped.
The prime minister is going to resign **according to** the BBC.

- *Check in the answer section and then give personal opinions about the following:*

  *global warming • third world poverty • the education system • vivisection*

## THE WORD WEB – PREFIXES

▮ *As we have already seen, the lexis can be extended by the use of prefixes and suffixes. Insert the following **negative** prefixes into the sentences: anti- ▪ dis- ▪ im- ▪ in- ▪ ir- ▪ un-.*

1. In fact, Tycho Brahe did not accept the Copernican system. He thought that the Earth was .......... mobile.
2. The coriolis force, which explains the direction of wind patterns, is clockwise in the northern hemisphere and .......... clockwise in the southern hemisphere.
3. Many people who are colour blind are .......... aware of it.
4. Crime statistics are frequently .......... accurate as so many crimes are never reported.
5. The typical .......... abilities of Alzheimer's disease include loss of memory, anxiety and social withdrawal.
6. There is no way of proving it, but it is highly .......... probable that the sun will not rise tomorrow.
7. Before changing any of the components, all electrical equipment should be .......... connected.
8. The development of electronic communication is making distance ............. relevant.
9. According to Greek legend, Odysseus attached himself to his ship because the songs of the Sirens were .......... resistible.
10. Glycol is an ..........freeze, that is to say, it lowers the freezing point.

### *5.5. Web search*

▮ If you are interested in Black holes, big bangs and singularity, try the Stephen Hawking site:

➢ http://www.hawking.org.uk/

▮ For further information about the Griffon vulture contact:

➢ http://www.hawk-conservancy.org/**priors/griffon.htm**

### *Word search*

▮ What are the most important words in the *Key points*? Find examples in context from the web and report back.

## *Self evaluation – exit test*

▌ *Fill in the gaps.*

1. **Be** .................... using rechargeable batteries, what other different ways are there of storing energy? *(apart from)*
2. The combustion of methane can produce an undesirable product, **na** ............. carbon dioxide, which is responsible for global warming. *(that is to say)*
3. **De** .................... its numerous spectacular successes, magnetic resonance imaging is not entirely satisfactory when applied to proteins surrounded by water molecules. *(although it has had ...)*
4. The evidence has often been contradictory, **ne** .......................... , hypnosis is finding numerous medical uses. *(yet)*
5. **As** ......................... , animals who survive in desert habitats tend to be small. *(generally – 3 words)*
6. Oral administration of insulin does not reduce blood sugar, **wh** .................... orally administered corosolic acid can. *(while, on the other hand)*
7. **Ob** ................ , when dealing with toxic and hazardous material, robots offer great advantages. *(clearly)*
8. The gas containers are kept underground, **th** ........... minimising temperature change. *(by that means)*
9. Environmental concerns will **do** .................... increase in the years to come. *(certainly)*
10. The comet travels at 75 kilometres per second, **he** ............. it creates shock waves when it enters the atmosphere. *(consequently)*

# 6. Time – present & past

*An essential function of language is sequencing events – organising data chronologically. This often poses a problem for learners because* ***"time"*** *can be expressed in different ways in different languages. For instance, the English expression* ***"She has been working"*** *may not correspond to any literal, word-for-word translation in another language.*

*The tenses are often accompanied by characteristic* ***time markers*** *– that is to say, adverbs and other expressions which give supplementary information confirming the choice of tense.*

## Self evaluation – entry test

▌ *Put the verbs in brackets into the appropriate tense.*

*Example:*

*Several attempts ............................. to identify the virus.* (already to be made)

→ *Several attempts* ***have already been made*** *to identify the virus.*

1. Biologists ............................................. for a long time that there is some kind of electrical communication system in plants. *(to know)*
2. The researchers .......................................... for the results of the clinical trials. *(now to wait)*
3. Fermi .......................................... as professor of theoretical physics at Rome University for more than 10 years when he was awarded the Nobel Prize. *(to work)*
4. This is the first time scientists ....................................... material on Earth created by recent supernovae. *(to find)*
5. Slowly but surely, the world's rain forests .................................. irrevocably damaged by global warming. *(to be)*
6. As soon as I ....................................... I will telephone you. *(to finish)*
7. Einstein ....................................... in the Soviet Union. *(never to work)*
8. Victims of Alzheimer's disease ............................. from a loss of memory and judgement. *(to suffer)*
9. By 1400 BC, the earliest geographers ................................................. the shores of the Mediterranean Sea. *(already – to map)*
10. It is alleged that the Roman emperor Nero played the violin while the city .......................................... . *(to burn)*

# *Functions & Grammar*

## KEY POINTS – ORGANISING TIME: THE PRESENT & THE PAST

→ *There are four present tenses and four past tenses.*

## PRESENT TIME

### *1. Present simple*

| Example | Meaning |
|---|---|
| *The newspaper **says** ...* | The "general" present. |
| *He likes Ann. She **drinks** coffee.* | Opinions and habits. |
| *She **lives** in Turin.* | The "status quo". |
| *He **leaves** for work at 7 o'clock.* | Habitual actions. |
| *Water **freezes** at 0°C.* | Scientific facts. |

*TYPICAL TIME MARKERS*
*(N.B. – Time markers may be implicit)*

every day · usually · often · sometimes

### *2. Present continuous*

| Example | Meaning |
|---|---|
| *Look! It **is raining**.* | **On-going** present time. |
| *Mary **is trying** to finish her work.* | Actions happening now. |
| ***At the moment**, he **is working** in London.* | **Temporary** actions in the present. |

*TIME MARKERS*

now · at the moment · currently · at present · temporarily

### *3. Present perfect simple*

| Example | Meaning |
|---|---|
| *She **has already finished** her work.* | It is important **now** / a surprise. |
| *He **has broken** his leg.* | The **result** is important – he can't walk **now**. |

| Example | Meaning |
|---|---|
| *I **have just** finished.* | The finishing is part of the **present**. |
| *I **have never been** to Miami.* | In my life – **up to now**. |
| *He **has worked** in Madrid **since** 1999.* | From then **till now** – it is not history. |
| *I **have seen** him twice **this week**.* | The time span is the present – **this** week – not **last** week. |

*TIME MARKERS*

- just G. Notes 13 ▪ recently ▪ already ▪ not yet
- ever ▪ never G. Notes 14 ▪ so far ▪ up to now
- since 1999 ▪ for 3 years
- this week ▪ this month

### *4. Present perfect continuous*

| Example | Meaning |
|---|---|
| *He **has been living** in Paris for several months.* | An **on-going** situation – not yet completed. |
| *They **have been studying** the question **for years**.* | **Non-stop** – up to the present. |
| *She **has been working** in Bordeaux.* | **Temporary** present – up to now. |

*TIME MARKERS*

for 10 years ▪ for a long time ▪ since 1999

## PAST TIME

### *1. Past simple*

| Example | Meaning |
|---|---|
| *I **went** to the cinema last week.* | Past, **finished** actions. |
| *In 1865, Pasteur **discovered** the theory of microbes.* | Dates – **"History"**. |
| *I **saw** her briefly a couple of hours ago.* | Past action considered as **no longer important**. |
| *When I **was** a child ...* | Memories. |

*TIME MARKERS*

yesterday ▪ two days ago ▪ last week ▪
in 1970 ▪ in the 18th century ▪ during the war

## *2. Past continuous*

**Example**

*She **was trying** to finish a letter.*
*While he **was eating** the meal, the TV imploded.*
*At the time, he **was living** in London.*

**Meaning**

Past **duration**.
Two past actions – one **interrupted** by another.
**Temporary** past.

*TIME MARKERS*

while · when

## *3. Past perfect simple*

**Example**

*As soon as he **had finished** his meal, he went out.*

**Meaning**

The **first** of two past events.

*TIME MARKERS*

after · as soon as · when

## *4. Past perfect continuous*

**Example**

*They **had been living** in Cairo for about ten years when the war broke out.*
*He **had been working** on the problem for years.*

**Meaning**

The first of two actions – past action with duration.
Stress on the **action**.

*TIME MARKERS*

when · after · for a long time · during this period

# *Examples in context*

### *THE MEDIA AND MEDICINE*

*The text below discusses the potential dangers of the mediatisation of medical knowledge.*

**starter**

- **Explain to your partner what you understand by "mediatisation".**
- **Give recent examples of mediatisation in medicine.**
- **Positive effects – negative effects?**

- *Draw an arrow connecting the verb and the verb form.*
  *(N.B. – There are passive forms[G. Notes 15] in the text)*
- *Underline the time markers or contexts justifying the verb forms (sometimes the markers are implicit).*

PRESENT SIMPLE ○

PRESENT CONTINUOUS ○

PRESENT PERFECT SIMPLE ○

PRESENT PERFECT CONTINUOUS ○

PAST SIMPLE ○

PAST CONTINUOUS ○

PAST PERFECT SIMPLE ○

○ Breast cancer **kills** – everyone knows that. However, does the message always get across? Over recent years, there has ○ been a certain number of cases which **have** clearly **shown** the danger of the mediatisation of scientific information in the general press.

○ The heated discussion which **is** currently **taking** place concerning the effectiveness of mammography is an important warning for us all. At the beginning of the month, a Danish research ○ team published an article which severely **criticised** six different studies of mammography screening for breast cancer that had been carried out over the last three years. The article maintained ○ that the test groups **had not been** properly **matched** and concluded that the results were virtually worthless. The team, ○ which **has been working** in an area called "evidence based ○ medicine", **aims** to provide independent advice for health care workers.

However, a spokesman for the Imperial Cancer Research Fund said that such alarming reports are potentially very dangerous ○ as women who **were intending** to be screened were likely to change their mind after reading the article. Errors in the protocol of certain research studies do not mean that all previous studies are invalid. He pointed out that so far, the vast majority of large scale ○ studies **have** clearly **demonstrated** that, for women in the 50-70 year age range, early detection of breast cancer can reduce mortality rates by as much as 25 per cent.

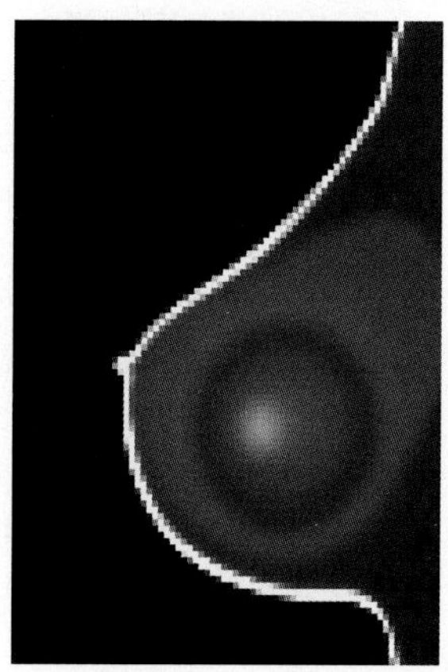

**TALKING POINT**

- Explain to your partner "does the message get across?" (line 1).
- What criticism did the Danish group make of the 6 studies?
- Explain what the Danish group is trying to do.
- Why, according to the Imperial Cancer Research Fund, is the report dangerous?

# Exercises

## 6.1. Exercise

*A. Insert the time markers into the sentences (some can be used in more than one place) and write the tense of the verbs in the column on the right:*

*IT IS A FACT THAT • WHILE • THE NEW SCIENTIST REPORTS THAT • CURRENTLY • PREVIOUSLY • BUT WITH LITTLE SUCCESS SO FAR • THIS YEAR • NOWADAYS • OVER THE LAST 20 YEARS • RECENTLY*

1. A major problem for health authorities is that .............................. rats and mice **are becoming** increasingly resistant to poisons designed to kill them.
2. Two balloonists were killed ...................... **they were carrying** out tests in Australia.
3. Britain **has** ................................ **decided** to relax its restriction on carbon dioxide pollution from 150 to 200 parts per billion.
4. ........................................................ geologists **have managed** to trace the shift of the Earth's magnetic poles by analysing lava deposits.
5. Victor Lorenzo from the National Centre of Biotechnology in Madrid **has been trying** to develop genetically engineered plants to combat toxic metal pollution .......................................................................... .
6. The theory of plate tectonics suggested that the world was older than scientists **had** ...................... **thought**.
7. ........................................................ detergents **dissolve** hydrocarbons, thereby making it easier for bacteria to break them down.
8. The government **is** ................................. **considering** whether to ban the use of depleted uranium in weapons.
9. There **have been** more than 20 cases of cholera reported in the Philippines .................................................... .
10. ...................................................... weather forecasts **have been** gradually **becoming** more accurate thanks to enhanced computers.

*B. This text is based on a job advertisement from the meteorological office. Supply the required tenses.*

The Meteorological Office ........................................ *(to seek)* a highly qualified physicist to join our world renowned research department which ......... ...................................... *(to play)* an essential role in developing key weather forecasting and display systems. Amongst recent projects we .................... ............................. *(to be involved)* in developing an integrated meteorological processing system for Thailand and in configuring display systems for use on Royal Navy ships. Currently, we .................................... *(to work)* on the integration of web technology and geographical information systems and also in the exploitation of data from a new geostationary satellite. Candidates .................................... *(to be expected)* to have excellent communication skills and the ability to work in a team. Preference will be given to those who .................................... *(to have)* at least 2 years' relevant experience in industry.

## *6.2. Sports that kill*

*The violence and danger of certain sports is doubtless what makes them attractive to some. 90% of professional boxers will suffer from brain trauma, while parachutists know that there are no second chances. Now, there appears to be a new sport to be added to the danger list – speleology.*

**starter**

**• What sports are particularly dangerous? Why do people do them?**

- *Read the text once and summarise it to your partner in not more than 4 sentences.*
- *There are 3 verbs in the passive. First mark them with a "P" in the box on the right and indicate the agent (by whom). Then write the tenses and the most appropriate time marker from the list below (markers may be used more than once):*

  *(a) THE FIRST OF TWO PAST ACTIONS • (b) CURRENTLY – AT THE MOMENT • (c) THE ACTION IS PROBABLY NOT FINISHED, IT IS IMPORTANT • (d) USUALLY – AS A RULE • (e) A LAW OF NATURE • (f) A CONTINUOUS PAST ACTION – INTERRUPTED BY ANOTHER ACTION • (g) RECENTLY – THE INFORMATION IS NOT OUT OF DATE • (h) FINISHED – PAST ACTION – SOME TIME AGO*

Speleology is one of those new outdoor sports that **is** 1
**growing** fast in popularity. It **has been estimated** 2
that in the UK alone, more than 20,000 people
practice the sport. However, according to a team of
researchers from Northampton University College
who **have been studying** data on air conditions in 3
underground caverns, the sport could be far more
dangerous than **is** commonly **realised**. The research 4
**was sparked off** when one of the team, who was a 5
keen speleologist, decided, while he **was exploring** a 6
cave, to bring back an air sample to the laboratory for

analysis. After it **had been analysed**, he found to his 7
astonishment that it contained extremely high and dangerous levels of radon gas. The explanation is, in fact, quite simple. Due to the decay of uranium in granite, radio-active gases **form** and, as they cannot 8
escape from the underground caverns, build up to very high concentrations.

The Nottingham team **has shown** that speleologists 9
spending 40 hours per year underground receive radiation doses of up to 4 millisieverts – this is 4 times as high as the annual safety limit. Even worse however, is the situation of guides and instructors. Many of them **have been working** for 10
several years and may spend annually up to 800 hours underground. In such cases, they are likely to have received five times as much as the authorised safety level for radiation workers.

**TALKING POINT**

You will doubtless be surprised to learn that one of the sports with the highest mortality rate in the US is golf.

- Can you suggest an explanation?

## *6.3. Cosmology – past and present*

*There have been three main peaks of achievement in the history of cosmology. The foundations were laid in antiquity when Aristotle, Hipparchus, Ptolemy and others were the first to begin to reason in terms of natural law, to offer mathematical explanations and to propose models.*

■ *Read the text and answer the questions at the end.*

**starter**

- **What three things do you know about Aristotle? – what did he believe about the universe? – what was the contribution to cosmology of Galileo (a), Newton (b)?**
- **Explain to your partner how spectroscopy can aid cosmology.**

It is Aristotle who has probably had the greatest influence on the history of Western science. His decisive contribution was made while he was living in Athens where he set up the "lyceum" (BC 335) after he had returned from Alexandria. It must be remembered that, at the time, the only tools available for scientific research were mathematics and the naked eye. It is, therefore, hardly surprising that certain of his and his contemporaries' ideas proved to be so utterly wrong, for instance, the belief

that the moon was inhabited or that the universe consisted of just the four elements – earth, air, fire and water. Nevertheless, the ancients were also often right. It was they who worked out many of the fundamental notions of cosmology: the causes for eclipses, that the Earth was a sphere, that the orbit of the moon was circular. They even managed to calculate, with a reasonable degree of accuracy, the radius of the Earth – notions that scientists have been using ever since.

One measure of how much Aristotle achieved is that it took almost 1,900 years for the next breakthrough to occur. It was in the 16th and 17th centuries that Copernicus, Galileo and Newton, backed by the powerful new theories of dynamics and gravitation and also, of course, the revolutionary new tool, the telescope, opened up the way for the heliocentric universe. It was the refracting telescope that gave Galileo access to new data showing that the surface of the moon was not smooth and that satellites orbited Jupiter.

Four hundred years later, cosmology **is living** through another golden age. Over the last 80 years, a whole set of new paradigms **has been developed**. The theories of relativity, quantum mechanics and the notion of the expanding universe have opened up new perspectives. At the same time, we now have at our disposal the extraordinary power provided by modern data gathering technology. Spectroscopy, radio astronomy and satellite technology increase the hard data that can be fed into the new models. To take just one example, the Hubble telescope **has** dramatically **enlarged** the universe. The "Hubble deep field" consists of 300 images which **were taken** in 1995 over a period of 10 days. It maps just one small part of the sky, revealing clusters of galaxies stretching back millions and millions of years to when the universe was just 10% of its current age. Never before has so much data been available, never before have the theories been so powerful.

*Hubble deep field*

### QUESTIONS

**1. Paragraph 1**

The theme of the paragraph is cosmology in antiquity. Consequently, nearly all the verbs are in the past tense. However, there are five exceptions – two verbs in the present perfect and three verbs in the present. Find the verbs and explain to your partner:

a) why the present perfect is used;

b) the use of present tense in the middle of the text.

**2. Paragraph 2**

Underline the tenses used. What comment can you make?

**3. Paragraph 3**

Check through the Key points again (p. 70) and associate the verb forms in **bold** with meanings.

## *6.4. Checkpoints*

IN OTHER WORDS

**Definitions – generalisation and clarification**

*Use the following pattern:*
"X is **basically** Y ... **in other words** ... Z ..."

*Example:* a drawback
*"A drawback is **basically** some sort of disadvantage, **in other words**, a weakness."*

- *Give a definition of the following words:*
  *a letter ▪ a drug ▪ a nose ▪ petrol*
- *Look at Exercise 6.3 and find a word that you can define in the same way.*

BACK TO BASICS

**"To transform / to turn"**

- *Answer the questions.*

What does a dynamo do?
(transform / mechanical energy / electrical energy)

.......................................................................................

....................................................................................... .

What did alchemists want to do?
(turn / base metal / gold)

.......................................................................................

....................................................................................... .

- *Check your answers.*
- *Give four examples of transformations (e.g. Fahrenheit ... a nuclear reactor ...)*

## THE WORD WEB – SUFFIXES

- *Form adjectives with the suffixes: -able ▪ -al / -ial ▪ -ful ▪ -ic ▪ -ine ▪ -ish ▪ -ive ▪ -less.*

Diamond is a form of pure *(crystal)* .............................. carbon which has been formed under great heat and pressure and brought to the surface of the Earth by *(volcano)* ........................ activity. It is the hardest *(nature)* ........................ substance in the world with a very high *(refract)* ......................... power giving specific *(optic)* ....................... properties, above all, a particularly clear and brilliant reflection of light.

The most *(value)* ........................ diamonds are completely *(without colour)* ............................ . They are, however, extremely rare; the majority having a *(slightly yellow)* .......................... or *(slightly green)* .......................... colour caused by different mineral impurities and gases. Diamond feels cold to the touch as it dissipates heat very quickly, hence, checking thermal conductivity is a *(rely)* ............................ method of detection. Cheaper synthetic diamonds are now being made for *(industry)* ......................... applications. These are particularly *(use)* ........................ for cutting tools.

### 6.5. Web search

- Make a web search for statistics and information about the dangers of sport. Make a 3 minute OHP presentation.
- What is the latest news on Hubble?

### Word search

- Search the web for 5 examples of the present perfect continuous, using head words such as: STUDYING ▪ WORKING ▪ ATTEMPTING ▪ EXPECTING.

  ➢ *Example : "have been studying"*

  Report back on the context in which the words were found (time markers ...).

## Self evaluation – exit test

- *Supply the most appropriate verb form.*

1. Throughout history, society ........................................... the existence of mental disorders. *(to recognise)*
2. The government ................................................ what action to take when the first soldiers were killed. *(to consider)*
3. You can see the results already. It is quite obvious that the new technology ............................................. the way people think. *(to influence)*

4. By the end of the second World War, they .......................................... airline technology considerably. *(to improve)*
5. At last, after all these years and thanks to satellite photographs, scientists ............................................ the spot where the meteorite fell. *(to identify)*
6. Currently, BP ..................................... for oil in 9 different countries. *(to drill)*
7. So far, no government ....................................................... to ensure full employment. *(to manage)*
8. While they ........................................... the stars of the Milky Way, they accidentally found a new galaxy. *(to study)*
9. Predators ..................... prey and prey .............................. by predators – that is the law of nature. *(to eat – to be eaten)*
10. When, at last, Nero stopped playing his violin, Rome ............................... ............................ . *(to be utterly destroyed)*

# 7. Cause & consequence

*Axiomatically, science is concerned with questions of "Why?", "How?" and "What?" – in other words, with causes and consequences, with reasons and results. These functions can be expressed in a variety of ways, ranging from link words, to verbs and nouns. We have already seen some of these in a different context in Unit 5.*

## Self evaluation – entry test

- *Fill in the gaps.*

  *Example:*

  ***Th** .................... chlorophyll, $CO_2$ is **transformed into** oxygen.* (because of)

  → ***Thanks to** chlorophyll, $CO_2$ is transformed into oxygen.*

1. A superficial interpretation of statistics may **le** ...................... to erroneous conclusions. *(have as a consequence)*
2. The airports are being enlarged, **th** ................... we can expect an increase in the tourist industry. *(consequently)*
3. **Du** ................. rising temperatures, the average thickness of polar ice is only half as much as it was 10 years ago. *(because of)*
4. New data supplied by the human genome project is going to **sp** ................ a revolution in medical research. *(cause, start)*
5. In statistics, when the number of possible **ou** ................... is 0, it indicates that an event will never occur. *(consequences, results)*
6. The accident **re** ....................... two deaths from multiple organ failure. *(had as a consequence)*
7. Lake Geneva is becoming severely deoxygenated during the summer months **ow** .................. the hydroelectric dams built in the upper Rhone. *(because of)*
8. The $CO_2$ produced in respiration is a **by-** ............. of metabolism. *(collateral, secondary result)*
9. In surgical operations, serum rather than plasma is often used **si** .............. it is more readily available. *(because)*
10. New York City has spent $10 million on mosquito control, **th** ................. reducing viral health risks to the population. *(by doing this, thus)*

# Functions & Grammar

## KEY POINTS – CAUSE & CONSEQUENCE

### 1. Adverbs and conjunctions

▮ *Cause*

because of ▪ owing to ▪ due to ▪ on account of ▪ thanks to

➤ ***Owing to*** *his bad health, the minister was forced to resign.*

because ▪ as ▪ since

➤ ***As*** *he was ill, the minister was forced to resign.*

▮ *Consequence*

consequently ▪ therefore ▪ thus ▪ hence ▪ as a result ▪ thereby *G. Notes 11*

➤ *The minister was in bad health,* ***therefore*** *he was forced to resign.*
➤ *The minister resigned,* ***thereby*** *putt****ing*** *the government in difficulty.*

### 2. Verbs

▮ *Cause*

to cause ▪ result in ▪
lead to ▪ be responsible for ▪
bring about ▪ give rise to ▪
trigger (off) ▪ spark (off) *G. Notes 17*

➤ *Illness* ***led to*** *the minister's resignation.*

▮ *Consequence*

to come from ▪ result from ▪
arise from ▪ stem from

➤ *The minister's resignation* ***stemmed from*** *his bad health.*

### *3. Nouns*

▌ *Cause*

cause · reason · origin · source

➢ *The real* ***cause*** *of his resignation was bad health.*

▌ *Consequence*

- consequence · result · outcome · effect
- by-product · spin-off

➢ *The final* ***outcome*** *of the illness was the minister's resignation.*

**starter**

**• Ask your neighbour questions about scanning electron microscopes. How? – what for? – who? – when?**

## *Examples in context*

### *THE SCANNING ELECTRON MICROSCOPE (SEM)*

▌ *Read the description and find synonyms for the words in* ***bold.***

**As** the wavelength of visible light is approximately 4,000 angstrom, this means that there is a lower limit to the resolution of optical microscopes. To obtain higher resolution, shorter wavelengths are required. Electrons used in SEMs have wavelengths of 0.5 angstrom, **hence** it is possible to visualise molecules and even atoms.

Samples cannot be scanned unless they are dry (to prevent vaporisation) and electrically conductive. **As a result**, organic materials must be coated with a metallic layer, such as gold.

**Thanks to** the scanning pattern, a 3-dimensional image of the surface structure can be obtained.

The suggestion that electrons might be regarded as a form of wave motion and used for microscopy **stems from** the work of Louis de Broglie (1924), as an **outcome** of his research into quantum mechanics. The first SEM was built in 1933.

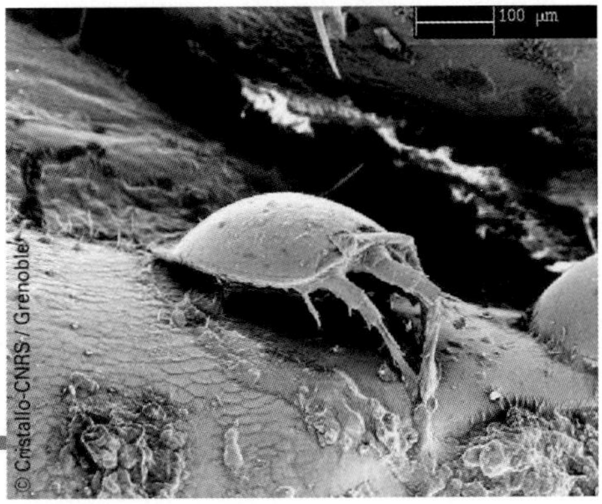


*Dust mite (Acari)*

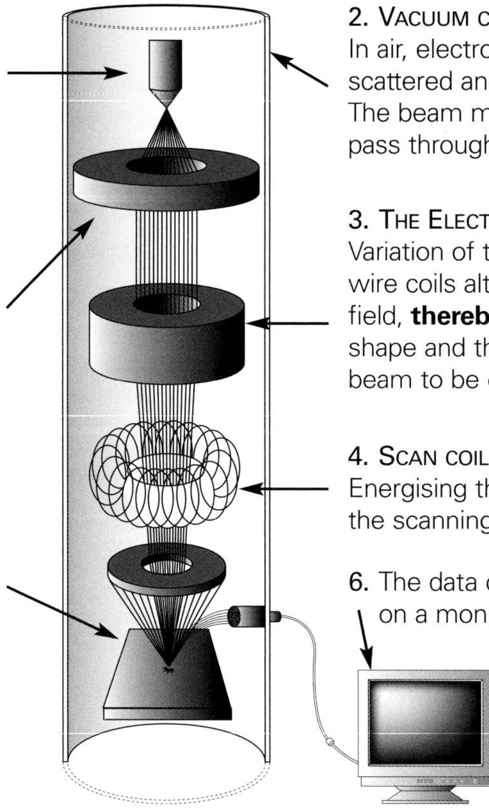

1. THE ELECTRON GUN
This functions as the electron source. A voltage is applied to a tungsten cathode, heating it up and **thus** liberating electrons.

The strong attractive force of the anode **results in** the formation of an electron beam which passes through the anode.

2. VACUUM COLUMN
In air, electrons are ionised, scattered and slowed down. The beam must **therefore** pass through a vacuum.

3. THE ELECTROMAGNETIC LENSES
Variation of the current in the wire coils alters the magnetic field, **thereby** allowing the shape and the focus of the beam to be controlled.

4. SCAN COILS
Energising the coils **triggers** the scanning function.

5. TARGET
The electron beam strikes the target, **giving rise to** interactions and liberating X-rays, back-scattered electrons and secondary electrons.

6. The data can be visualised on a monitor.

# *Exercises*

## *7.1. Exercise*

*A. Match the causes and consequences and insert the appropriate words:* *LEAD TO • HENCE • COMES FROM • OWING TO • ARISES • SINCE • WAS BROUGHT ABOUT • THANKS TO.*

1. The word "alcohol" .........................................
2. Genetic variation .........................................
3. Extra galactic stars are moving away from the Earth .........................................
4. Their numbers will increase .........................
5. Millions of lives have been saved ..................
6. The population explosion will ......................
7. He will certainly be travelling abroad ............
8. The formation of Gondwanaland .................
.........................................................................

a. the discovery of penicillin.
b. the Arabic "al-kuhl", a fine powder used as an eye cosmetic.
c. by the collision of the Earth's tectonic plates.
d. he now works for a petroleum company.
e. there is a red shift in the light. (the Doppler effect)
f. the fact that predators have been eliminated.
g. famine and epidemics throughout the world.
h. when mutations occur in genes and chromosomes.

*B. Complete the sentences.*

1. The increase in temperatures will **lead to** ................................................ ..........................................................................................................

2. As the **outcome** of the experiment was totally unexpected, they ...................... ..........................................................................................................

3. The strike was **sparked off** by ........................................................................ ..........................................................................................................

4. Diseases spread **on account of** ....................................................................... ..........................................................................................................

5. The huge amount of water being withdrawn from the river Jordan **is responsible for** .................................................................................................... ..........................................................................................................

6. The serious shortage of organs to be transplanted has **given rise to** ................ ..........................................................................................................

7. Monkeys, mice and men share a great number of genes. This **stems from** the fact .................................................................................................... ..........................................................................................................

8. One of the **by-products** of a higher standard of living is ............................. ..........................................................................................................

## *7.2. How to zap lightning*

*The Key points are written in* ***bold.***

- *Ask questions about the phrases underlined (i.e. the underlined phrase is the answer to your question).*

**starter**

- **What do you know about Benjamin Franklin – who? – where? – when? What was his famous experiment with electricity?**
- **Explain to your neighbour how lightning works.**

The development of protection systems against lightning strikes is currently arousing renewed interest in the world of physics. The occurrence of lightning and the extent of the damage it **causes** is far greater than is commonly realised, with an estimated 6,000 strikes per minute on the surface of the Earth and with 2 strikes per sq km annually for France. Not surprisingly, much of the financial backing for the research comes from the electricity companies. This **stems from** the fact that the power lines of the electricity grids are particularly vulnerable. Other sensitive sectors, like the nuclear and aviation industries, are also concerned **as** electronic control devices are especially liable to damage. Globally, the cost of lightning is high. It **is** not only **responsible for** thousands of deaths and injuries each year, but also for extensive damage to buildings and it is the **origin** of the majority of forest fires throughout the world.

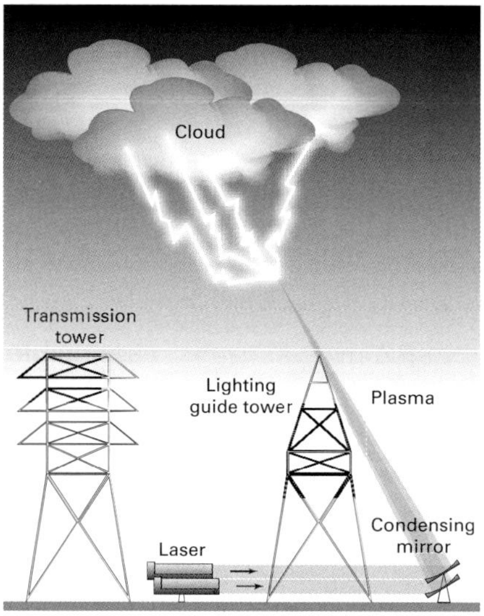


There have been various attempts in the past to address this problem, including the launching of small rockets carrying thin conducting wires. However, the unit cost per rocket is high, the failure rate considerable and furthermore, in densely populated areas, the technique is potentially hazardous. A more promising line of approach appears to be the use of laser technology. One of the important features of laser beams is that on collision with air molecules they displace electrons, **thereby** creating ions. In this way, the laser beam generates a path of ionised plasma which acts as a conductive channel and can **thus** pilot the immense surge of current towards a safe spot on the ground.

Researchers from the Institute for Laser Technology in Osaka, Japan, have recently managed to **trigger** a natural lightning discharge of 20,000 MW. Two carbon dioxide lasers were used, delivering 1 kJ of energy in 50-ns pulses in each beam. In order to protect the system, the beams were reflected by an array of mirrors, while the lightning strike was earthed via the tip of a discharge tower.

Certain problems persist however. When actuating the discharge, timing is critical. **Hence**, it is necessary to have access to extremely accurate real time data with regards to the state of charge of the electric field so that the precise moment of breakdown can be determined.

## *7.3. Blind spots*

**starter**

- **Give five different causes of blindness.**

*Many would say that sight is the most precious sense we have. But, because of our genetic make up, it would seem that it is something that a great many of us are destined to lose.*

▮ *Fill the gaps with the following words:*

*ON ACCOUNT OF • HENCE • RESULTING IN • SINCE • OUTCOME • STEMS FROM • BY-PRODUCT • TRIGGER • THUS • IS BROUGHT ABOUT*

Age-related macular degeneration (AMD) is a degenerative disease affecting the central portion of the retina, known as the macula. The macula, which has a diameter of no more than 5-6 mm, plays an essential role in vision, ..................... it has the highest concentration of photoreceptive cells and is the part of the retina used for detailed vision and reading.

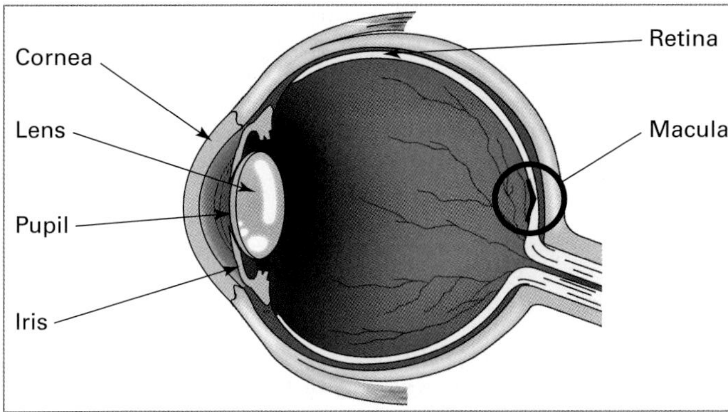


High density of light sensitive nerve cells. Degeneration reduces central vision required for reading, driving, etc.

AMD affects primarily people over the age of 60. It is estimated that, world-wide, between 25 and 30 million suffer from AMD, with a 30% risk of getting the disease by the age of 75. Inevitably, ....................................... the ageing population, the ratio is particularly high in the developed countries.

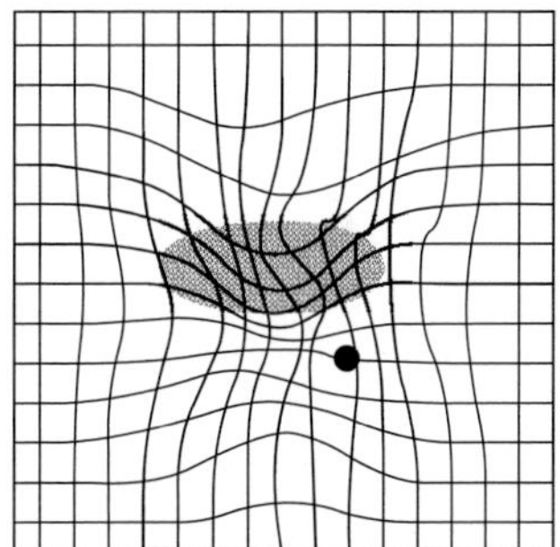

*Visual distorsion*

There are basically two forms of AMD. The most common form is "Dry AMD", which ........................ a failure of the retinal pigment, epithelium, to evacuate nutrients and wastes, called "drussen". These accumulate in the form of yellowish retinal deposits as a ........................... of the conversion of light into nerve signals and so prevent the photoreceptors from functioning properly. This form of the disease is relatively mild, ...................... there is only slight visual loss.

The incidence of "Wet AMD" is, by contrast, considerably lower, corresponding to less than 10% of the cases. It ............................................ by the pathological development of new blood vessels (neovascularisation) beneath the retinal tissue.

*Blind spots in the central cone*

This proliferation can .......................... certain harmful consequences, including haemorrhages which burst through the retinal layer and leak blood or fluid into the retina. The retinal surface is ............... deformed and the photoreceptors and macula are damaged .............................. blind spots of the central cone of vision and significant visual loss through distortion. The final ............................ is that patients are no longer able to read, to drive a car or even to recognise familiar faces.

**TALKING POINT**

Answer the questions without consulting the text.
- Why is the macula so important for vision?
- Why will the cases of AMD increase?
- What are the causes of dry AMD?
- What is neovascularisation and its results?

## 7.4. Checkpoints

**IN OTHER WORDS**

**Definitions – defining professions**

*Use the following pattern:*
"An X is **a person whose job is to** do Y ..."

*Example:* a banker
*"A banker **is a person whose job is** to run a bank."*

- *Define two of the following words:*
  *a manager ▪ a dentist ▪ a biologist ▪ an electrician*
- *Make two more definitions of your own.*

**BACK TO BASICS**

**"To raise / to rise – to lay / to lie"**

- *These word pairs are often confused. Complete the sentences with the correct verb (present tense only).*

1. The doctor told the patient to ................ on her side.
2. They decided to .................. the temperature in the incubator.
3. Please, will you .................. the book on the table?
4. As the gas gets hotter, the balloon slowly ............. .
5. It was Mendel (1822-1884) who helped to ............. the foundations of modern genetics.
6. The results ...................... a number of interesting questions.
7. If the temperature .................. , the average speed of the molecules is increased.
8. It is up to you – the decision ................. with you.

- *Suggest an explanation to distinguish the pairs and then check in G. Notes 18.*

### The word web – verb formation

- *Prefixes like "over- • under- • un-" can be used to modify the meanings of verbs. Here, they express the notions of "too much", "not enough", "not at all".*
  *Example:* *Natural resources may be **over**exploited, **under**exploited or **un**exploited.*

1. The photograph was almost white. It had been ................ **exposed**.
2. Low farm prices are a direct consequence of ................ **production**.
3. Cancer is characterised by ................ **checked** cell growth, leading to tumours that damage the surrounding tissue.
4. If the hypothalamus is damaged, the rat will ............ **eat** and become obese.
5. Some educationalists claim that unless exceptionally intelligent children are put in special classes, they will ................... **achieve**.
6. Liberal economists maintain that there are too many ................ **employed** workers in the public sector.
7. Leonardo da Vinci has a reputation as artist and scientist ................ **matched** by any other man.
8. Human beings have a tendency to ................ **estimate** to what extent their ideas are their own.
9. A direct cause of the Bhopal catastrophe in India was that the operating procedures were sub-standard and the plant was chronically .............. **staffed**.

### 7.5. Web search

- The geography of lightning. Consult:
  ➢ http://science.nasa.gov/ (enter < lightning geography > as search words)
- Find out ways of treating AMD:
  ➢ http://www.macula.org**/treatment/index.html**

### Word search

- What are the 6 most important words in Units 5-7 (*Key points*)? Search the web for *Examples in context* and make a 6-question test for your partner along the lines of the *Entry tests*.

## Self evaluation – exit test

- *Fill in the blanks.*

1. Ceramics are well-suited to resisting heat **ow** ................ the strong chemical bonds that hold them together. *(thanks to)*
2. The molecules move less and **th** .......................... take up less space. *(thus)*

3. The new laws will inevitably **sp** ........................ a controversy. *(cause, start)*
4. To a certain extent, Freud's theory **st** ........................ from his observations of dreams. *(originated in, arose from)*
5. Theoretical research into lasers has had considerable **sp** .................. for eye surgery. *(positive consequence)*
6. The disease **ar** ................ from a developmental failure in the brain. *(has as its origin)*
7. Before the discovery of antiseptics, the **ou** .................. of surgical operations was very often fatal. *(result)*
8. It was the development of more advanced stone tools that **tr** ........................ the first human migration out of Africa, 1.7 million years ago. *(caused, started)*
9. Unless it is checked in some way, the virus will ultimately **br** .................... the death of the host cells. *(be responsible for, cause)*
10. The current rate of deforestation is having a direct **ef** ............. on wildlife. *(consequence)*

# 8. HYPOTHESIS

*A fact is something certain. It can be proved. It exists. Science, however, is not only concerned with what is already known, it is also very much concerned with what remains to be discovered. Exploring zones of doubt and ambiguity, making hypotheses and building models are essential functions of scientific activity.*

***Hypothesis** can be expressed in three main ways:*

- *by conditionals,*
- *through the use of certain conjunctions, adverbs and verbs,*
- *by modals (see Unit 9).*

*In this section, we focus on the different forms and uses of the conditional. Conditionals link two ideas – a hypothetical cause and its result.*

*Compare:* ➤ *I gave her some medicine when she was ill.*
➤ ***If** she was ill, I **would** give her some medicine.*

*In the first sentence, the illness is a fact. In the second it is only a hypothesis. In the first sentence the patient gets some medicine. In the second, she doesn't.*

## Self evaluation – entry test

▮ *Supply a suitable verb form or conjunction.*

*Example:*

*If oil prices increased, air travel ......................... more expensive.* (to become)

→ *If oil prices increased, air travel **would** become more expensive.*

1. If water is boiled, it ...................................... into steam. *(to be transformed)*
2. The U.S. Geological Survey predicted that if the stress on the San Andreas fault increased, there ........................... an earthquake of magnitude 5.5 to 6. *(to be)*
3. According to Morrison, the dinosaurs would not have become extinct if an asteroid ........................................... with the Earth. *(not to collide)*
4. If the red light begins to flash, it .................................. that the machine has overheated. *(to mean)*
5. Provided the smoke has been detected, the alarm ........................... . *(to go off)*
6. If you went by plane, the journey ............................ less than an hour. *(to take)*
7. As soon as phosphorus is exposed to ultraviolet light, it .................................. luminescent. *(to become)*
8. If Galileo had not withdrawn his claims, he ............................................. . *(to be burned)*
9. You must follow the instructions carefully, otherwise there ............................... an accident. *(to be)*
10. ............. you oxygenate the water, those fish will die. *(if you do not)*

# *Functions & Grammar*

## KEY POINTS – CONDITIONALS

### *1. Verb forms*

→ There are four different forms of the conditional.

▌ *The timeless conditional*

*IF + PRESENT / PRESENT PERFECT + PRESENT*

➢ ***If*** *water* ***boils****, it* ***produces*** *steam.*
➢ ***If*** *water* ***has boiled****, it* ***is*** *safe to drink.*

**Meaning**

Conditions which are **invariably true** – therefore timeless.
Typically, this form is used to express **scientific facts** and **logical links**.

▌ *The first conditional*

*IF + PRESENT / PRESENT PERFECT + FUTURE (WILL)*

➢ ***If*** *you boil the water, it* ***will produce*** *steam.*
➢ ***If*** *the low atmospheric pressure* ***continues****, there* ***will*** *be rain.*

**Meaning**

**Potential** future events and situations.
Used for **predictions**, **potential consequences** and **warnings**.

▌ *The second conditional*

*IF + PAST + CONDITIONAL (WOULD)*

➢ ***If*** *it* ***snowed****, she* ***would*** *not come.*
➢ ***If*** *I* ***had*** *more money, I* ***would*** *help you.*

**Meaning**

**Speculation**, **unreal** or **imaginary situations** which are not very likely to happen.
N.B. – The difference between the first and the second conditional is **not** a difference in time – it is a difference in the **probability** of the **condition**.

### The third conditional

*IF + PAST PERFECT + PAST CONDITIONAL (WOULD HAVE + P.P.)*

- ***If*** *Napoleon* ***had invaded*** *England, French* ***would have become*** *the language of science.*
- *He* ***would have*** *avoided the accident if he* ***had left*** *earlier.*

**Meaning**

Reference to events and results in the past that **did not occur** because the conditions were **not fulfilled** [G. Notes 19].

## 2. Conjunctions

→ "If" is not the only conjunction used to introduce conditions.

*POSITIVE CONDITIONS*

if · provided / -ing · on condition that

*NEGATIVE CONDITIONS*

unless · otherwise

- *We will go swimming tomorrow* ***unless*** *it rains.*

## 3. Lexical expressions

→ There is a restricted number of lexical expressions which can have a conditional meaning.

- a requirement · a prerequisite
- to depend on · to require
- it is necessary · essential

- *My visit* ***depends on*** *the weather.* (if the weather is bad, I won't come)
- *Hygienic conditions are a* ***prerequisite*** *for surgical intervention.*

## *Examples in context*

### *CLIMATE CHANGE*

**starter**

**• Give some examples of phenomena which seem to indicate that the climate is changing.**

▮ *Look at the examples and add hypotheses of your own (try changing the order, using negative and interrogative forms).*

*A.* ***Timeless conditionals*** *– scientific statements and logical propositions*

*Australia is the driest continent. Some biologists claim that water requirements for agriculture are exhausting the soil and the country is heading for ecological collapse.*

**If** there **is** a shortage of rain, deserts **spread**.
**If** vegetation **dies**, the wind **erodes** the soil.

............................................................

............................................................

............................................................

............................................................

Christiane Guiraudie

Sifoto

*B.* ***First conditional*** *– predictions, warnings*

*The effects of global warming are particularly visible in the Arctic.*

**If** the temperature **does not stop** rising, the **icebergs will melt**. The albedo[1] **will decrease** if the ice cap **becomes** smaller.

............................................................

............................................................

............................................................

............................................................

*C.* ***Second conditional*** *– speculation, imaginary situations*

*Motor vehicles cause greenhouse gases. It has been suggested that the only solution is for the government to drastically restrict the use of private cars.*

1 Albedo: proportion of light reflected from the (Earth's) surface.

**If** the use of private cars **was** restricted, the tourist **industry would collapse**. Most of the out-of-town supermarkets **would close if** car travel **was** forbidden.

.....................................................

.....................................................

.....................................................

.....................................................

.....................................................

D. ***Third conditional –***
*past events that did not occur*

They **would** probably **have adapted** better **if** their brains **hadn't been** so small. **Would** the Dinosaurs **have survived if** the climate **had not changed**?

.....................................................

.....................................................

.....................................................

.....................................................

.....................................................

.....................................................

## *Exercises*

### *8.1. Exercise*

*A. Explain the difference in meaning between the two sentences to your partner.*

1. a) If **you get** a Nobel prize, **you receive** a gold medal, a diploma and a large sum of money.
   b) If **you get** a Nobel prize, **you will receive** a gold medal, a diploma and a large sum of money.

2. a) If the anti-pollution measures **become** law, cars **will be** more expensive.
   b) If anti-pollution measures **became** law, cars **would be** more expensive.

3. a) If oil **was discovered** in Ireland, the standard of living **would change**.
   b) If oil **had been discovered** in Ireland, the standard of living **would have changed**.

*B. Conditional chains*

*Example:*

If the vein was blocked ................

**a)** If the vein was blocked, there **would** be a lack of oxygen in the brain.

↳ **b)** If there **was** a lack of oxygen in the brain, the cells **would** die.

↳ **c)** If the cells **died**, you **would** be paralysed.

▮ *Choose the hypothesis that you find most interesting **(only one)** and write a chain of consequences.*

***1. TIMELESS CONDITIONALS***
*(logic and scientific propositions)*

If animals have no predators ... ▪ If babies cry ... ▪ If the wind is too strong ...

a) If ..............................................................................................................

b) If ..............................................................................................................

c) If ..............................................................................................................

***2. FIRST CONDITIONAL***
*(future events, predictions, warnings)*

If you switch on the heater ... ▪ If people eat too much ... ▪ If urban pollution increases ...

a) ..............................................................................................................

b) ..............................................................................................................

c) ..............................................................................................................

***3. SECOND CONDITIONAL***
*(speculation, imaginary situations)*

If I was unemployed ... ▪ If ice did not float ... ▪ If they set up a space station on the moon ...

a) ..............................................................................................................

b) ..............................................................................................................

c) ..............................................................................................................

***4. THIRD CONDITIONAL***
*(past events which did not occur)*

If I had been born in Ethiopia ... ▪ If iron had never been discovered ... ▪ If Columbus had not discovered America ...

a) ..............................................................................................................

b) ..............................................................................................................

c) ..............................................................................................................

*C. Rewrite the sentence using a conditional. Indicate in the box which sort of conditional you have used, e.g. timeless, 1st conditional, 2nd conditional or 3rd conditional. N.B. – Avoid using modals (must / could, etc.).*

1. It was Malthus who pointed out that there was a link between population growth and the danger of famine.
   Malthus warned that if the population continued to grow, *(there to be)* ......................................................... .
2. To become a member of the Antarctic research team, it is imperative to be single.
   You have to be single if *(to want)* ................................
   ......................................................................... .
3. The continued production of progesterone by the ovaries depends on fertilisation taking place.
   Provided fertilisation occurs, *(the ovaries)* ....................
   ......................................................................... .
4. You didn't get the job for one reason; you hadn't got enough work experience.
   If you had had more work experience, *(you)* .................
   ......................................................................... .
5. Selection to go on a Russian space mission entails learning Russian.
   If you were chosen for the space mission, *(to have to)* .......
   ......................................................................... .
6. Millions of people were saved thanks to Penicillin.
   Unless they had developed Penicillin, *(to die)* ................
   ......................................................................... .
7. Pasteur realised that the destruction of micro-organisms depended on heating milk to 57°C.
   Pasteur realised that if milk was heated, *(to be destroyed)*
   ......................................................................... .
8. Pterosauria had very primitive wings. Scientists assume that they lived on cliffs by the sea as this is the only way to explain that they learned to fly.
   Unless they had lived by the sea, Pterosauria *(not to learn)*
   ......................................................................... .

## *8.2. Near Earth Objects*

**starter**

**• What is the difference between an asteroid and a comet?**

*Life on Earth cannot last for ever. Sooner or later, either the Sun will cool, or more dramatically, the Earth will be destroyed by a collision with an object from outer space.*

- *Locate the 4* ***timeless conditionals*** *in the text.*
- *Reformulate the phrases in* ***bold*** *using a* ***negative 3rd conditional.***
  *Example: If they* ***had not*** *spott****ed*** *the asteroid, they* ***would*** *not* ***have raised*** *the alarm.*

In 1997, astronomers reported that an asteroid 1.5 km across might come into collision with the Earth in the year 2028. Fortunately, **this warning turned out to be a false alarm**, but the outcome was that it sparked off research at an international level into NEOs, (Near Earth Objects). **A task force was set up by the UK government** with three main directives. First of all, it was to attempt to identify the facilities required for obtaining reliable data to improve our understanding of the nature of NEOs and to assess the likelihood of a collision. Secondly it was to examine the feasibility of potential counter-measures and finally, it was to make recommendations of how international co-operation might best be facilitated. The following text is an extract from the final report.

Asteroids and comets consist of the remains and debris of the formation of the solar system about 4.5 billion years ago and range in size from small stones to rocky or icy masses nearly 1,000 kilometres across. If the trajectory of an asteroid or a comet intersects the orbit of the Earth or is within 0.3 Astronomical Units, (1 AU = distance Earth-Sun) it is labelled as a "NEO". It is not, however, classified as "potentially hazardous", unless it comes within 0.05 AU (7.5 million kilometres) of the Earth and its diameter attains 150 m. So far, 258 potentially hazardous objects have been located.

*Eros*
*a 33 km long asteroid*

Asteroids are made up of different carbonaceous materials, rocks (silicates) or metal. In structure, they may be solid masses of stone or iron, or comprised of clusters of rocks held together only by their own weak gravitational forces. They are not spherical in shape and may spin as they travel.

Comets, on the other hand, consist essentially of dust-covered ice. If their trajectory brings them close to the sun, the gases evaporate, freeing dust, and thus forming the tail which can sometimes be seen with the naked eye. The numbers and dimensions of NEOs can be worked out, either directly, using data gathered from ground-based telescopes or, alternatively, it can be derived from calculations based on crater impacts on the Moon or the planet Mercury.

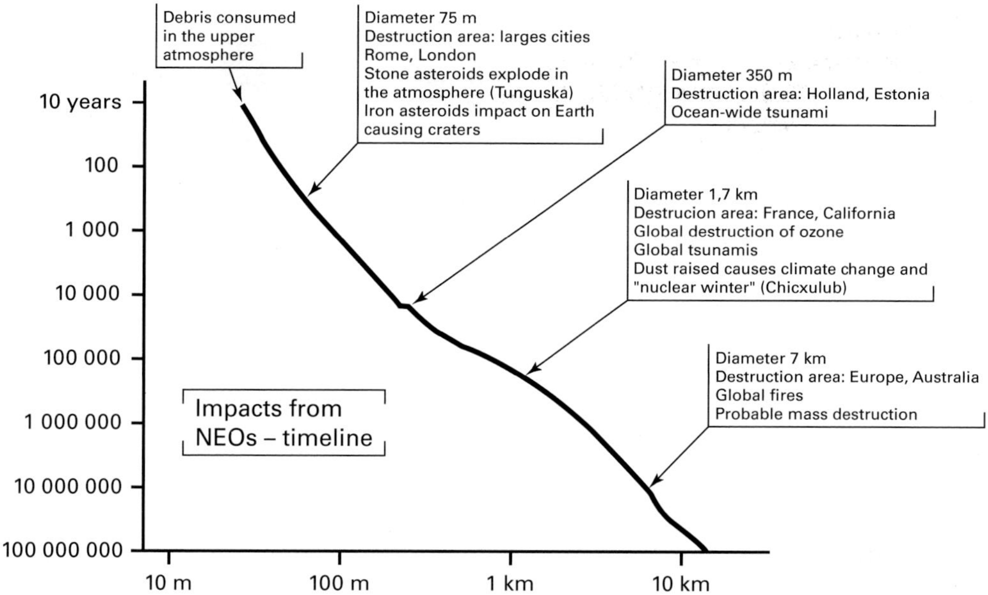


Since its formation, four and a half billion years ago, the Earth has been subject to a non-stop stream of debris from outer space. Daily, hundreds of tonnes of dust enter the upper atmosphere and each year, larger objects of a few meters in diameter do likewise. Provided they have sufficient mass, these objects may reach the ground before being consumed and therefore, are potentially hazardous. Every century or so, there are bigger impacts whose destructive capacity is proportional to their mass (see figure).

The best known are the impacts that allegedly caused the extinction of the dinosaurs 65 million years ago (Chicxulub, Mexico) and, more recently, the Tunguska blast in 1908, **which fell in the middle of the Siberian forest**, flattening 2,000 sq km, an area equivalent to greater London. It should not be forgotton however, that this bombardment of Near Earth Objects **is one of the prerequisites to life on Earth**, for without the carbon and water from space, there could be no life as we know it on our planet.

TALKING POINT

- As a class, find five different things that you would like to know about NEOs.

## 8.3. Tomorrow's technology

*What is the most important question of all? Doubtless, "What will the future be like?". In a recent issue of the "Technology Review" from the Massachusetts Institute of Technology the editors listed areas of emerging technology that they believe will have the greatest impact during the next decade.*

**starter**

**• What is your guess for the future? Suggest one or two interesting social changes resulting from new technology that might happen in the next 20 or 30 years.**

▮ *What does progress depend on? Rephrase the words in **bold**. Use the first conditional (PRES + WILL) and the following conjunctions in turn: UNLESS • PROVIDED • OTHERWISE • ON CONDITION THAT.*
*Example: **Unless** they **develop** better algorithms, the project **will** fail.*

### ① BRAIN-MACHINE INTERFACES

Implanting sensors in the cortex will open the way to the interpretation of electrical activity so that thought processes can be converted into actions.

RESEARCH REQUIREMENTS
• Improved algorithms for interpreting electrical activity in the brain.
• Progress also depends on the development of **reliable and safe implant techniques**.

POTENTIAL USES – Brain-machine interfaces would allow disabled or paralysed people to control wheel-chairs, write e-mails, etc. In the long term, accurate control of artificial arms should be possible.

### ② BIOMETRICS

Biometrics is concerned with developing systems that can recognise unique biological features so that individuals can be reliably identified.

RESEARCH REQUIREMENTS
• More sophisticated search algorithms and pattern recognition software will be needed.
• **Huge data bases will have to be set up** and storage capacity developed.

POTENTIAL USES – Current identification methods are not secure for electronic transactions. Biometric software can already identify finger prints, retinal patterns, voice patterns, and facial features. In the near future, digital codes and other passwords could be replaced by biometric identification.

### ③ MICROPHOTONICS

Photonic crystals and photons can be compared to semiconductors and electrons. Depending on the wavelengths and the design of the crystal, they can be used to bend, to split or to reunite photons. As these crystals do not scatter or absorb light, they are significantly faster and more efficient.

RESEARCH REQUIREMENTS
• Identification and cheap synthesis of electro-optical polymers which have the appropriate physical properties.
• **Improved amplification and signal regeneration techniques will also be required.**

POTENTIAL USES – The fibre optics network for telecommunications is on the point of saturation. Transmitting data at speeds approaching that of light means that a 1,000 times as much data could be transmitted.

### ④ MICROFLUIDICS

This field is concerned with research at the level of the nano or picolitre. Once understanding has been attained at a micro-scale, many basic functions of analysis, synthesis and diagnosis could be done automatically.

RESEARCH REQUIREMENTS
The main prerequisites for progress in this area are :
• Improved interfaces.
• **A breakthrough in chip miniaturisation.**

POTENTIAL USES – High speed analysis of DNA, automatic analysis and synthesis, detection of gene mutation and drug-delivery techniques.

TALKING POINT

- Which of the above-mentioned technologies do you find least / most interesting? Why?

## 8.4. Checkpoints

IN OTHER WORDS

**Definitions – if + then**

*Use the following pattern:*
"**If you want** to do X, **then you** use Y."

*Example:* a credit card
*"**If you want to** withdraw money from the bank, **then you use** a credit card."*

- *Define these words:*
  *a map ▪ a fax ▪ a switch ▪ a parachute*
- *Make two definitions of your own.*

BACK TO BASICS

**"Hard / hardly"**: are you sure you know what these words mean?

- *Write an example of each, showing the different meanings.*
- *In what ways are these words different from each other?*
- *Check in the answer section.*

THE WORD WEB – VERBS MEANING "PERFORM"

- *The verbs "DO ▪ MAKE ▪ TAKE" can all have the meaning of* **perform***. But which word should be used? It depends on the context.*
  *Example: He .................. a major* **error** *in his calculations. (made)*

1. Much more information is required before any **action** can be .................. .
2. They have .................. **arrangements** for another meeting early next month.
3. Most of the **damage** was .................. by the fire that followed the explosion.
4. We are getting nowhere. We must .............. a completely different **approach**.
5. There is very **little** that can be .................. to reduce the danger of floods.
6. The sonic boom is caused by the **noise** .................. by the shock wave.
7. It is the government's responsibility to ........... **something about** the shortage of skilled workers.
8. Enormous **progress** has been .................. in metallurgy over the last 50 years.
9. The government is .................. **measures** to improve food safety.

### *8.5. Web search*

- Find a graph on the web and make a 3 minute OHP presentation showing
  - either: future patterns and tendencies (2nd conditional),
  - or: past developments (3rd conditional).
- Find answers for the 5 questions you asked in Exercise 8.2 (*Talking point*). You could try the British National Space Centre:

  ➢ http://www.nearearthobjects.co.uk/ (select FAQs)

  or alternatively, the NASA FAQs:

  ➢ http://neo.jpl.nasa.gov/**faq.html**

### *Word search*

- If you made a mistake with "hard / hardly" (*Back to basics*), find four contrastive samples from the web.

## *Self evaluation – exit test*

- *Either replace the "if" forms by appropriate terms, or write in the required tense for the verbs.*

1. The radiation level is not dangerous ......................... protective clothing is worn. *(if)*
2. If the water .............................. within 24 hours, there will be little danger of contamination. *(to be pumped out)*
3. The report warned that the Yellow River ............................ if they continued to irrigate on this scale. *(to dry up)*
4. She agreed to come, but only on ........................ that they paid the travelling expenses. *(if)*
5. If passengers had worn seat belts there ............................................. half the number of road deaths last year. *(to be)*
6. If a pilot undergoes a force of 4 g for more than a few seconds, the resulting symptoms ..................... from visual troubles to total loss of consciousness. *(to range)*
7. Repairs carried out by the crew would have been impossible if the experiment ...................................... on an unmanned spacecraft. *(to take place)*
8. No one knew whether the epidemic ................................. or not. *(to spread)*
9. Heat generation will be so great that it will lead to thermal shock ................ high quality ceramics are employed. *(if not)*
10. The subject must be willing to co-operate, ....................... hypnotic trances seldom occur. *(if not)*

# 9. MODALITY

*In the previous unit we looked at how conditionals are used to express doubt and hypothesis. Another linguistic tool used for this function is modality. The modals are a small set of auxiliaries which behave quite differently from other verbs and convey a different sort of information. Unlike most verbs, modals do not refer to facts about the real world but give the speaker's **opinion** as to the **possibility, probability**, and **expectancies** of a given situation or action.*

*As always in language, there are alternative ways of expressing modality, including adjectives, adverbs and non-modal verbs.*

## Self evaluation – entry test

▮ *Choose the most appropriate term.*

1. X-rays are potentially dangerous and .................... be used on pregnant women.
   **a.** will not **b.** could not **c.** might not **d.** should not
2. In 1555, Nostradamus predicted the end of the world for AD 3797. Most people think this is ................ .
   **a.** expected **b.** feasible **c.** unlikely **d.** doubtless
3. If there is a reduction of the area of the habitat, a forest .................... lose up to 50% of its species.
   **a.** ought to **b.** must **c.** may **d.** expects to
4. The best acoustic qualities require natural sound. That is why, ideally, recording studios .................. be designed to have a normal degree of echo.
   **a.** may **b.** might **c.** could **d.** ought to
5. An intoxicated person is 4.5 times as .................... to die in a motor-vehicle accident as the statistical mean.
   **a.** possible **b.** expected **c.** feasible **d.** likely
6. Most scientists now agree that the extinction of the dinosaurs .................................... caused by an asteroid impact.
   **a.** is expected to have been **b.** must have been **c.** would have been **d.** might have been
7. It ..................... be realised that the conventional segregation of zoology and botany is meaningless as many lower organisms are neither plants nor animals.
   **a.** should **b.** may **c.** will **d.** could
8. As oil becomes scarcer, there .......................... be an increase in prices.
   **a.** expects to **b.** will doubtless **c.** might **d.** can
9. The estimation of the total number of species that exist in the world varies enormously. Some say there ................ be 100 million, others suggest 5 million.
   **a.** can **b.** should **c.** would **d.** might

→ *In the following example all the answers are correct. Explain the different meanings.*

10. The computer has crashed, it .............................. ......................................... due to a short circuit.
    **a.** must have been **b.** may have been **c.** could have been **d.** is

# *Functions & Grammar*

## KEY POINTS – MODALITY

### *1. The meaning of modals*

- Modals are a special category of words. They include: **can / could**, **may / might**, **must**, **will / would**, **should / ought to**.
- Most modals have at least 2 meanings – a simplified presentation is given below *G. Notes 21*.
- Modals give a different sort of information from other verbs. In an ordinary verb phrase when you say "The volcano has erupted" you are giving information about the **volcano**. With modals, the information is not about the **action**, it tells us whether the **speaker** estimates that the action is **probable**, **possible**, or **advisable**.

  ➢ *The volcano **may** erupt.* (I think there is a 50% chance of this happening)
  ➢ *The inhabitants **should** leave the valleys.* (I think it would be a good idea)

■ *WILL*

➢ *The sun **will** rise at 5.32 tomorrow.* (this is a fact – there is no possible doubt)

**Meaning** – Total certitude about a future event – probability "100%".
**cf.** – It is certain …

■ *MUST*

➢ *There **must** be ice on the moon.* (I am convinced, but I have no proof)
➢ *She's absent – she **must** be ill.* (it is the only logical explanation)

**Meaning** – Almost total certitude – probability "90%".
**cf.** – I am almost sure …

■ *MAY*

➢ *The volcano **may** erupt next year.* (perhaps it will erupt, perhaps it won't)

**Meaning** – There is a reasonable chance – probability "50%".
**cf.** – Perhaps … maybe …

■ *MIGHT*

➢ *It **might** erupt next year. (it is possible, but I would be rather surprised)*

**Meaning** – The difference between **might** and **may** is slight in modern English. However, **might** frequently expresses the notion of "reduced probability". That is why it is often followed by "but …" – probability "25%".
**cf.** – Perhaps, but … it is just possible …

**▮ *SHOULD / OUGHT TO***

- *You **should / ought to** help old ladies cross the road.* (if you are a good person)
- *You **should** turn off the electricity at night.* (if not, you will waste electricity)
- *You **should** read this book.* (it is a good book – it would be a mistake not to read it)
- *The letter **should** arrive tomorrow.* (if nothing abnormal happens)

**Meaning** – The primary meaning of **should / ought to** is **"what is right, good, normal"**.
**cf.** – It would be a good idea … it is advisable / desirable … it is to be expected / if nothing goes wrong … normally / theoretically / in principle …

**▮ *CAN***

- *Satellites **can** detect objects with a diameter of 10 cm.* (it is feasible, technically possible …)
- *He **can** speak German.* (he has the capacity, the knowledge …)
- *He **can't** answer the question.* (it is too difficult …)

**Meaning** – Unlike the previous examples, **can** and **could** do not express **probability**, but **feasibility** – what is physically, technically or intellectually possible. The feasibility is 100%.
**cf.** – To be able to … to succeed in …

**▮ *COULD***

- *A short-circuit **could** be responsible for the break-down.* (there are several possible causes – this is one of them)

**Meaning** – **Could** expresses the idea that something is technically possible, but that it will not necessarily happen. It is just one hypothesis.
**cf.** – It is a possibility … perhaps … maybe …

**N.B.**

*The distinctions in meaning between "could", "may" and "might" are very small. In practice, when speaking of probability and possibility, they are used almost interchangeably.*

- *Someone is knocking on the door. It **may / might / could** be the postman.*

### *2. Future and past time*

- **The future –** As modals give the speaker's assessment of the situation at the time of speaking, they can be used to talk about the future.
  - ➤ *He may get a job in Turin next year.* (I think **now** that there is a reasonable chance of this happening **next year**)
- **The past –** Past modality is expressed by using the past infinitive.

| *SUBJECT* + | *MODAL* + | *HAVE* + | *PAST PARTICIPLE* | |
|---|---|---|---|---|
| She | **must** | **have** | **telephoned** | last night. |
| He | **could** | **have** | **come** | yesterday. |
| She | **may** | **have** | **finished** | already. |

### *3. Alternative expressions*

to suppose • assume • to presume • to expect

it is probable • possible • feasible • likely / unlikely • doubtless / doubtful

➤ *The introduction of screening procedures for all donors means that infection through blood transfusion is now extremely **unlikely**.*

➤ *In classical physics, it was **assumed** that all observers obtained identical measurements.*

## *Examples in context*

### *THE POWER OF THE RISING SUN*

*Not only do fossil fuels threaten the biosphere, but in time, they will inevitably run out. Governments are, at last, beginning to take much more seriously the need to replace them by alternative forms of energy.*

**starter**

- **What do you think are the most promising alternative fuels today?**

▌ *Read the text and then match the modal forms (in **bold**) with the most appropriate description:*

*(a) IT IS NOT TO BE EXCLUDED, THERE IS SOME CHANCE OF THIS • (b) THIS SEEMS TO BE THE ONLY POSSIBLE EXPLANATION • (c) IT IS FEASIBLE • (d) IT IS CERTAIN • (e) PERHAPS • (f) IT IS A TECHNICALLY ACCEPTABLE HYPOTHESIS • (g) IN PRINCIPLE*

Faced with the problem of ensuring future energy supplies, the Japanese Ministry of Economy, Trade and Industry (METI) plans to launch a geostationary orbiting solar power station to collect solar energy to be transmitted back to Earth. They believe that operations **can** start by 2040.

The Space Solar Power System **will** be placed in orbit at an altitude of 36,000 km and weigh 20,000 tonnes. It is to be equipped with 2 solar panels, 3 km in length and 1 km wide and will be capable of generating 1 gigawatt of energy. The energy will be converted into microwaves before being beamed back to ground-based receiving antennae. It is estimated that the total cost of the enterprise **should** be in the region of 1.8 billion euros.

There are several advantages of producing energy in space. Exposure to solar energy is uninterrupted and, as there is no cloud or atmospheric dust, the intensity of solar radiation is 8 times as great as on Earth. In addition, solar power stations will help reduce the emission of greenhouse gases from fossil fuels.

Nevertheless, a certain number of questions have been raised concerning the project. First and foremost is the problem of cost. Preliminary estimations suggest that the huge investment means that the cost per kWh **could** be three times as high as the current cost of conventional power sources in Japan. There are also concerns that such high power densities on ground stations **may** lead to health problems. Although the plan is to locate the receiving station in remote, mountainous regions, Molly Macauley, author of a NASA report on the subject, believes that the long term effects of such high power densities **might** well pose a problem.

What is significant, however, is that Japan is willing to spend such enormous sums of money on such a futuristic project. This is a clear indication that the government **must** now be taking the issue of future energy supplies and environmental problems very seriously indeed.

# Exercises

## 9.1. Exercise

A. *Write 3 sentences referring to the **present** and 3 sentences referring to the **past** using the modals (see photos on the next page):*

*SHOULD / OUGHT TO • COULD • MIGHT • MUST • CAN • MAY*

*Example:*

*photo (a)* → *She **ought to** take his pulse. (present)*
*photo (b)* → *The sea level **must** have gone down. (past)*

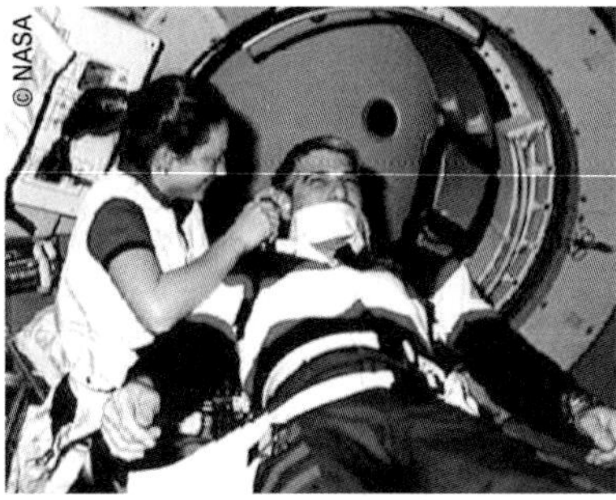


*(a) Medical emergency in space – simulation*

*(b) Abandoned boat*

*(c) Asbestos decontamination*

*(d) Cellular phones*

*(e) Travelling in Mongolia*

*B. Present or future time*

▌ *Rewrite the sentences using the most appropriate modal:* SHOULD / OUGHT TO • COULD • MIGHT • MUST • CAN • MAY.

*Example: Kate is not at home. It is **almost certain** that she is at work.*
*→ She **must** be at work.*

1. In the Kalahari desert, **it is possible** for the temperature to range from freezing at night to more than 44°C during the day.
   The temperature ................................................................................................ .
2. **I am convinced** that this is the right solution.
   This ................................................................................................ .
3. Improved telescopes mean that, in the next few years, **we will theoretically** see great progress in astronomy.
   In the next few years, we ................................................................................................ .
4. It has been claimed that the new techniques **will perhaps** enable doctors to detect cancer cells with absolute accuracy, but more research is needed.
   The techniques ................................................................................................ .
5. It is currently estimated that **it would be possible** for farmers to use 15% of the salt deserts for growing crops.
   Farmers ................................................................................................ .

*C. Past time (MODAL + HAVE + PP)*

*Example:* ***Perhaps*** *he telephoned yesterday evening,* ***but I don't think so****.*
→ *He* ***might have*** *telephon****ed*** *yesterday evening.*

6. No one is quite sure of the exact figures, but the 1918-1920 Spanish influenza epidemic **almost certainly** killed more than 30 million people.
The epidemic ........................................................................................ .
7. The computer crashed. His work was lost because he hadn't saved it. **He made a mistake**.
He ........................................................................................................ .
8. Faced with the crisis, the minister **had several alternatives**. One of them was to resign, but he didn't.
The minister .......................................................................................... .
9. What was the cause of the accident? **Perhaps** the pilot misunderstood the instructions from the control tower.
The pilot ................................................................................................ .
10. As he was in hospital when the accident happened, it is **impossible** that he caused it.
He ........................................................................................................ .

## *9.2. Of mice, monkeys and men*

▮ *Give an explanation of each of the words in bold. Check in the Key points if necessary.*

**starter**

**• What recent examples of genetic modification have you heard of?**

A team from Oregon University, headed by Professor Schatten, has produced the first genetically modified primate, a rhesus monkey called ANDi ("Inserted DNA" spelled backwards).

The gene used was a green fluorescent protein from a jelly-fish. So far, ANDi has not shown any signs of fluorescence, but this is not totally **unexpected**; the most **likely** explanation being that the expression of fluorescence has been delayed because of problems of manipulation or maturation.
The new gene however, **ought to** pass on the fluorescence to any future offspring.

© Oregon University

According to Schatten, "we are at an extraordinary moment in the history of mankind". He and his team are confident that GM monkeys **will** provide valuable experimental models for a range of major diseases. As monkeys are genetically closer to humans than mice, he believes that this research **may** speed up the development of new treatments for diseases such as HIV and Parkinson's. In the immediate future, Schatten hopes to insert other types of genetic markers that **can** be tracked with magnetic resonance or PET scans.

Other scientists, however, are more sceptical, fearing that this success will lead to a needless surge in experiments on primates. According to Patrick Bateson, chairman of a Royal Society Committee, "there is no reason to **assume** that this type of research will provide the bridge between mice and men. Although it is possible that medical benefits **might** result from producing genetically modified monkeys, it is important that this sort of work **should** be subject to strict monitoring for any potential harmful effects".

While most people seem to have few problems with genetically altered mice, "monkeys are a little closer to home", says Terri Lomax, an Oregon State University plant geneticist. The genetic engineering of primates raises serious ethical issues and many people **must** be wondering exactly where this is leading us. David King of the campaign against human genetic engineering in London, fears that it **could** end up in a new form of eugenics where we start "designing our own children according to our caprices".

TALKING POINT

- In twenty years' time, will we be "designing children according to our caprices"?

### *9.3. Tsunamis*

**starter**

**• What is a tsunami? – where? – why? – when? Exchange questions with you partner.**

*Insert the appropriate words:*

*MAY HAVE BEEN • CAN • MUST BE • CAN BE • MAY • ESTIMATED • COULD (1-7)*
*SHOULD • UNLIKELY • SUPPOSING • DOUBTLESS • MUST HAVE BEEN • WILL • MIGHT • ASSUMED (8-15)*

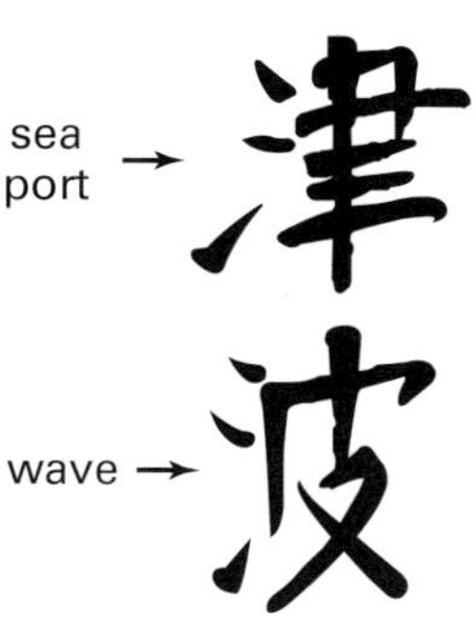


Tsunamis (the word is Japanese in origin) *(1)* ................ among the most potentially dangerous natural hazards threatening mankind. They ........................ caused by a wide range of geological disruptions, including submarine landslides, volcanoes and earthquakes. They occur most commonly, but not exclusively, in the Pacific Ocean, triggered by the subduction of tectonic plates along fragile seismic fault lines. More than 80 tsunamis have been recorded since 1990.

When large-scale underwater seismic tremors occur, the disruption of the seabed causes a corresponding displacement of water masses. The resulting waves .................. attain several hundred kilometres in length, travelling at speeds of up to 800 kph. The speed and amplitude of the tsunami depend on the depth of the water. This means that while travelling across oceans, the waves often attain no more than 40 cm in height, which explains why they often go unnoticed by deep sea shipping. As they approach the sea shore, however, and the sea bed begins to slope upwards, their speed is reduced and their amplitude increased. In extreme cases, waves of 30 meters in height have been reported. Because of the high population density along most coastal regions, their damage potential is immense and low-lying islands ............. be utterly submerged. In the 1883 tsunami, caused by the Krakatoa eruption, it is .......................... that more than 36,000 people .................................. killed.

Recent research by Simon Day of University College, London and Steven Ward of the University of California suggests that the *Cumbre Vieja* volcano in the Canary Islands ................... well present a major tsunami threat.

Day and Ward have shown that a crack has developed in the steep mountain side dominating the sea. It is *(8)* ......................... that this ................................ caused by the 1949 eruption. As a result, the entire west face of the mountain has become unstable and is now sliding at a rate of about 1 cm per year towards the sea. ................ that the mountain does collapse, a mass of several billion tonnes ................. be dumped, within a few seconds, directly into the sea, producing a giant tsunami.

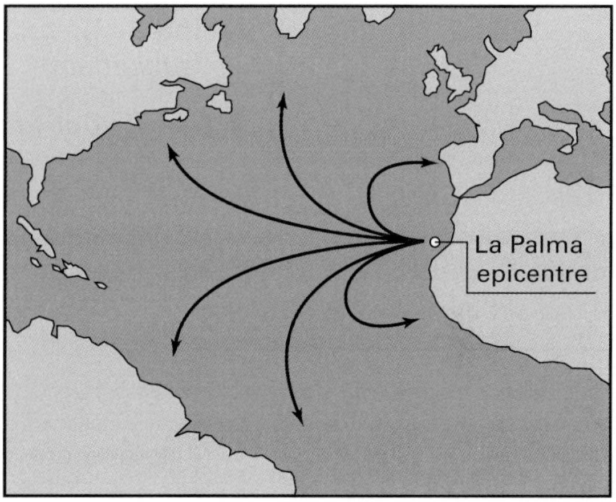


According to the model that Day and Ward have developed, it is ................. that the trajectory will be a straight East-West line across the Atlantic. It seems more probable that it will be slowed down by the shallow water near La Palma and then spread out in an arc, curving southwards towards Africa and northwards towards the European coastline.

At the moment, the volcano is quiescent and there ............... be no real danger for the present. However, a future irruption, which .............. occur at anytime within the next few hundred years, would ....................... generate an ocean-wide disaster.

## *9.4. Checkpoints*

In other words

**Definitions – alternative uses: either / or**

*Use the following pattern:*
"You can use an X **either** to Y **or** to Z."

*Example:* a scanner
*"You can use a scanner* ***either*** *to photocopy* ***or*** *to read a text."*

- *Define the words below:*
  *a Landrover • water • the money • a computer*
- *Now define two words of your own in the same way.*

**BACK TO BASICS**

### ❽ Information ... advice ... news ... equipment ...

▮ *Complete these sentences.*

1. I will send you all ........................................ by fax tomorrow. *(information)*
2. The .............. from Madrid ...... bad. *(news + to be)*
3. I would like some more ..................... about the programme. *(advice)*
4. Three ...................................... have just arrived. *(equipment)*

▮ *Check your answers in the grammar section.*

**THE WORD WEB – MULTI-WORD VERBS**

▮ *Complete with the most suitable phrase:*

*SMOKING ▪ A TOOTH ▪ THE EXAM PAPERS ▪ THE ELECTRICITY ▪ A DIFFICULT JOB ▪ PRODUCTION ▪ TO PREVENT A CONFLICT ▪ THE MEAT*

▮ *Provide the definition:*

*INCREASE ▪ STOP THE SUPPLY ▪ REMOVE ▪ INTERVENE TO HELP ▪ DISTRIBUTE ▪ STOP / ABANDON ▪ DIVIDE INTO SMALL PIECES ▪ ACCEPT RESPONSIBILITY*

| | *Definition* |
|---|---|
| to give out .......................... | ▶............................ |
| to give up .......................... | ▶............................ |
| to take on .......................... | ▶............................ |
| to take out .......................... | ▶............................ |
| to step up .......................... | ▶............................ |
| to step in .......................... | ▶............................ |
| to cut up .......................... | ▶............................ |
| to cut off .......................... | ▶............................ |

## *9.5. Web search*

▮ A tsunami occurred in the Mediterranean in 1979. It started at Nice. Consult the web and make a report.

You could use < tsunami 1979 Nice > as a search string.

▮ Solar power – Geothermal power – Wind power – Fuel cells.

Divide the class into 4 groups – each gives a 5 minute OHP presentation on one form of alternative energy.

### *Word search*

- Search the web for examples of past modals in the field of animal experimentation. Try the following sorts of search strings:

  < "could have already" monkey experimentation >
  < "should have known" mouse laboratory >
  < "may have been" cat test >

*N.B. – The modal string should be between inverted commas.*

## *Self evaluation – exit test*

- *Fill in the missing words (sentences 1-6 are modals).*

1. He .................. come by bike, but I would be surprised – it is raining. *(perhaps)*
2. Palaeontology is at the cross-roads. The question is, which way .................. we proceed from here? *(is it best)*
3. He .............................. realised his mistake as soon as he put down the telephone. *(it is almost certain)*
4. Nanotubes .......................... be inserted through the cell membranes to act as sensors. *(a possible solution)*
5. Prehistoric man ................................ discovered the therapeutic value of medicinal plants by trial and error. *(perhaps this was the case)*
6. Any significant change in the climate ..................... involve vast movements of population. *(inevitably)*
7. In these models, we **as** ......................... that future avalanches will occur under circumstances similar to those in the past. *(suppose)*
8. In fact, there is no real technological problem. The question is whether or not it is economically **fe** .............................. . *(possible)*
9. As **ex** .......................... , sustained electro-shocks affected the appetite and memory of all six rats. *(predicted, thought probable)*
10. It is generally acknowledged that, in the coming years, the most exciting scientific developments are **li** .................. to occur in biology. *(will probably)*

# 10. Purpose & process

*This unit deals with two closely linked concepts:* ***purpose*** *and* ***process****. Purpose is concerned with the question of* ***why*** *or for* ***what reason*** *something is done or exists, while process describes* ***how,*** *or* ***the manner*** *in which it is done.*

*Process is frequently associated with the passive form. This is discussed more thoroughly in Unit 11.*

## Self evaluation – entry test

▮ *Supply the missing words.*

*Example:*

*The* ***go*** .............. *of the Cancer Research Fund is to provide financial backing for research teams.* (objective)

→ *The* ***goal*** *of the Cancer Research Fund is to provide financial backing for research teams.*

1. As far as public transport is concerned, the **ta** ................ is to extend the tram network by 25 km within the next 6 years. *(goal, objective)*
2. The infection causes an inflammation which blocks the artery **su**.................... blood to the appendix. *(providing, feeding)*
3. To survive on land, reptiles had to develop a skin which was relatively impermeable to water **so** .............. prevent desiccation. *(in order to – 3 words)*
4. The **ai** .............. of the Government's population policy is to bring about a fundamental change in the demographic pattern. *(the objective)*
5. When predators are withdrawn from the area, the number of dominant species increases, **th** .................. reducing diversity. *(by doing this, thus)*
6. It was Canadian scientists who first proposed and **de** ........................ the experiment. *(made the plan)*
7. A complete survey of the surface of the Earth has been carried out **by** ............. high-resolution satellite photography. *(using, thanks to – 3 words)*
8. The escape velocity, which is 40,250 kph, **en** ............... a rocket to overcome the Earth's gravitational pull. *(permits)*
9. It was only in 1947 that women were first **al** ................. to become full members of Cambridge University. *(permitted)*
10. The machine was badly damaged **th** .................... negligence and lack of maintenance. *(because of)*

# *Functions & Grammar*

## KEY POINTS – PURPOSE & PROCESS

### *1. Purpose*

→ Purpose is concerned with questions of **"why"** or for **"what reason"** something is done.

▌ *Nouns*

the purpose • function • use

➢ *Metal is increasingly used in architecture for structural **purposes**.*

the aim • goal • target • objective

➢ *The main **objective** of hydrology is to study the physical and chemical processes of the water cycle.*

▌ *Verbs*

it is designed to / for[G. Notes 23] • is devised to / for • is planned to / for • is aimed to / for • is responsible for

➢ *The new safety measures were **designed to** reduce the risks of contamination.*

➢ *A cooling system was **devised for** the preservation of clinical specimens.*

it functions (as) • operates (as)

it provides • supplies

➢ *The haemoglobin **provides** the extra oxygen.*

▌ *Other expressions*

in order to / so as to • so that

→ **N.B.**

- ***"In order to / so as to"** have basically the same meaning as **"to"**. They are merely stronger ways of expressing the idea of purpose.*

- ***"So that" is followed by a clause composed of subject + verb.***

  ➢ *Platinum contacts should be used **to** prevent oxidisation.*
  ➢ *Platinum contacts should be used **in order to / so as to** prevent oxidisation.*
  ➢ *Platinum should be used **so that oxidisation can be prevented**.*

## *2. Process*

→ Process is concerned with questions of **"how"** or **"in what way"** something is done.

▌ *Adverbial and prepositional phrases (see Unit 5)*

by means of · through · thanks to · via

➢ *The brain was damaged **through** lack of oxygen.*

therefore · thus · thereby

➢ *He switched off the computer, **thereby** losing all the data.*

▌ *Verbs*

to enable · make (it) possible (for) · allow · permit

➢ *It is the carbon compounds that are responsible for the chemical reactions that **enable / make it possible for** the cell to grow.*
➢ *Visibility was poor – the plane was not **allowed / permitted** to land.*

**N.B. – Meaning**

- ***"To enable / to make possible"** have the primary meaning of making something feasible or physically possible.*
- ***"To allow / to permit"** have the primary meaning of making something possible by giving authorisation or permission.*

*However, in modern English, the meaning of **to allow / to permit** is often extended to physical possibility.*

| | | |
|---|---|---|
| The Erasmus grant | **enabled**<br>**made it possible for**<br>**allowed**<br>**permitted** | him to go on studying |

## *Examples in context*

**starter**

**• The steam engine – the industrial revolution: when? – who? – what? – consequences?**

### *AN 18TH CENTURY WATER PUMP*

*This rather eccentric and highly impractical 18th century design for a hydraulic power project reminds us to what extent the pre-industrial world was handicapped by lack of power systems.*

■ *Answer the questions following the text.*

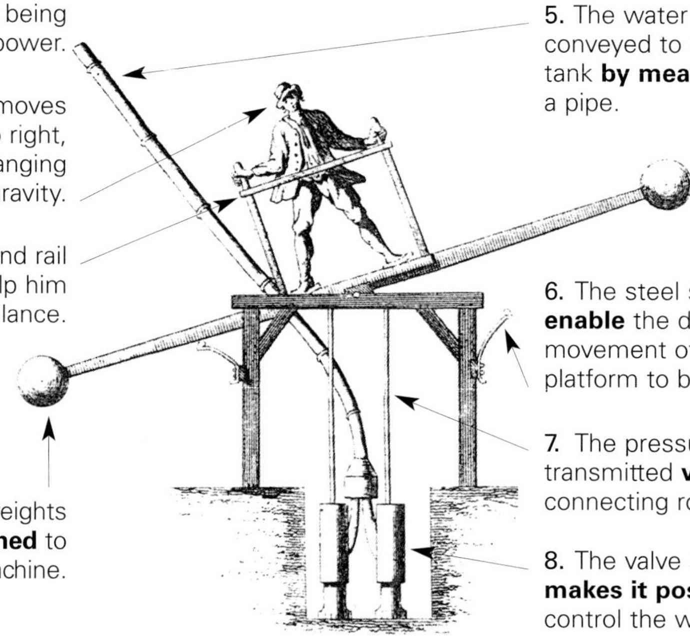


9. In the past, it was essentially the lack of power systems that was **responsible for** industrial stagnation.

■ *Write questions corresponding to each statement, using the expressions in brackets.*

*Example: The machine is designed to pump water.* (what / be for)
→ *What is the machine for?*

1. (what / human being / provide) ..........................................................................
2. (how / machine / operate) ..........................................................................
3. (how / man / keep his balance) ..........................................................................
4. (what / counterweights / do) ..........................................................................
5. (what / water pipe / be for) ..........................................................................

6. (what / steel springs / do) ..............................................................................
7. (in what way / pressure / be transmitted) .......................................................
8. (what / valves / control) ..................................................................................
9. (what / responsible / industrial stagnation) .....................................................

# Exercises

## 10.1. Exercise

*A. (Purpose) Insert the required word or expression: MAKE IT POSSIBLE • PROVIDES • RESPONSIBLE FOR • SO THAT • PURPOSE • AIMS • DESIGNED • IN ORDER TO.*

1. It is a new generation of artificial organs specifically ........................................ to be implanted in patients with diabetes.
2. The Akosombo dam on the Volta river ........................................ hydroelectric power to Ghana and neighbouring countries.
3. A small bit of specialised tissue, called the sinoauricular node, is ............................. initiating the heartbeat.
4. The software will ................................................ to detect the virus before any harm is done.
5. Cadmium can be used .................................... lower the melting point of alloys.
6. The sensors are orientated .............................. cosmic $\gamma$-rays will be detected.
7. It should be pointed out that quantum mechanics was originally introduced for the .................................. of explaining chemical facts.
8. Biochemistry, like other sciences, ............ at quantifying or measuring results.

*B. (Process) Draw arrows to link the phrases.*

1. The main advantage of sexual reproduction is that it **enables** ...
2. The particles then collide with gas molecules in the atmosphere, **thereby** ...
3. Earth-orbiting satellites have **made it possible** ...
4. In all probability, he got the job **through** ...
5. The acoustic wave enters the ear and the information is transmitted to the brain **via** ...
6. If the infection is **allowed** ...
7. The cancerous cells are transmitted to the other organs **by means of** ...

a. exciting them and causing luminescence.
b. to determine with accuracy the path and speed of the Gulf Stream.
c. the blood stream.
d. to spread, there will be thousands of deaths.
e. an advertisement.
f. a species to adjust and adapt to changing conditions.
g. the auditory nerve.

### *10.2. Sleeping pilots and chaos theory*

*Why are there accidents? Where does the responsibility lie? One of the uses of technology is to devise ways and means of reducing the consequences of human error.*

▮ *Fill in the gaps with the following words:*

*SO THAT • OBJECTIVES • BY MEANS OF • ENABLES • DESIGN • DEVISE • PROVIDE • MAKES IT POSSIBLE TO • IS RESPONSIBLE FOR*

**starter**

- **Give examples of both major and minor accidents.**
- **Were they brought about by faulty technology or human error?**
- **Was any action taken as a result of the accident?**
- **Give examples of how technology can be used to increase safety.**

Despite the thousands of parts which are used in the construction of aeroplanes, very few air-crashes are caused by component failure. It is, in fact, human error that ........................................ 80% of air accidents. This explains why one of the primary ..................... of the aircraft industry today is to ............................... ways of improving these figures. One area of particular concern is pilot fatigue. This problem is far more widespread than is commonly realised and Dr. Mark Rosekind claims that "70% or more pilots say that they have fallen asleep at least once while piloting". Fatigue is particularly linked to the crossing of time zones which can severely disturb the circadian rhythm.

© Kakuichi Shiomi

*Normal voice pattern*

The Japanese company, Electronic Navigation Research Institute (ENRI), is currently in the process of developing a monitoring system which will be able to ..................... early warning of fatigue .............................. voice recognition techniques.

© Kakuichi Shiomi

*Fatigued voice pattern*

Biological functions, such as blood pressure, heart-beat and voice, have a fractal structure which can be identified. Under stress or fatigue, these physiological manifestations undergo change and consequently, as can be seen in the figure, the pattern alters, gradually losing its structure and becoming chaotic. By using the mathematics of chaos theory, Kakuichi Shiomi, chief researcher of ENRI, has been able to ............ software which ................ these minute distinctions to be identified ................ the pilot's voice pattern can be matched with a control model of an alert voice. It takes no more than 10 seconds for data samples to be processed which means that fatigue can be measured in real time without interfering with the normal activity of the flight crew.

According to Shiomi, the system ........................................... detect tiredness in test subjects 10 to 20 minutes before they become aware of it themselves.

TALKING POINT

- The uses of non-intrusive, real time, fatigue predictors obviously extends far beyond the field of aviation. For what else could they be used?
- Describe the flow chart of the ENRI system (below) to your partner.

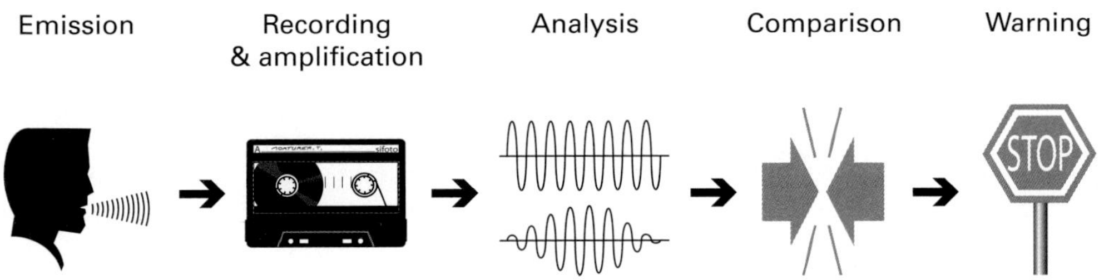


## *10.3. Tactical deception[1] in upper primates*

**starter**

- **Are animals intelligent? If so in what way? Give examples.**

*Descartes assumed that animals were merely "automata" and that thought was uniquely a human activity. Nowadays, scientists tend to be more concerned with similarities between human beings and animals. They point to parallels in neural structure, behaviour patterns and the use of tools. The text below gives examples of a less well-known similarity: the capacity of animals to be "dishonest".*

- *When you have finished reading the text, write questions referring to the words in **bold**.*
- *Draw the missing figure.*

Byrne and Whiten have documented a large number of cases of what they call "tactical deception" among primates. This has enabled them **to give a precise description** of "machiavellian strategies", whose primary aim appears to be **to mislead**[2] other members of the group and so gain advantage. Three main classifications are proposed.

1. ACTIVE CONCEALING – In such cases, animals can be observed to adopt unusual behaviour, **thereby successfully hiding their intentions** from others in the group. Hans Kummer, a Swiss primatologist, describes the following case. The hierarchy of hamadryas baboon harems is maintained by a single dominant male who forbids

1 To deceive / deception: to cause someone to believe something that is not true.
2 To mislead: to lead someone to a wrong conclusion, to deceive.

females to seek contact with other males. On one occasion, a young female baboon, who could clearly be seen by the dominant male, began shifting position very slowly **so as to approach a young male** sitting behind a rock. The whole process took about 20 minutes. Once she was behind the rock, while keeping her head and the upper part of her body visible to the dominant male, she immediately began to groom[3] the young male.

?

2. ACTIVE MISLEADING – Woodruf and Premack conducted an experiment in which chimpanzees behaved with the clear objective of intentionally **mislead-ing laboratory assistants**. Food was placed inside one of two containers in the presence of the chimpanzees. **A wire grid** however, made it impossible for them to get access to the food. Two human assistants were introduced one after the other on the food side of the grid. The first assistant was "friendly"; that is to say, when the chimpanzees indicated in which container the food was, he would take the food and share it with them. The second assistant, however, behaved in an "unfriendly" manner. After being shown where the food was, he ate it all himself. After a short number of trials, the chimpanzees learned to give a "dishonest" reply to the unfriendly human by pointing to the wrong container.

3. COUNTER DECEPTION – It sometimes happens that a monkey becomes aware that he is being misled by another. Byrne and Whiten describe a case where the victim appears to react accordingly by taking counter measures, apparently devised **to neutralise the deception**.

When a certain chimpanzee (A) realised where a banana was hidden, he would immediately walk away **with the apparent purpose of encouraging the rest of the group to do likewise**. As soon as the others had left, he would return to eat the hidden food. After some time, however, one member (B) of the group seemed to realise what was happening. This chimpanzee then pretended[4] to leave with the others – but in fact remained hidden behind a tree **in order to keep watch**. As soon as the first monkey returned to take the banana, he rushed back, seized it and ate it.

3 To groom: when an animal cleans or picks out the parasites from the hair of another animal.

4 To pretend: to mislead by acting as if something is true when it is not.

Examples such as these appear to support the hypothesis that the upper primates are aware that **information** can function as a tool and be used to manipulate the actions of others. It suggests that animal behaviour is far more complex than previously supposed and may often be a result of conscious decision making.

TALKING POINT

- What is chimpanzee (A) "thinking"? What is chimpanzee (B) "thinking"?

## *10.4. Checkpoints*

IN OTHER WORDS

**Definitions**
**Purpose: designed + turn / transform + into**

*Use the following pattern:*
"It is an X **that has been designed to transform** Y **into** Z."

*Example:*
*"A photoelectric cell is a device **that has been designed to turn / transform** light **into** electricity."*

- *Define the following words:*
  *a turbine • a solar panel • a voice recognition program • a loudspeaker*
- *Now make two more definitions of your own.*

BACK TO BASICS

These word pairs are frequently mixed up.

| | | |
|---|---|---|
| TO GROW | —— | TO GROW UP |
| TO REALISE | —— | TO CARRY OUT |
| LAST | —— | LATEST |
| EXPERIENCE | —— | EXPERIMENT |

- *Explain to your partner the difference in meaning.*
- *Match these words with those above:*
  *bus • clinical tests • scientific • flowers • suddenly • personal • child • news*

### THE WORD WEB – MORE SUFFIXES

- *Provide the missing suffixes, changing the stem of the word if necessary. Some are used more than once: -able • -acy • -ence • -hood • -ic • -ing • -ity • -ive • -ment • -tion.*

EARTHQUAKES AND VOLCANOES

One of the main reasons that earthquakes are so *(destroy)* ......................... is that there is no *(rely)* .................. method of predicting their *(occur)* ..................... . This means that they strike suddenly and without *(warn)* ..................... . Although enormous amounts of money have been spent on earthquake research, so far there has been little *(improve)* ............................. in the *(accurate)* .......................... of prediction.

By contrast, scientists do have the *(able)* .......................... to predict certain other geological activities, such as volcanoes, with a *(reason)* ........................... degree of success. Prior to the Mount St Helens' *(erupt)* ......................... in 1980, ground *(deform)* ....................... were reported and *(seismography)* ............................ *(record)* ........................... clearly indicated that *(volcano)* .......................... activity was present. Consequently, vulcanologists were able to announce the *(likely)* .......................... of the event within a time-scale of a few months.

### *10.5. Web search*

- Make a report on aviation crashes:
  ➤ http://www.airdisaster.com**/statistics/**
- Search the web for an illustration of a process. Make a 3 minute OHP presentation.

### *Word search*

- Collect 6 sentences using the string: < "make it impossible" chimpanzee >.

## *Self evaluation – exit test*

- *Fill in the gaps according to the definitions given in brackets.*

1. The main risk is that the laser beam may damage the structure of the cells surrounding the **ta** ........................ . *(objective, goal)*
2. It is essentially **th** ........................ research and development that aviation safety can be enhanced. *(via, as a result of)*
3. This 12-month course will **en** ............ students to gain a broader perspective of fundamental aspects of microbiology. *(allow, let)*
4. The sample can be maintained at low temperature **by** .......................... a large cryo-vacuum container. *(thanks to – 3 words)*

5. Weather conditions are very similar to those found in an anticyclone; as the air rises, there is cooling and condensation and **th** ........................ clouds are formed. *(consequently, so)*
6. Preliminary calculations predict that fluorescent imaging could **ma** ................ ............................. to detect 1-micron samples. *(permit – 3 words)*
7. The **pu** ................ of the Mars Society is to further the goal of the exploration and settlement of the "red planet". *(aim, objective)*
8. The first step involves acquiring the information needed to **de** ............... treatments or cures for these diseases. *(elaborate, design)*
9. The liquid must be heated slowly **so** ..................... avoid sharp variations in temperature. *(in order to – 3 words)*
10. The money will be used to help fishermen in Liberia buy equipment, **th** .......... reducing their dependence on foreign aid. *(as a result of this action, in this way)*

# 11. IMPERSONAL FORMS

*One of the most striking features of scientific English is the intensive use of the* ***passive*** *and other* ***impersonal forms****. The passive form alone accounts for roughly 35% of all verbs found in general scientific texts. What is the reason for this? By using the passive, the focus can be placed on the action – on "****what*** *was done" and not "****who*** *did it". Science is not particularly interested in the actor ("I", "you", "she"). It is the action or result that matters.*

## Self evaluation – entry test

▌ *Complete the sentences with a passive form.*
*Example:*
*In 1911, Amundsen discovered the South Pole.*
→ *In 1911, the South Pole* ***was discovered*** *(by Amundsen).*

1. The UK government has sent research teams to the Antarctic since as far back as 1923.
→ *Since as far back as 1923, research teams* ...have been sent...
2. It was only in 1943, during World War II, that the government set up the first regular station.
→ *It was only during World War II that the first regular station* ...was set up...
3. The first stations were set up because enemy shipping was using the whaling bases for shelter.
→ *The first stations were set up because the bases* ...were being used...
4. Medical care in the Antarctic is crucial. Not many people know how this is organised.
→ *It* ...is ~~not~~... *not widely* ...known...
5. In an emergency, evacuation is always costly and sometimes impossible. Hence BAS (The British Antarctic Survey) have taken measures to avoid it.
→ *Measures* ...have been taken to avoid evacuation...
6. BAS provides a 24 hour telemedicine support service via satellite telephone.
→ *A 24 hour telemedicine support service* ...is provided...
7. Currently, BAS is recruiting medical staff to work in the Antarctic.
→ *Medical staff* ...is being recruited to work in Antartic
8. Prior to posting, BAS will give specialist training to all selected candidates.
→ *Specialist training* ...will be given...
9. Candidates will have to master unfamiliar techniques such as dentistry, taking and processing X-ray films and plastering[1].
→ *Unfamiliar techniques* ...will have to be mastered...
10. Before applying, potential candidates should realise that contracts of employment may stretch for a period of 33 months.
→ *It* ..............................

1 Plastering: to immobilise a broken bone with gypsum.

# Functions & Grammar

## KEY POINTS – IMPERSONAL FORMS

### 1. The passive

Why is the passive so common in scientific, administrative and formal written English? It is because these registers are concerned with **processes and events** more than they are with the actors. The active form, however, is much more common in literature and the spoken language where it is people who are the focus of attention. In the following example, it can be seen how the transformation from active to passive **evacuates** the actor[G. Notes 25].

➢ *The doctor removed the* ***cataract***.

*The* ***cataract*** *was removed.*

By placing the complement at the beginning of the sentence, it is the importance of the action (the subject + the verb) that is stressed.

*Note – Passives and modals*
***The passive is frequently used in conjunction with the modals.***

➢ *Huge amounts of energy* ***must be used*** *to break atomic bonds.*
➢ *Thanks to ice-nucleating bacteria, artificial snow* ***can be produced*** *in greater quantities.*

### 2. Impersonal forms: it

The impersonal form can also be expressed by using "it" as a subject. The following patterns are particularly frequent in academic English:

*IT + PASSIVE VERBS EXPRESSING OPINIONS AND BELIEFS + THAT ...*

(it is often said ▪ it is widely believed ▪ it is commonly thought ▪ it is sometimes maintained ▪ it has been suggested ...)

➢ ***It is*** *sometimes* ***maintained*** *that the movement of the stars influences our lives.*

*IT + MODAL PASSIVE + THAT ...*

(it should be realised that ▪ it must not be forgotten that ▪ it could be said that ...)

➢ ***It should be noted*** *that a similar heating process has been used before.*

*IT + TO BE + ADJECTIVE + TO / THAT CLAUSE*

(it is impossible ▪ it is important ▪ it is essential ▪ it is crucial ...)

➢ ***It is important to*** *remember to switch off the computer.*
***It is important that*** *you remember to switch off the computer.*

### 3. "-ing"

The "**-ing** form" is a powerful way of expressing impersonal ideas. Notice that the action **(verb + -ing)** is frequently introduced at the front of the sentence.

➢ *We require 4,000 million bits to record 45 minutes of hi-fi stereo.*
*__Recording__ 45 minutes of hi-fi stereo requires 4,000 million bits.*

➢ *We can increase conductivity if we reduce the temperature.*
*__By reducing__ the temperature, conductivity can be increased.*

## Examples in context

### BRIDGE BUILDING

*N.B. – These examples are all illustrations of the modal passive (see Unit 9).*

▌ ***The staff and collaborators of an engineering company are discussing the possibility of getting a bridge finished according to schedule. Who says what?***

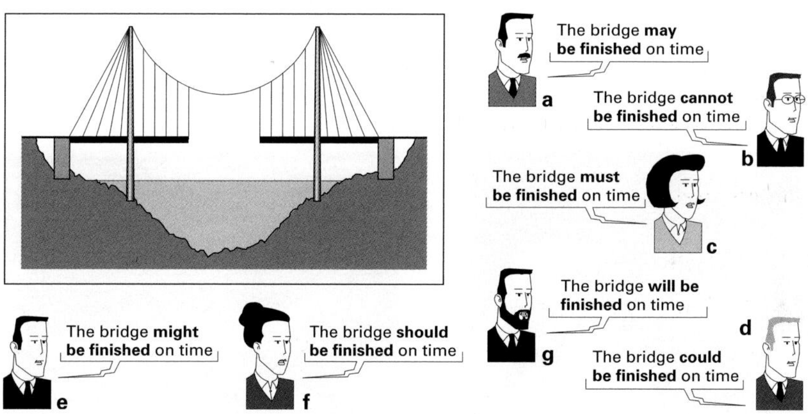


| | |
|---|---|
| 1. The manager of the firm c | – *It is essential – if it is not completed, the firm will go bankrupt.* |
| 2. The chief engineer, in charge of the project g | – *The person is completely confident.* |
| 3. The 2nd engineer a | – *Perhaps it will be completed, perhaps it won't. He/she doesn't want to take a decision.* |
| 4. A spokesperson for the firm speaking to the press f | – *In theory – unless there is a major problem. He/she is speaking in careful, reassuring terms.* |
| 5. The third engineer e | – *A pessimist: it is just possible, but he doesn't think it likely.* |
| 6. An outside advisor from Manpower d | – *At the moment things don't look very good. But if you decide to employ our know-how, then it will be possible.* |
| 7. An outside consultant who has been called in to do a feasibility study b | – *We have detected a fundamental fault in the design. It is technically impossible.* |

# Exercises

## 11.1. Exercise

*A. "All generalisations are dangerous, even this one", said Alexandre Dumas fils. We can make them more acceptable by qualifying them.*

*Match the phrases.*

1. It is hardly ever acknowledged that ...
2. It is sometimes claimed that ...
3. It is commonly thought that ...
4. It is seldom admitted that ...
5. It is widely believed that ...
6. It has often been suggested that ...

a. the rich are too rich and the poor are too poor.
b. efficient government is impossible in a democratic society.
c. after the age of 55, the accident rate of surgeons increases sharply.
d. the stars influence our health.
e. incest is not uncommon in Western Europe.
f. university examination procedures are unreliable.
g. simple people are more honest than intellectuals.

*B. Make qualified generalisations about the photos.*

*Women*

*Dolphins*

*Apples*

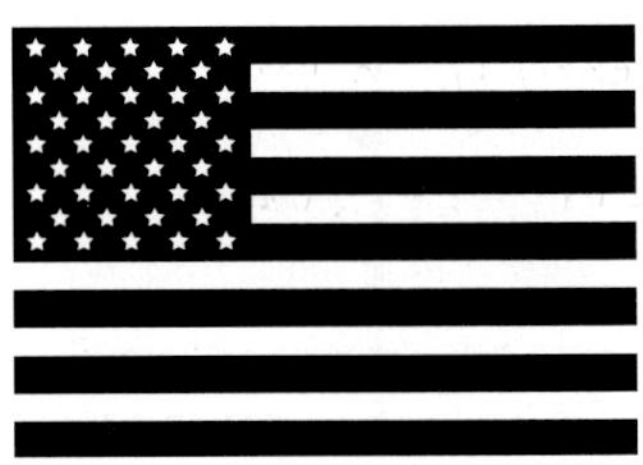

*Americans*

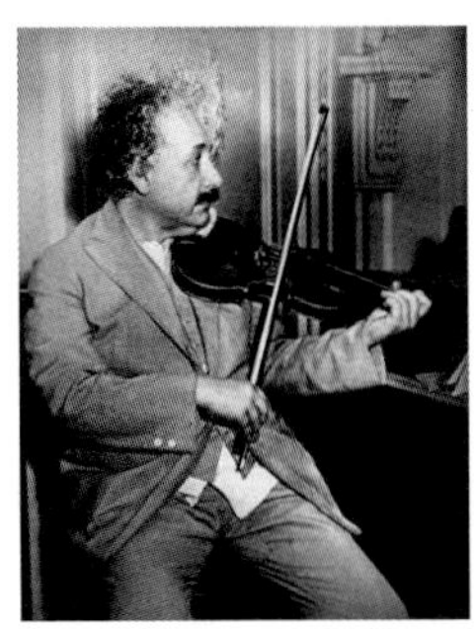

*Scientists*

*C. Make two qualified generalisations of your own.*

### *11.2. "e-noses" and tuberculosis*

*The more sophisticated technology becomes, the more it spreads to areas which, in the past, were the sole responsibility of human beings. This text offers just one more example of machine replacing man.*

**starter**

- **Human beings have five senses: hearing, sight, smell, taste and touch. With your partner, give examples of technological devices employed to replace the natural organs.**

- *Reformulate the underlined phrases with passive forms.*
- *There are 6 phrases written in **bold**. Suggest the missing agent **(by whom / by what)**.*

**It is reported** from Cranfield University that a research team is developing an electronic nose using artificial smell sensors to detect tuberculosis-carrying bacteria. The device **has been modelled** on techniques that were first pioneered by the food production industry to recognise smells in industrial food production.

Underlying this new technology is the principle that certain materials are reactive to the environment. Molecules in vapours, for example, may bind to materials causing changes in fundamental properties, such as electrical conductance. In "e-noses", the most commonly used materials are metal oxides or polymers, the latter being particularly favoured as it is possible to engineer their molecular structure for specific applications with great precision.

In the Cranfield project, an array of polymeric thin film sensors, not more than a few microns thick and responding in ppm (parts per million), **are enclosed** in a hermetically sealed[2] container. A circulation pump ensures the airflow of the previously gasified sample via the inlet and outlet pipes. An electric current is passed through the sensors which transduce the acidic chemical quantities into electrical signals. The unique signature of the gas **can then be identified** after processing the data with pattern recognition software and matching it to a memory bank.

The Cranfield project, which analyses samples of patients' sputum[3] and lung material containing potential TB bacteria, is a significant breakthrough in medical technology. Foremost among its advantages is that it speeds up the detection process considerably, returning results in four hours compared to the two days taken by conventional methods. Besides being faster, the device provides much more comprehensive results; different strains of bacteria present in the sputum spray **can be immediately distinguished**. Up until now, biologists have had no other option but to grow laboratory cultures which then **have to be analysed** under a microscope in a process that may take as much as six weeks.

If the "e-nose" proves successful, in the long term it would constitute a very significant advance in the fight against TB. The disease kills around three million people each year and is on the increase in Europe owing to growing poverty. It is in the UK that the highest number of cases is recorded, with a rate of almost 4,000 per year. This corresponds to a 20% increase over the last 10 years.

---

2 Sealed: closed.

3 Sputum: saliva and mucus.

TALKING POINT

- Draw a flow chart of the different stages of the process (paragraph 3). Cf. Exercise 10.2.

### 11.3. Looking after mummy

**starter**

- **What do you know about mummification? – who? (apart from the Egyptians) – why? – how? – when?**

*The discovery of chemical processes is not new. It dates back more than 4,000 years to the ancient civilisations of Egypt, Mesopotamia and China. The mummification carried out by the Egyptians to preserve bodies for the after-life was in fact one of the first large-scale industries with a chemical basis. It has been estimated that up to 730 million bodies were mummified before the practice died out in AD 700.*

▌ *Fill in the gaps by transforming the active verbs into passives.*

If the Egyptian mummies survived for more than 4,000 years, it is not merely because of the remarkable skill of the ancient Egyptians in preserving bodies, it is also due to the excellent storage conditions in which they ................................... . Inside the tombs of the Valley of the Kings, there was no human presence and so the air was relatively sterile, the atmosphere dry and the temperature extremely stable. In a more hostile environment, organic materials ............................ easily, and once transferred to museums, these fragile objects are vulnerable to attack from insects, micro-organisms and atmospheric pollution. This is particularly true in busy metropolises, such as Cairo, with its exceptionally high oxidant and particulate levels, coupled with the daily pressure of thousands of visitors. It is unfortunately true to say that it is often in museums that irreparable damage ........................... to our oldest and most precious cultural treasures.

With the help of the Getty Institute, a prototype display case ................................ at the "Instituto de Conservacion", in Madrid, for the Royal Mummy Collection in the Egyptian Museum in Cairo. The project had the triple aim of producing a case that would control biological damage, would provide optimum display conditions, while ensuring that the cost per unit was kept as low as possible.

The prototype .................................. using a 3,000 year-old Egyptian mummy as a model. The woman was approximately 40 years old when she died and, judging from the expensive mummification treatment and by the layer of gold over her eyes, it ............................... that she was from a rich family.

1 People kept the mummies.

2 It is possible for the environment to damage organic materials.

3 Pollution is doing irreparable damage.

4 Engineers have designed a display case.

5 Designers developed the prototype.

6 It is possible to assume this ...

The mummy was decaying fast because of severe contamination by "Daedalea beinnes Fries", a fungal species. After a preliminary sterilisation by γ-ray radiation using cobalt-60, the mummy was placed in a hermetically sealed display case and the air replaced by nitrogen at low relative humidity.

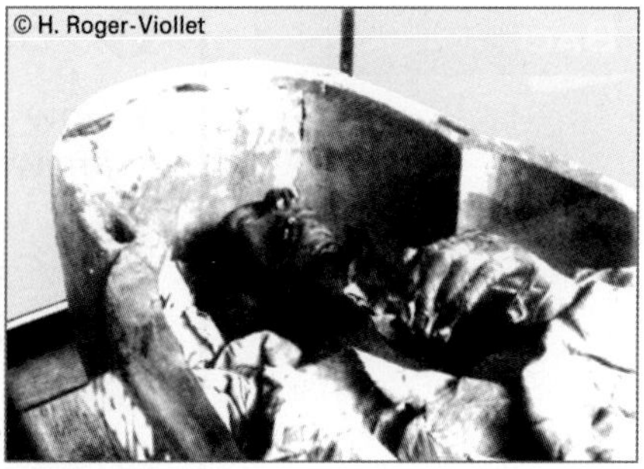


Nitrogen environments provide one of the most effective places for the conservation of organic objects since the gas is inert and all microbiological activity ...................... to a halt, in an oxygen-free atmosphere. Unlike common fumigation systems, nitrogen ............................................. and it is also safe and inexpensive.

Although, ideally, all oxygen ................................. this in fact ................................ to be impractical because of air leaks, estimated at 20 ppm per day. However, provided the residual concentration can be maintained within a 0.1%-0.2% range, satisfactory results ................................

The project has been an overall success and the display cases which ......................................... locally are being exported to India.

7 This brings microbiological activity to a halt.

8 It is possible to handle nitrogen easily.

9 It is desirable to remove all oxygen.

10 Engineers have shown this.

11 It is possible to obtain satisfactory results.

12 The Egyptians are now manufacturing the cases locally.

## *11.4. Checkpoints*

IN OTHER WORDS

**Definitions – duration**

*Use the following pattern:*
"An X **is a period during which** we do Y ..."

*Example:* an eclipse
*"An eclipse is the **period during which** the Earth is in the Moon's shadow."*

- *Define the following words:*
  *weekend ▪ Ramadan ▪ hibernation ▪ semester*
- *Give two examples of your own.*

K TO BASICS

Check your knowledge of numbers.

▮ *How do you say the following (write down your answers)?*

| | |
|---|---|
| *NUMBERS* | *47* |
| | *93,673* |
| | $9^{-6}$ |
| *DATE* | *02.03.2005* |
| *TELEPHONE* | *530065* |
| *PRICE* | *it costs € 100* |
| *DECIMAL* | *0.503* |
| *TIMES* | *2.30* |
| | *5.45* |

## THE WORD WEB – VERB FORMATION

*The prefixes "en-" and the suffixes "-ise" can be used to form verbs (see Unit 3). The general meaning is **"to transform – to change – to make something have this feature".***
*Examples: to **en**force ... to modern**ise***

▮ *Supply the required verb form.*

1. When other analgesics have failed, morphine is used to .................... pain in terminal cancer. *(minimum)*
2. Research in physics and chemistry in the US was considerably ..................... by the arrival of European refugees in the 1930s. *(rich)*
3. The seating capacity and wingspan of the new Airbus has been considerably .......................... . *(large)*
4. Plants that have been ....................... can be found in Precambrian coal. *(fossil)*
5. The firm has .......................... in the manufacture of heat resistant polymers. *(special)*
6. It is the investment in research and development since the war that has ........................ French manufacturing exports to expand at such an enormous rate. *(able)*
7. Huntingdon's disease is ................................ by uncontrolled movements, dementia, and death within 20 years of onset. *(character)*
8. The most urgent question is how to ...................... that nuclear weapons do not spread. *(sure)*

### *11.5. Web search*

- What exactly are the different techniques that have been used for mummification? You could try:
  - ➤ http://www.bbc.co.uk**/history/ancient/egyptians/mummies_01.shtml**
- Find information about the British Antarctic Survey (see *Entry test*):
  - ➤ http://www.antarctica.ac.uk/

#### *Word search*

- Make a web search for generalisations. Use search strings like:

  < "it is often suggested" >

  < "it is commonly thought" >

  < "it is seldom admitted" >

## *Self evaluation – exit test*

- ***Neo-organs are man-made, engineered tissues which can replace malfunctioning and deficient organs. Reformulate the sentences using an impersonal form.***

1. They are currently testing bone-growth hormones capable of regenerating bony tissue.

   → *Currently, hormones affecting the growth of bones ............................... .*

2. They have not yet completed the clinical trials.

   → *So far, ................................................................................ .*

3. It is important to bear in mind that tissues more than a few millimetres thick require blood vessels.

   → *It should be remembered that ............................................. for thick tissues.*

4. Most people acknowledge that Judah Folkman has played a key role in neo-organ engineering.

   → *It .................................... that a key role ................................ by Judah Folkman.*

5. In 1972, Folkman discovered that developing tumours need their own blood vessels to supply themselves with nutrients.

   → *The importance of blood vessels to developing tumours .......................... in 1972.*

6. Folkman suggested that we could use specific molecules to slow down the growth of tumours.

   → *Folkman suggested that* ................................................................ *to influence the growth rate of tumours.*

7. Up to now, they have only examined blood vessel growth thoroughly.

   → *So far, only* ........................................................................................ .

8. One solution is to use injectable polymers to convey bio-active molecules.

   → ................................................ *in order to convey bio-active molecules is a potential solution.*

9. Reports have said that more than 30,000 people die each year because of liver failure.

   → *It* ......................................................... *are more than 30,000 deaths per year.*

10. As the population ages, hospitals will need more and more replacement tissue.

   → *Clearly, as the population gets older,* ....................................................
   ................................................................ .

# 12. COMPOUND NOUNS & ADJECTIVES

*In this last unit we look at* ***compound nouns*** *and* ***adjectives****. These are groups of two or more nouns or adjective which are combined to express a complex single idea.* ***Compounds*** *are widely used in scientific and technological English as they allow new concepts with multiple meanings to be expressed in a concise way.*

*There are a large number of frequently used formulaic compounds: "Greenhouse effect", "Geneva Peace Conference", "gamma ray detector" but there is no definitive list as combinations are always being "invented" to express new concepts.*

## Self evaluation – entry test

▌ *Replace the phrases by more concise, compound forms.*

*Example: A thermometer containing mercury*
→ *A* ***mercury thermometer***

1. Cells which are sensitive to light
→ ..........................................................

2. A satellite which is for espionage and is geostationary
→ ..........................................................................................

3. An engine which burns petrol
→ .......................................................

4 A crater of a meteorite which is 2 metres wide
→ ...............................................................................

5. A system of injection which is controlled by computer
→ ...........................................................................................

6. A rate of unemployment which increases fast
→ ..............................................................................

7. A technician for research in the field of microbiology (who is senior)
→ .................................................................................................................

8. A conference which lasts four days
→ .............................................................

9. A victim of a landmine with one leg
→ .............................................................

10. A family with three children
→ ..................................................

# *Functions & Grammar*

## KEY POINTS – COMPOUND NOUNS & ADJECTIVES

### *1. Compound nouns*

As you know, nouns can be modified in several different ways:

| | | |
|---|---|---|
| 1. ADJECTIVES | ▶ *a big / a general / a private / a mental ...* | *hospital* |
| 2. POSSESSIVE FORMS | ▶ *St Mary's / a children's ...* | *hospital* |
| 3. "-ING" PARTICIPLES | ▶ *a teaching / a smoothly-running ...* | *hospital* |
| 4. PAST PARTICIPLES | ▶ *a well-built / a modernly-equipped ...* | *hospital* |

However, it is very important to understand that nouns can also be modified by other **nouns**, i.e. these nouns function as if they were adjectives. These constructions are called **compound nouns**.

| | | |
|---|---|---|
| 5. NOUN MODIFIERS | ▶ *a research / a city / a prison ...* | *hospital* |

- Compound nouns are used to refer to specific, identifiable objects or concepts. They are extremely common in scientific and specialised English because they make it possible for complex notions to be expressed in a concise, elegant way. Compare:

  ***X-ray therapy*** *and* ***a therapy using rays which are in the category X*** *G. Notes 27*

- Compound nouns are frequently difficult to understand. Why? It is because the order is the **inverse** of what is usual in many languages. This is particularly clearly illustrated by acronyms.

  *UNO* → *ONU* *(United Nations Organisation)*

  *NATO* → *OTAN* *(North Atlantic Treaty Organisation)*

  The reason that the order is inverted is because the **principal** meaning of a compound noun is in the **final** word.

  *Example:* *What is a "robot control technology"?*
  It is a **technology**.
  ↳ It is a **technology** designed to control.
  ↳ It is a **technology** designed to control robots.

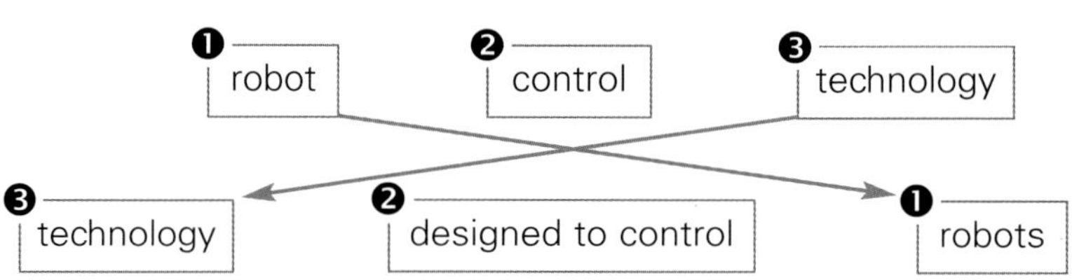

- Modifying nouns have the same function as adjectives. This explains why they do not take an **"-s"** (with some exceptions[G. Notes 28]) – **even after numerals**.

  ➢ *a four **door** car ▪ a 20 **euro** note ▪ a 5 **man** crew ...*

- There is no definitive list of compound nouns. As new ideas develop, new compound nouns are "invented" to correspond to specific purposes. Supposing that NASA required a new tool to detect radon gas on Mars. A new word (which, doubtless, has never been used before in the history of the language) can be invented to describe this tool:

  ➢ *a remote controlled Mars radon detector*

- The rules for spelling compounds are not fixed:
  - sometimes they are written as one word ➡ *a wavelength*
  - sometimes they are linked by a hyphen ➡ *an X-ray*
  - and sometimes they are written as two words ➡ *a radon detector*

## *2. Compound adjectives*

There are three different forms:

- The **"-ing"** form
  The present participle of the verb can be used as a modifier.

  ➢ *a **hard-working** student (he/she works hard all the time) ▪ an **amplifying** system ▪ a **warning** device ▪ a **distinguishing** feature ...*

This form refers to a typical, defining characteristic.

- The past participle may also be used.

  ➢ *a **well-written** report (the report was written well **by** someone) ▪ a **well lubricated** machine ▪ a **pre-tested** drug ▪ **widely-used** techniques ...*

This form has usually a **passive** meaning (i.e. you can add "by") and refers to something already done, something in the past.

- A small number of compound adjectives are formed by adding **"-ed"** to a **noun** (the nouns act as if they were verbs).

  ➢ *a cold-**blooded** animal ▪ a red-**haired** girl ▪ a two-**winged** insect ▪ a twin-**engined** plane ▪ a 6-**wheeled** lorry ...*

# Examples in context

## LIFE SCIENCES LABORATORY EQUIPMENT (LSLE)

*Advanced technology uses compound forms (and acronyms) massively. The text below illustrates the typical jargon that is being developed in the space industry and elsewhere.*

- *In the figure of the AFS-2 on the left, all the words are either 2 or 3 word compound forms. Check.*
- *In the specifications, on the right, there is 1 compound form with 9 elements, 1 with 6 and 3 with 3 elements. Find and underline them.*

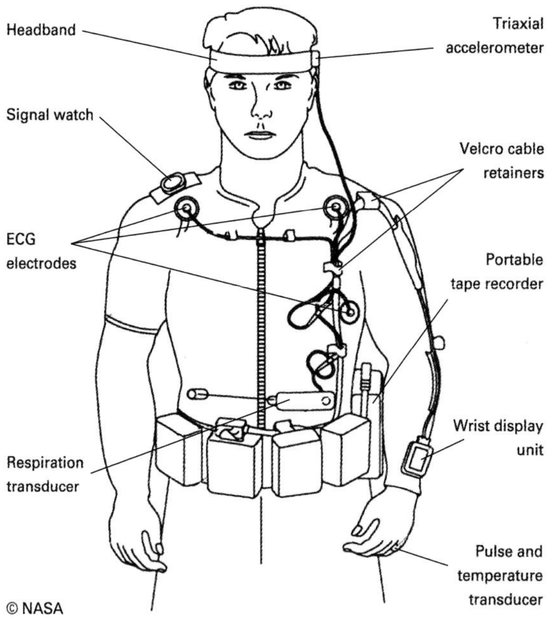


© NASA

**AFS-2 THE AUTOGENIC FEEDBACK SYSTEM**

***Specifications***

*The AFS-2 is a light-weight, battery-operated, fully ambulatory physiological monitoring system that allows complete freedom of motion for users. It is designed to enable astronauts to monitor their own physiological data and alter their physiological responses to counteract the effects of space motion sickness.*

***WEIGHT:*** *2 kg*

***POWER:*** *four 9-volt lithium thionyl chloride batteries*

***SENSORS:***
*Blood volume pulse (1-200 ± 0.5)*
*Skin temperature (70-99.9 ± 1°F)*
*Skin conductance level*
*(0.5-50 μMHOs ± 2%)*
*Respiration (40-60 breaths / min)*
*Electrocardiography (40-180 beats / min)*
*Acceleration (± 0.25 G ± 5%)*

# Exercises

## 12.1. Exercise

*A. Expand the five compound nouns below by making full definitions.*

*Example: They have introduced new **"aviation fuel tests"**.*
*→ That is to say, **tests** which are carried out on **fuel** that is used in **planes**.*

1. Caffeine boosts **rat brain activity**.
2. The weight of the bridge was borne by a **25 tonne concrete column**.

3. Yellow fever has a **3-6 day incubation period**.
4. The ship was sunk by a **remote controlled underwater mine**.
5. Antarctic fish can only survive because of **protective anti-freeze proteins**.

*B. Put all the 10 compounds in part A) and part B) in the correct column in the box (the first one, "rat brain activity", has been done for you).*

| | |
|---|---|
| a) purpose (what is it for?) | |
| b) is made of / contains | |
| c) location | 1, |

6. Plasma can be defined as **electrically conducting ionised gas particles**.
7. They manufacture **high-temperature fuel cells**.
8. The majority of the children were suffering from an **insect-transmitted eye disease**.
9. The bike had a **reinforced aluminium alloy frame**.
10. They are developing new **avalanche victim search strategies**.

*C. Using the words below, give **4-stage definitions** of these words:*

*(1) A THERMOMETER • (2) A GEIGER COUNTER • (3) A BUS SERVICE • (4) NASA • (5) A TELEPHONE • (6) A PACEMAKER • (7) AN ENCYCLOPAEDIA • (8) A VIRUS*

*Example:*
What is a "mouse"?
**1.** You could say a mouse is an **interface**.
↪ **2.** It is an interface which is used for **computers**.
↪ **3.** It is <u>an interface which is used for computers and is **controlled by hand**</u>.
↪ **4.** That is to say, <u>**a hand controlled computer interface**</u>.

*You should start here:* → ❶

| ❸ | ❷ | ❶ |
|---|---|---|
| **hand-controlled** | **computer** | **interface** |
| α-ray | transport | bank |
| disease | carrying | device |
| information | detection | organism |
| heat | measurement | instrument |
| heart | research | system |
| space | muscle | organisation |
| paper | data | regulator |
| passenger | transmission | appliance |

*D. With your partner make as many 3-term compound nouns as you can from the selection ( start with the final word of the compound noun).*

| 3 | 2 | 1 |
|---|---|---|
| mouse | community | cell |
| large-scale | reforestation | project |
| computer | space | programme |
| alarm | triggering | station |
| process | training | simulation |
| laboratory | temperature | control |
| 6-man | blood | technology |
| | | equipment |

## *12.2. Landmines – the Dervish*

**starter**

**• What five things can you say about landmines? Pool your ideas with your partner.**

*The UN estimates that anti-personnel mines kill 24,000 people each year, while at least 450,000 are injured. Present mine-clearing techniques are exceedingly dangerous, slow and expensive. In Kuwait alone, after the Gulf War, eighty four mine-clearers using hand held detectors were killed and it can take up to 80 days for one person to clear a hectare.*

▮ *Answer the questions at the end of the text.*

Faced with the growing number of deaths due to anti-personnel mines, Stephen Salter, Professor of Engineering Design at the University of Edinburgh, has designed a low-cost mine clearing vehicle called a "Dervish".

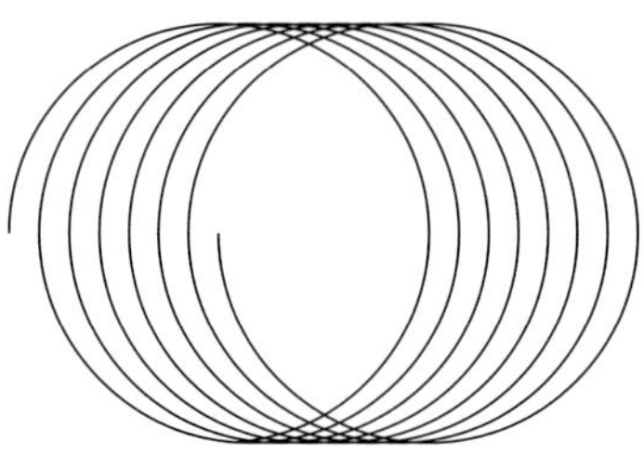

*The pattern of the Dervish's tracks*

It is a remote controlled 3 wheeled robot with wheels set at 120 degrees so that it spins as it moves forward. This means that the wheels cover every 3 cm of ground in almost concentric circles clearing a 5 m wide mine-free path. The wheels, actuated by three computer-controlled hydraulic pumps, powered by a 350 cc electricity generator are made of hardened Swedish steel alloy, each one weighing 80 kg. As the weight distribution resembles that of the human body, the load triggers the mine on its passage.

The Dervish has an open, tetrahedral frame to reduce the profile for mine blasts and the engine is shielded by a protective V-shaped case suspended at the apex.

The Dervish is extremely versatile and can operate on open, uneven or moderately sloping ground. Its foremost advantage, however, is that it has a 5 square metre per minute clearance capacity – more than 1000 times faster than hand clearance.

The Dervish has certain limitations. Mines which are hidden by obstructions or those at the bottom of steep craters and holes remain untouched, and its performance drops sharply on hard, frozen ground or if the mines are faulty.

*The Dervish mine-detector*

Nevertheless, at a cost of under $16,000, the Dervish brings a new capability to mine clearance programmes operating under restricted budgets in post-conflict situations.

▮ *Answer the questions according to the text using **one** word only.*

1. What did Professor Salter design? ............................................................
2. What is a Dervish? ............................................................
3. As it advances, what does it clear? ............................................................
4. What actuates the wheels? ............................................................
5. What is it powered by? ............................................................
6. What are the wheels made of? ............................................................
7. What reduces the force of the blasts? ............................................................
8. What shields the engine? ............................................................
9. What is the Dervish's strongest point? ............................................................

## 12.3. Intracytoplasmic sperm injection

*Research involving human embryos is, justifiably, one of the most sensitive areas of modern medical research for it poses fundamental ethical problems about scientific responsibility.*

**starter**

**• Suggest two or three ways in which medically assisted fertilisation might be genetically or socially dangerous.**

▮ *Supply the appropriate compound nouns.*

Infertility rates are far higher than is commonly appreciated, with some estimates suggesting a figure as high as 17% for European populations. Last year, in the US alone, as many as 20,000 couples sought aid from ........................................ ........................... *(technologies which concern fertilisation and which are assisted).* There is a wide range of different causes for infertility. In the large majority of cases, the problem stems from a ................................ *(a count of sperm which is low),* i.e. less than 10-15 million sperm per ml of semen (normal range – 50 million). This affects one out of thirty males in Western Europe. The complete absence of sperm, however, is relatively rare, affecting no more than 1 per thousand. Advanced in vitro techniques have represented a major breakthrough for the treatment of severe male infertility by reducing the need for the couple of turning to ......................................... *(sperm from donors who are outside (the couple))*. One example of such techniques is ICSI, Intracytoplasmic sperm injection, pioneered in 1992 by Drs. Van Steirteghem and Devroey from the Free University in Brussels, in which a single sperm is injected directly into the cytoplasm via a ...................................................................... *(pipette which is made of glass and is controlled by a computer)*. This technique offers ........................................................ *(rates of success of implantation of 65%)* and, as a result, is one of the ............................................. *(areas which are growing the fastest)* in infertility treatment. However, recent research carried out by Sherman Silver, director of the ....................................... *(centre for infertility which is in the town of St Louis)* in Missouri, has confirmed earlier worries about potential dangers of embryo manipulation.

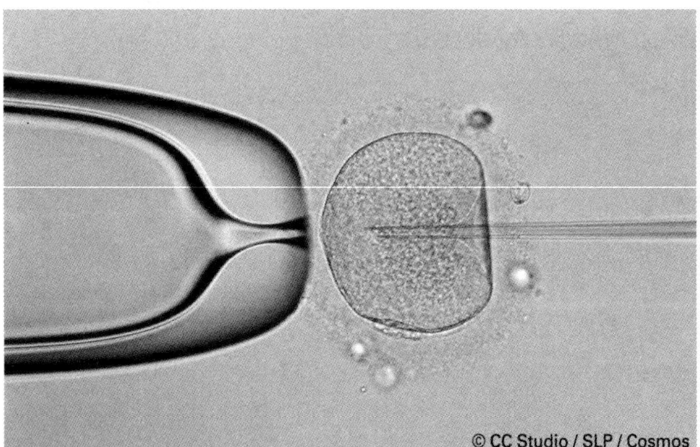


*Sperm injection by pipette*

The findings of one study, concerning four boys born using ICSI, revealed that the Y chromosomes of all four subjects had a deficiency on the long arm of the chromosome, pointing to the likelihood of ................................................................ *(defect of the sperm which is related genetically)* being passed on to male children, thus making them infertile like their fathers.

This raises at least two separate ethical issues. On the one hand, is it acceptable to allow genetic deficiencies to be knowingly transmitted? On the other, what ........................................... *(effect in a term (period) which is long)* could this have on the ................................................ *(pool of genes of humans)*?

TALKING POINT

- Some people maintain that the danger to the gene pool is a minor problem that need not be taken seriously. What do you think?

## *12.4. Checkpoints*

IN OTHER WORDS

**Definitions – purpose**

*Use the pattern:*
"X **means** to do Y **so that** Z occurs."

*Example:* to monitor
*"To monitor **means** to systematically collect data **so that** progress can be checked."*

- *Define these words:*
  *to diet ▪ to hurry ▪ to examine ▪ to sum up*
- *Find a word in Exercise 12.3 that can be explained in the same way and ask your neighbour to define it.*

BACK TO BASICS

**"The / a"**: do you know how to use the article?

- *Complete the text about scorpions with **the** / **a** / **Ø**.*

1. Douglas Gaffin is ...... zoologist working at ...... Oklahoma University. One of his fields of expertise is ...... arachnid ecology.
2. ...... scorpion is ...... nocturnal animal and its study is facilitated as it fluoresces under ...... ultraviolet light at ...... night.
3. The species is extremely resistant. Desert scorpions can withstand ...... high temperatures of up to 47°C which kill other desert arthropods, while other sorts of scorpion can be frozen for weeks and within ...... few hours, return to normal levels of ...... activity.
4. After ...... sexual activity ...... females sometimes eat ...... male.
5. The venom of some species found in ...... Middle East, ...... South Africa and ...... Philippines can be highly dangerous as it contains ...... neurotoxins which attack ...... nervous system and can cause ...... death.

## THE WORD WEB – MORE MULTI-WORD VERBS

▮ *First match the sentence with the definition and then insert the appropriate particles: FORWARD • THROUGH • UP • ON • DOWN • AWAY • OFF • OUT.*

1. He opened the letter and **threw** ........ the envelope.
2. Have you got time to **look** ............ my essay before I hand it in?
3. At the end of the meeting, William **put** .................. a new suggestion.
4. Due to the force of gravity, the space vehicle **speeds** ........ as it approaches the planet.
5. They **carried** ........ talking for at least half an hour after he had left.
6. As the speed of the molecules decreases, the gas **cools** ........... .
7. His hand-writing is terrible. It is difficult to **make** ........ what he has written.
8. I am not free for the appointment on Friday. We must **put** it ........ till the following week.

a. to propose
b. to distinguish
c. to get rid of
d. to cancel / delay
e. to continue
f. to check / examine
g. to lose heat
h. to accelerate

### *12.5. Web search*

▮ Find a specifications list or an image of a process. Make a 3 minute OHP presentation (cf. *Examples in context*).

▮ Do you know what an aardvark is? It is a **four legged, termite-eating animal**. Find out more about it.

### *Word search*

▮ Search the web for five 4-word compound nouns using head words like "technique", "system", "process" ...

## *Self evaluation – exit test*

▮ *Form compound nouns corresponding to the following definitions.*

1. A module for travelling in space designed for three men
   → ..........................................................................................................

2. A program which sequences genes
   → ...........................................................................

3. Techniques for survival over a period of time (term) which is long
   → ..........................................................................................................................

4. Research into drugs which is oriented towards profit
   → ...........................................................................................

5. Levels of dioxide of carbon which rise
   → ......................................................................

6. A tube that is made of steel with a diameter of 88 millimetres
   → ........................................................................................................................

7. Cells which cause cancer and destroy bones
   → ...............................................................................

8. A period for trials which lasts four days
   → ......................................................................

9. Techniques which sensor and are controlled by satellites
   → .................................................................................................

10. An insect that has six wings and four legs
   → ............................................................................

# Using the Overhead Projector

*Being able to use the OHP is an important skill to master. Students sometimes think that this is difficult, but in fact, it is relatively easy to make a high quality and elegant presentation. There are several reasons for this:*

- *as the speaker, you know your subject well;*
- *if you forget what you were going to say, the transparency supplies notes to remind you of the next point;*
- *you become easier to understand, as what you say is reinforced by visual communication.*

This section consists of four parts:

1. A brief review of the most common forms of graphic support followed by exercises so that you can practise using OHP presentation structures.
2. A model OHP presentation.
3. Pair work practice.
4. A "reference bank" of functions to help you prepare your presentations.

## Part 1

*Answer the question using the phrases in brackets.*

***Figure A – Table***

CAUSES OF UNNATURAL DEATH
STATISTICAL PROBABILITY
USA

| | |
|---|---|
| Road accident | 1 : 100 |
| Homicide | 1 : 300 |
| Fire | 1 : 800 |
| Firearms accident | 1 : 2,500 |
| Aircraft crash | 1 : 20,000 |
| Flood | 1 : 30,000 |
| Snake bite | 1 : 100,000 |

Source: *Nature* – 1994 (adapted)

1. What does the table show?
*(figure A / provide / comparative data / probability)*

.......................................................................................

....................................................................................... .

2. Where is the information concerning causes of death located? *(indicated / left hand column)*

.......................................................................................

....................................................................................... .

3. What can you say about the source of the data? *(as you can see / bottom left hand corner / data / first published)*

.......................................................................................

....................................................................................... .

***Figure B – Bar chart***

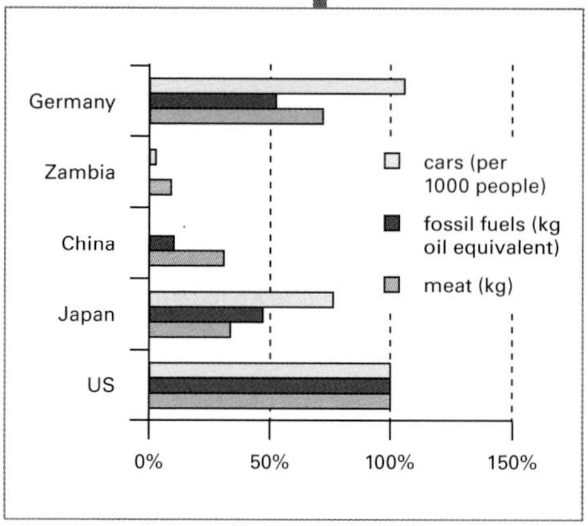


***Per capita consumption***
*% of US consumption – 1997*
Source: World Resources Institute (adapted)

4. What is shown on the horizontal axis? *(per capita / can be seen)*

..........................................................

..........................................................

.......................................................... .

5. What does the graph show about developing countries?
*(basically / the poorer countries are ...)*

..........................................................

.......................................................... .

6. What can you say about the consumption of meat in Zambia and the US? *(roughly / ten times as much)*

..........................................................

.......................................................... .

***Figure C – Line graph***

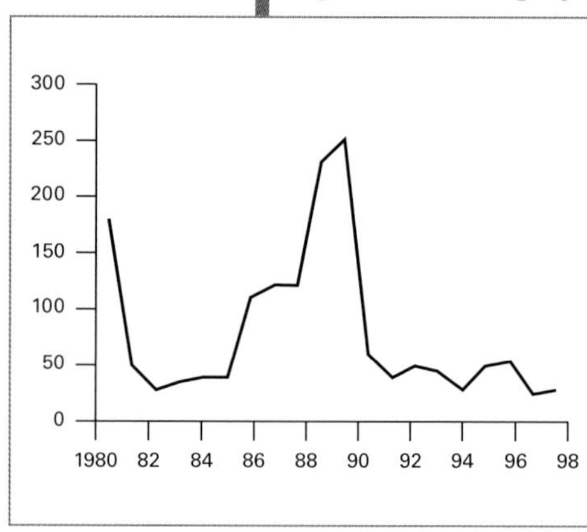


***Incidence of measles in the US (‰)***
*(comprehensive vaccination campaigns were stopped in the early 1980s and reintroduced in 1989)*
Source: National Immunisation Program – 2002 (adapted)

7. What happened between 1982 and 1986? *(to begin with / slow but steady / increase / curve / rise / sharply)*

..........................................................

.......................................................... .

8. What happened in 1986?
*(after / sharp / increase / level off)*

..........................................................

.......................................................... .

9. What happened in 1989? *(immediately after / attain / peak / fall / abruptly)*

..........................................................

.......................................................... .

10. What happened after 1990?
*(from then on / virtually / die out)*

..........................................................

.......................................................... .

11. What do the different sectors of the pie chart show?
*(correspond / distribution)*

..............................................................

.............................................................. .

12. Compare the risks of artificial and natural radiation.
*(clearly / far greater)*

..............................................................

.............................................................. .

13. Compare the danger of radiation from cosmic and radon sources.
*(roughly / seven times as ...)*

..............................................................

.............................................................. .

***Figure D – Pie chart***

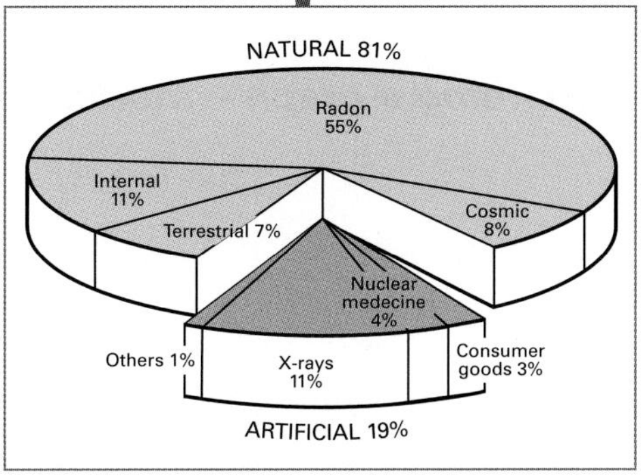


***Natural and artificial sources of radiation. USA – annual dose – 1987***

Source: National council on radiation protection (adapted)

***Figure E – Flow chart***

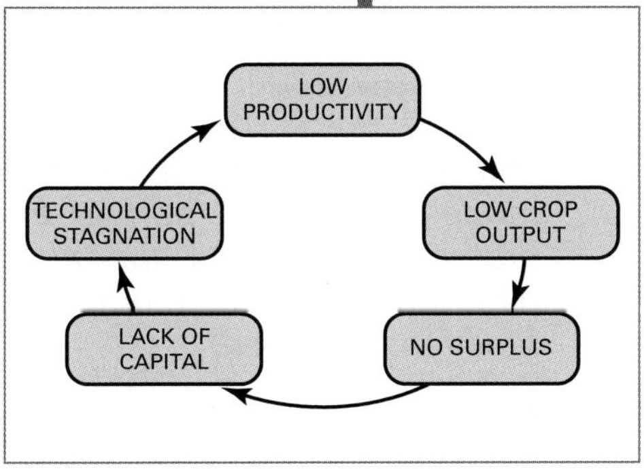


***Agriculture – the vicious circle of underdevelopment***

Source: Elements of human geography. Allen and Unwin – 1985 (adapted)

14. Describe the first 4 stages of the vicious circle using the following framework:

"Since productivity is low, this means that

.............................................................. .

Consequently, ..................................

..............................................................

available which accounts for ................

.............................................................. .

Inevitably, this situation leads to ............

.............................................................. ."

## Part 2

## *Describing a graph – model*

***Medical care (France).***
***Average annual spending per capita***
Source: INSEE – 1999 (adapted)

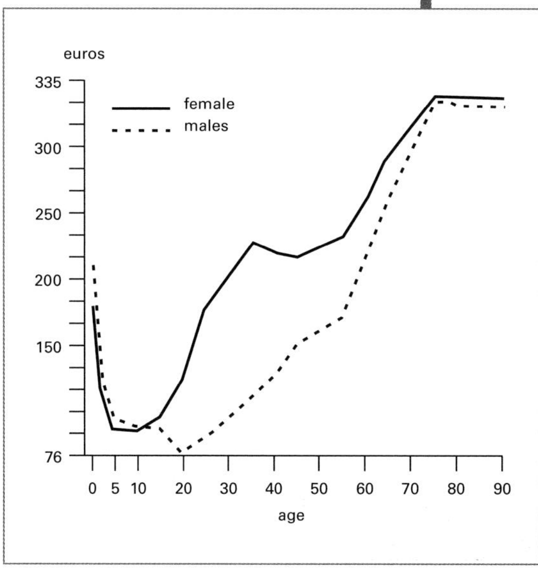


*The graph on the left and the model of the first part of an oral description on the next page illustrate how, in practice, functions are used.*

■ *When you have finished studying the two documents, look at the graph again and with the help of the reference bank (p. 156) describe the graph to your partner using as far, as possible, new functions.*

FRAMING

**Good morning. Well**, what I would like to discuss with you today is the **problem of rising medical expenses**, and **with particular with reference to** the situation in France.

TOPIC & FOCUSING

RELEVANCE OF TOPIC

**As you know, over the last 40-50 years**, there has been a steep increase in medical expenditure and governments are now faced with a major political problem of finding ways of financing the health services.

ORGANISATION & SEQUENCING

**To begin with**, we will look at a line graph, giving comparative data for male and female expenditure during a normal life span. This will be **followed by** a short commentary and **finally**, I will go on to discuss some of the causes and consequences of this state of affairs.

The line graph in the figure is **adapted from INSEE 1999** and gives comparative data for the average annual per capita expenses for men and women in France. **As can be seen**, age is indicated at 10 years intervals on the horizontal axis, while annual costs are shown in euros on the vertical axis on the left hand side – **here**.

SOURCE

REFERENCE TO VISUALS

GENERALISATION & APPROXIMATION

**Basically**, what the graph shows is that, in the first few years of life, there is a tendency for medical costs to be **similar** for the two sexes.

COMPARISON

REFORMULATION

**That is to say, the younger people are the more** medical care they need so, as can be expected, immediately after birth spending is high (**roughly** 200 euros).

LINK WORD

DETAILED DATA DESCRIPTION

**However**, over the next 5 years, the **curve drops steeply** for both sexes and then **levels off** until the age of 10.

CHRONOLOGY

**At this stage** the two curves separate. The bottom curve – here – for males, continues to drop until the age of 20, where it reaches its lowest point of approximately 80 euros. **From then on**, it rises **slowly but steadily** in function of age, with a **slight** acceleration after the age of 55.

MODIFICATION

# Part 3

## A. Pair work

- *Chose any one of the figures below that you would like to describe.*
- *Then, make a list of functions that you wish to learn from the different sections of the "reference bank" (p. 156).*
- *Improvise an OHP presentation to your partner using your list as notes.*

Here is an example of the sort of list you could make:

➤ *Well • This figure illustrates • With particular reference to • As you know • To begin with • Then • And finally • The data comes from ...*

***Pseudoscience – belief in astrology and the paranormal. USA – 1998***

Source: LEDA – http://leda.law.cornell.edu/leda/ (adapted)

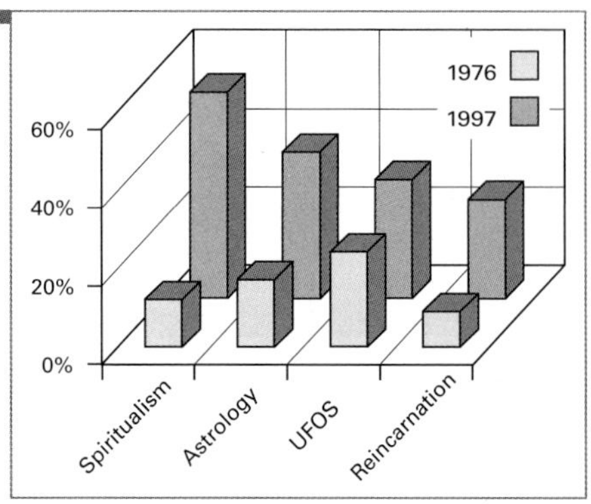


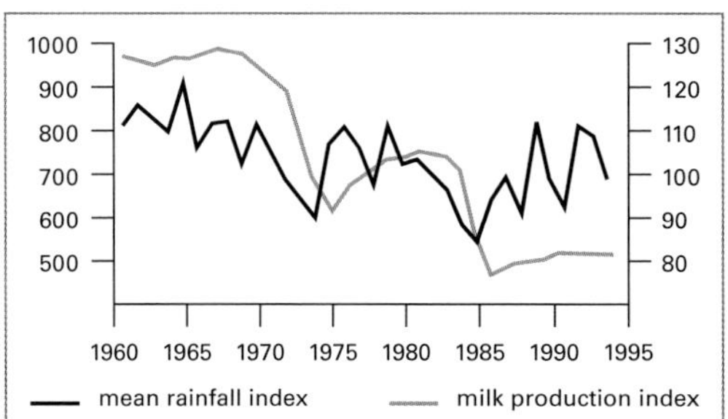


***Index of rainfall and milk production. Niger, Mali and Chad***

Source: FAO (adapted)

***Induced abortion rates – 1990-1997 (France)***

Source: Drees (adapted)

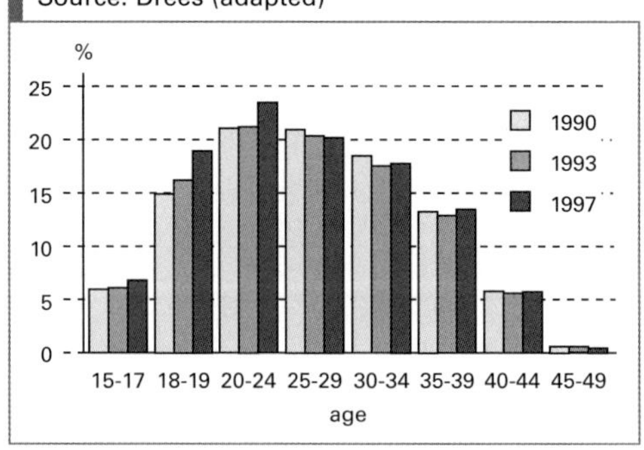


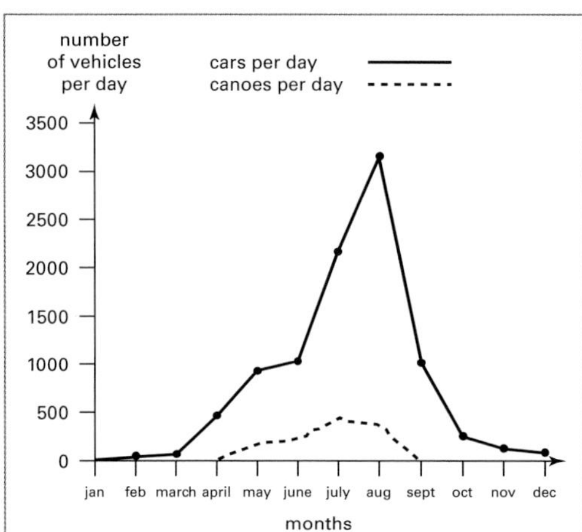


***Seasonal car and canoe traffic in the "Gorges de l'Ardèche"***

Source: P. Mathias, personal communication

***The problem of obesity: body mass for men and women in the UK***

Source: http://www.annecollins.com – 2003 (adapted)

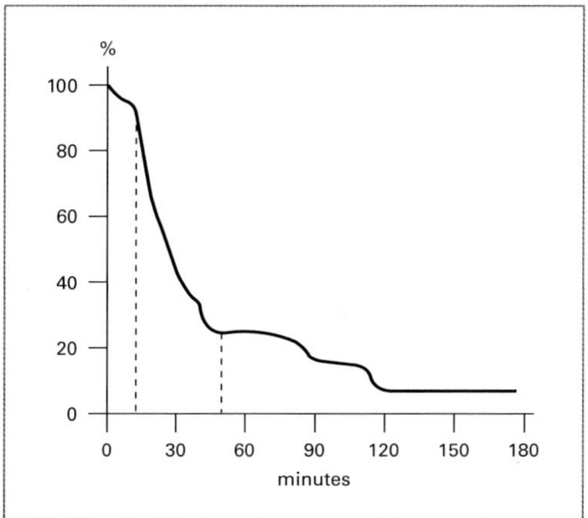


***Avalanches – probability of survival after burial***

Source: Fédération française de la montagne et de l'escalade – 2003 (adapted)

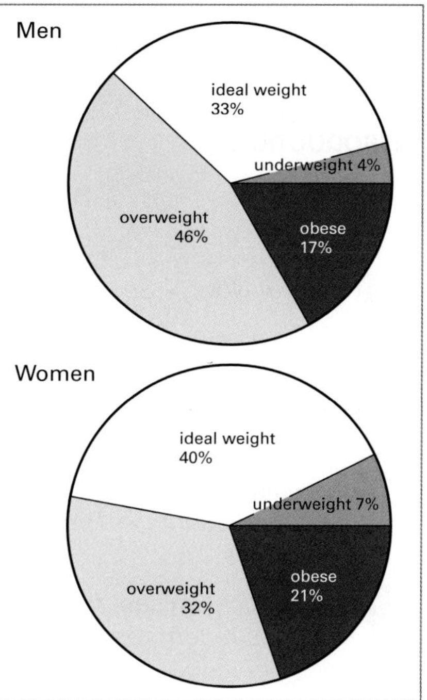


## B. *Making a good OHP presentation – the golden rules*

- *Work in pairs. Make a list of what you consider to be the five most important and the two least important pieces of advice.*

### The golden rules of OHP presentation

1. Never write more than 2 running lines of text.
2. Shift your eye contact from one person to another.
3. Don't forget to explain diagrams, units, sources, etc.
4. Prepare your final sentence – it is not easy to end elegantly.
5. Never hold notes in your hand – you will end up by reading and become incomprehensible.
6. Diagrams and graphic elements are not just decoration. Make sure that you use them dynamically.
7. To speak fluently, you must use the structures in the reference bank.
8. Make sure that your writing is large enough to be read by all.
9. Respect the time limit for the talk scrupulously.
10. Choose a subject which interests you personally and which you would like to communicate to others.
11. Before you start, make sure that your transparencies are in order.
12. A good rule to follow for OHP presentation is "tell them what you are going to tell them – tell them – tell them what you have just told them".
13. Turn off the OHP when you are not using it.
14. Be careful that you leave the audience time to read the information.
15. When referring to information on the OHP, make sure you use a pointer.
16. It is essential to have something interesting and thought-provoking in the introduction.
17. Make sure that your transparencies are not monotonous – vary the size of letters, use colours, boxes, arrows ...
18. You cannot make a good OHP presentation if you neglect body language.

# Part 4 – A functional reference bank

## INTRODUCTION

### 1. FRAMING

- *Well ▪ Now ▪ So ▪ Good morning ...*

### 2. THE SUBJECT

- *I would like to discuss / speak about ▪ I am going to talk about ▪ I would like to present ▪ The topic I have chosen is ▪ The issue I would like to discuss is ...*
- *The article raises the question of / is a report on / is an account of / outlines recent research on ... / discusses ways of dealing with ...*

### 3. FOCUSING

- *And more especially / specifically ▪ With particular reference to ▪ In relation to ▪ Laying particular emphasis on ...*

### 4. RELEVANCE

- *The reason that I have chosen ▪ As you know, medical expenses have a major impact on ... that is why ▪ Why talk about medical expenses? Well, it is because ...*
- *This is a striking example of ▪ It underlines one of the main problems ▪ The interest of the article lies in the fact ...*

### 5. PLAN / ORGANISATION

- *There are three main points ▪ Before going on to describe X, I would like to ...*
- *To begin with ▪ First of all ▪ In the first section ▪ I'll start by ...*
- *Secondly ▪ Then ▪ Next ▪ Afterwards ▪ This will be followed by ...*
- *Thirdly ▪ And finally ▪ And to end / conclude ...*

6. SOURCE AND REFERENCE

- *The information comes from ▪ It is adapted from ▪ The article was published in ▪ The talk is based on ...*
- *A survey was carried out in ▪ An experiment was designed to ...*

## GRAPH DESCRIPTION

7. REFERRING TO VISUALS

- *As you can see ▪ Here, on the bottom left hand corner ▪ This can be seen over here in the second column ...*
- *This curve illustrates ▪ The table illustrates ▪ The pie chart shows ▪ The figure ▪ Diagram ▪ Dotted line ▪ Shaded area ▪ The largest sector ...*

8. DESCRIBING A CURVE

- ***Rising** – The curve rises / increases / goes up / attains a peak ...*
- ***Falling** – The temperatures drops / goes down / decreases / declines / reaches a low point ...*
- ***Stability** – It levels off / reaches a plateau / stagnates / remains stable ...*
- ***Modification** – A sharp / steep / significant / considerable / unexpected / gradual ... fall ▪ It declines steadily / abruptly / dramatically / unexpectedly ... with minor fluctuations ...*

9. PATTERNS AND TENDENCIES

- *A general trend ▪ A growing tendency ▪ A slow but steady increase ▪ A clear pattern ▪ An overall improvement ▪ A swing ...*
- *The richer people are, the more energy they consume ...*

### 10. CHRONOLOGY

- *From then on / onwards ▪ Immediately after that ▪ At this stage ...*
- *Over the last few years ▪ Up to now ...*
- *In the near future ▪ Shortly ▪ Before long ▪ By the end of the year ▪ It is expected ...*

### 11. CONTRAST, COMPARISON & SIMILARITY

- *By contrast ▪ As opposed to ▪ Unlike ...*
- *However ▪ While ▪ Nevertheless ▪ On the other hand ...*
- *In the same way ▪ Similarly ▪ Likewise ...*
- *By comparison ▪ Compared to ▪ A great deal better ▪ Considerably worse ...*

## DISCUSSION

### 12. GENERALISATION & APPROXIMATION

- *Basically ▪ On the whole ▪ Generally speaking ▪ As a rule ...*
- *To a certain extent ▪ More or less ▪ Roughly ▪ Almost ▪ Virtually ...*

### 13. CAUSE & CONSEQUENCE

- *There are 3 main reasons; in the first place ▪ It is due to the fact ▪ Owing to ▪ Can be accounted for ...*
- *Since ▪ Because ▪ As ...*
- *This leads to / results in / brings about / triggers off ...*
- *Consequently ▪ Therefore ▪ Thus ▪ Hence ▪ Thereby ...*

### 14. Hypothesis

- *It can be assumed • It would appear likely that • In all probability / likelihood ...*
- *If the project is finished on time • Unless carbon emissions decrease ...*
- *This means there may be • It could well lead to • There might be ...*

### 15. Clarification & restatement

- *In other words • That is to say • What I mean by this is • To put it simply • For example • For instance • e.g. • Namely • Such as • This can be illustrated by ...*

## Concluding

### 16. Drawing conclusions

- *This means to say that • It suggests • It is a good / striking example of • It brings out / illustrates the importance • It underlines how important ...*

### 17. Recapitulation and finishing

- *To summarise • To go over the main points again • Basically, what I have tried to show ...*
- *Finally • As a conclusion • Last but not least • I would like to add just one last thing ...*
- *Are there any questions?*

# ANSWERS

## UNIT 1

### *Entry test*

1. height
2. amounts
3. range
4. weight
5. accurate
6. length
7. work out
8. slows down
9. average
10. root

### *Examples in context*

- roughly – approximately
- weight – mass
- slightly more ≠ much less
- wing span – distance from one wing tip to the other
- amount – quantity
- work out – calculate
- attained – reached
- cross-section – transversal dimension
- thick ≠ thin
- width – distance across

### *Exercises*

**➜ 1.1. – A**

1. It probably has a total length of approximately 2.2 km.
2. The central span is 856 m in length.
3. The width is 23.6 m.
4. Each tower is roughly 210 m in height.
5. The height is about 52 m.
6. Each tower weighs at least 20,000 tonnes.

**➜ 1.1. – B**

widens ▪ narrow ▪ extending ▪ high ▪ weight ▪ thin ▪ speeds ▪ amount ▪ average ▪ rate ▪ reached

**➜ 1.2. – A**

1. The average length of the fetus is almost 7 cm.
2. The weight ranges from 28 to 35 gm.
3. The circumference of the head is slightly over 8 cm.
4. The volume of the amniotic liquid is roughly 60 ml.
5. There is an odd number of fingers on each hand.
6. What is the width of the umbilical cord?
7. The nutrients are supplied through the narrow arteries.
8. The heartbeat can be monitored in the 9$^{th}$ week.
9. Blood vessels can be seen through the thin skin.

**➜ 1.2. – B**

1. At what stage does the heart begin to beat?
2. When does the fetus begin to monitor its own temperature?
3. Do male and female fetuses weigh the same?
4. In which week does the fetus begin to detect light?

**➜ 1.2. – C**

1. The bones begin to harden in the 13$^{th}$ week.
2. In the 4$^{th}$ week, the femur lengthens considerably.
3. After fertilisation, the wall of the uterus thickens.

### → 1.3.

- officially registered – recorded
- altitude – height
- measurement downwards – depth
- transversal measurement – cross-section
- measurement of volume – cubic
- opposite of thin – thick
- half the diameter – radius
- extent – scale
- precision – accuracy
- vary – range
- reached – attained
- nearly – almost
- average – mean
- quantity – amount
- zone – area
- delayed – slowed down
- which weighs a lot – heavy

### → 1.4. Checkpoints

IN OTHER WORDS ◄·······················

**Magma** is the hot, semi-liquid rock from a volcano.
**An island** is land which is surrounded by water.
**Famine** is when people die or are hungry because of a lack of food.
**The stratosphere** is a high layer of the atmosphere.

BACK TO BASICS ◄·······················

1. When did it become extinct / How long ago did …?
2. How much does it weigh / How heavy is … / What is the weight?
3. What did the specialists examine?
4. What runs very fast?

THE WORD WEB ◄·······················

1. wide / width / widen
2. measuring / measurements / measure
3. ranging / range / range
4. short / shortness / shortens
5. weak / weakness / weakens
6. equipped / equipment / equipped
7. red / redness / reddens [G. Notes 1]
8. heavy / weight / weigh

### *Exit test*

1. slightly
2. thin
3. inaccurate
4. stage
5. even
6. shallow
7. extent
8. monitoring
9. scale
10. strengthen

## UNIT 2

### *Entry test*

1. beats
2. swings
3. per
4. recurrence
5. rate
6. steadily
7. every
8. series
9. hourly
10. ratio

### *Examples in context*

- steady – regular
- rate – beat
- seldom ≠ often
- pattern – schedule, organisation
- set – group, series
- every second day – every other day
- range – vary
- swing – movement

**Aerobic Threshold running** – the upper limit of aerobic exercise just before lactate acid is produced.

## *Exercises*

### ➜ 2.1.

6. / d · 7. / c, a · 8. / b · 9. / e · 10. / a

11. / i · 12. / h · 13. / j · 14. / g · 15. / f

16. / o · 17. / k · 18. / l · 19. / n · 20. / m

### ➜ 2.2.

- **(1)** – waves which are reflected ...
- echoes. It is this ...
- periodically and are in ...
- range. As the bat ...
- rate increases ...
- per second ...
- series of genetic mutations ...
- **(8)** – pulses / frequencies used by bats ...
- frequencies / pulses than those ...
- usually used by other ...
- wavelength of 3 cm ...
- pattern of *"Tadarida teniotis"* ...
- random catches ...
- daily examination ...
- proportion of large insects ...

### ➜ Talking point

**Darwin** showed that evolution was a result of genetic mutations which were transmitted and then reinforced by natural selection. **Lamarck** believed that acquired characteristics could become hereditary and be passed on to the offspring.

### ➜ 2.3.

- repeated – recurrent
- rarely – seldom
- succession – series
- without method – randomly
- 1 : 10 – in / out of ten
- at a constant rate – steadily
- one after the other – alternating
- 2 times – twice
- little by little – gradually
- continual – non-stop
- from time to time – periodic
- pulsation – beat
- changes – fluctuations

**Treadmill** – a machine (for exercise) on which you walk without advancing.

### ➜ 2.4. Checkpoints

IN OTHER WORDS ◄··················

**A predator** is an animal which kills and eats other animals.
**A sonar system** is a system which uses echoes to locate objects.
**The skin** is a membrane which covers an animal's body.
**Food** is a substance which we eat to obtain calories.

BACK TO BASICS ◄··················

**Actually** – the sentence can be either **right** or **wrong**; it depends on what you mean. The sentence does **not** mean *"now / today / at the moment"* but it means *"you may be surprised to know / contrary to what most people think / in fact, the number is increasing"*.

THE WORD WEB ◄··················

1. rely on / f
2. carry out / a, d
3. consist of / b
4. set up / e
5. work out / d
6. involved in / g
7. accounts for / h
8. depends on / c, g

## *Exit test*

1. cluster
2. daily
3. pattern
4. seldom
5. recurrent
6. array
7. evenly
8. range
9. random
10. hardly

## UNIT 3

### *Entry test*

1. both
2. less
3. hotter
4. unlike
5. same as
6. enhances
7. spread / spreading
8. hair-like
9. improved
10. matching

### *Examples in context*

*The* ***Hindenburg crashed*** *in Lakehurst, New Jersey in 1937, coming from Germany. The crash was caused by an explosion due to a hydrogen leak. The Hindenburg carried essentially passengers. The competition of faster aeroplanes in the 1930s and their vulnerability to bad weather made Zeppelins less and less competitive.*

- underestimation ≠ overestimation
- heavier than ≠ lighter than
- lessens ≠ increases
- enhance ≠ reduce
- strengthened ≠ weakened
- foremost ≠ the least important
- lowered ≠ raised
- reduces ≠ increases
- major ≠ minor
- the fewer infrastructures there are, the cheaper ... ≠ the more infrastructures there are, the more expensive ...
- shortened ≠ lengthened
- leading ≠ secondary

### *Exercises*

**➜ 3.1. – A** (↦ *see G. Notes 4)*

1. warmer / -est
2. easier / -iest
3. more / the most expensive
4. less / the least expensive
5. thinner / thinnest
6. the more expensive a car is, the better it is
7. because it is unique

**➜ 3.2.**

- largest – biggest / greatest
- > little – less than
- closely match – are very similar to
- well-suited – suitable / adapted
- unlike – in contrast to
- 100 × > great – a 100 times as great as / a 100 times greater than
- warmer and more humid – hotter and wetter
- Mars-like conditions – Mars analog conditions / conditions comparable to Mars
- improved – better / enhanced
- major – main
- enhanced – better / more efficient
- to further – to extend / develop
- similar in shape to a U – U-shaped

**➜ 3.3.**

- improved – enhanced
- + good – better
- + versatility – more versatility
- increasing – raising
- worst ≠ best
- main – foremost
- + easy – easier
- – expensive – less expensive
- in contrast to – unlike
- + low – lower
- + accuracy – more accuracy
- match – suit
- 20 × > great – 20 times as great as / greater than
- more ≠ fewer
- extends – widens
- + far – further
- reduce – lessen

**➜ Talking point**

1. The material is programmed by forming it into the parent shape.
2. The temperature is raised.

3. As a result, crystallisation of the switching segment occurs.
4. The material can be bent into another configuration.
5-7. When reheated, it will switch back to the parent form at the transient temperature.

### → 3.4. Checkpoints

IN OTHER WORDS

**A rat** is similar to a mouse but much bigger.
**Diamond** is similar to glass but much harder.
**A village** is similar to a town but much smaller.
The climate of **Mars** is similar to Haughton but much colder in winter.

BACK TO BASICS

**To agree** – *"I do not agree (with you) that ..."* (N.B. – Do not put "**to be**" before agree: *"~~I am agreed that~~ ..."*)

THE WORD WEB

1. regulation
2. expand
3. standardisation
4. accumulates
5. explosion
6. pressure
7. generated
8. minimised
9. extension

### *Exit test*

1. neither / nor
2. enhanced
3. boost
4. match
5. spreading
6. weaken
7. unlike
8. twice as fast
9. the poorer people are, the less they eat
10. overheat

## UNIT 4

### *Entry test*

1. almost
2. steady
3. basically
4. relevant
5. widespread
6. roughly
7. minute
8. outstanding
9. reliable
10. steep

### *Examples in context*

- average – mean
- slightly – a little
- sharp – steep, sudden
- roughly ≠ exactly
- steep ≠ gradual
- steadily – regularly
- more or less – approximately
- virtually – almost
- entire – whole
- to a certain extent – partly
- on the whole – basically
- foremost – leading
- basically – fundamentally
- widespread – common

GRAPH

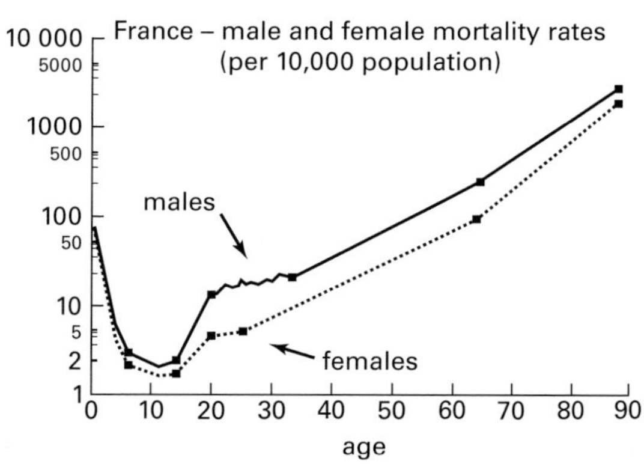

## Exercises

### → 4.1. – A

1. / g ▪ 2. / h ▪ 3. / j ▪ 4. / k ▪ 5. / b ▪ 6. / e ▪ 7. / f ▪ 8. / d ▪ 9. / a ▪ 10. / i ▪ 11. / l ▪ 12. / c

### → 4.1. – B

1. efficient
2. huge
3. basically
4. reliable
5. widespread
6. roughly
7. virtually
8. typical
9. thoroughly
10. outstanding
11. hardly any
12. to a certain extent / basically

### → 4.2.

- virtually – almost / practically
- tiny – minute
- major – leading
- massive – huge
- practically – almost
- extremely – exceedingly
- hardly – barely
- proper – real / appropriate
- efficient – reliable
- relevant – appropriate
- crucial – acute / real
- scarcely – hardly / barely
- utterly – entirely
- thorough – careful

### → 4.3.

- (1) – extensive – widespread
- key – crucial / foremost
- relatively – quite
- approximately – roughly
- constantly – steadily
- dependable – reliable
- leading – foremost
- careful – thorough
- (9) – essentially – basically
- nearly – almost / virtually
- relatively – fairly
- tiny – minute
- satisfactory – suitable
- practically – virtually
- tremendous, enormous – huge

### → 4.4. Checkpoints

IN OTHER WORDS ◄·····················

**An adolescent** is a young person, that is to say, someone who is not yet an adult.
**A bus** is a vehicle that carries people, that is to say, a means of transport.
**Cancer** is a disease caused by an uncontrolled growth of cells, that is to say, a tumour.
**An antibiotic** is a chemical product that can destroy viruses or bacteria, that is to say, a drug.

BACK TO BASICS ◄·····················

**Important** – "Important" should be used **only** in sentence 1.

→ *if you have made a mistake, check the meaning in the **G. Notes 6***

THE WORD WEB ◄·····················

1. / of ▪ 2. / at ▪ 3. / for ▪ 4. / with ▪ 5. / of ▪ 6. / to ▪ 7. / in ▪ 8. / in

## Exit test

1. major / main
2. roughly
3. virtually
4. slightly
5. extent
6. chief
7. reliable
8. suitable
9. whole
10. scarcely

## UNIT 5

### *Entry test*

1. thereby
2. namely
3. that is to say
4. moreover
5. in spite of
6. nevertheless
7. such as
8. hence
9. besides
10. as a rule

### *Examples in context* *(possible answers)*

- doubtless – clearly / in all probability
- that is to say – in other words
- despite – although he was suffering from
- as a result of – because of
- besides – not only did he / apart from
- as a rule – usually / generally
- i.e. – that is to say
- however – unfortunately / but the tracheotomy
- thereby – thus
- nevertheless – in spite of this

### *Exercises*

#### → 5.1. – A

1. / j • 2. / a • 3. / f • 4. / h • 5. / d • 6. / e • 7. / c • 8. / g • 9. / b • 10. / i

#### → 5.1. – B

1. actually
2. whereas
3. yet
4. despite the fact
5. namely
6. hence
7. thereby / hence
8. obviously / hence

#### → 5.2.

1. ... are the most powerful releases of energy within the solar system ...
2. ... 10-20 million K.
3. ... temperatures of 100 million K can be attained.
4. ... consists of ultraviolet radiation and X-rays.
5. They are converted into solar plasma heat ...
6. Accelerated particles ... electrons, protons and heavy nuclei ...
7. Particles take 36-48 hours to reach the Earth ...
8. ... only a small part of the energy arrives.
9. ... there is an effect on the magnetosphere and ionosphere.
10. ... radio communications are disrupted.
11. ... they cause magnetic storms.
12. The Earth's atmosphere is heated ...
13. The particles can damage electronic instrumentation ...

#### → 5.3.

- (1) – since / as
- as a result
- however
- namely
- furthermore
- whereas / however
- as / since
- (8) – therefore / hence
- such as
- although
- in fact
- besides
- naturally
- thereby / therefore / hence
- hence / therefore

#### → 5.4. Checkpoints

IN OTHER WORDS ◄·····················

**The solar system** – basically, the solar system consists of the sun and the 9 planets.
**A zoo** – basically, a zoo consists of a collection of animals for public display.

**A telescope** – basically, a telescope consists of a tube and a series of adjustable lenses.
**Water** – basically, water consists of two atoms of hydrogen and one atom of oxygen.

BACK TO BASICS ◄··········

**According to** – all the sentences are correct except sentence 3.
"According to" is rarely used to express one's **own** opinion.
→ *look at the **G. Notes 12** for more detail on how to express personal opinion*

THE WORD WEB ◄··········

1. immobile
2. anticlockwise
3. unaware
4. inaccurate
5. disabilities
6. improbable
7. disconnected
8. irrelevant
9. irresistible
10. antifreeze

### *Exit test*

1. besides
2. namely
3. despite
4. nevertheless
5. as a rule
6. whereas
7. obviously
8. thereby / thus
9. doubtless / doubtlessly
10. hence

## UNIT 6

### *Entry test*

1. have known
2. are now waiting
3. had been working / had worked
4. have found
5. are being
6. have finished / finish
7. never worked
8. suffer
9. had already mapped
10. was burning / burned

### *Examples in context*

- kills – pres. simp. – *everyone knows that* (general truth)
- have shown – pres. perf. simp. – *Over recent years*
- is taking – pres. cont. – *currently*
- criticised – past simp. – *At the beginning of the month*
- had not been matched – past. perf. simp. passive – *before they were tested* (implicit)
- has been working – pres. perf. cont. – *up to now* (implicit)
- aims – pres. simp. – *it defines what they are* (implicit)
- were intending – past cont. – *temporary duration in the past* (implicit)
- have demonstrated – pres. perf. simp. – *so far*

→ **Talking point**

- It is a fact – but is it clearly understood by everyone?
- They were not properly matched.
- Trying to provide independent scientific advice.
- The dangers of cancer outweigh the dangers of minor faults in protocols.

## *Exercises*

**→ 6.1. – A** *(possible answers – check in the Key points for tenses)*

1. nowadays / currently
2. while
3. recently
4. The New Scientist reports that
5. but with little success so far / over the last 20 years
6. previously
7. It is a fact that
8. currently
9. this year / over the last 20 years
10. Over the last 20 years

**→ 6.1. – B**

- is seeking
- has played / is playing / has been playing
- have been involved
- are working
- are / will be expected
- have had / have

**→ 6.2.**

1. pres. cont. / (b)
2. passive (by experts) / pres. perf. simp. / (g)
3. pres. perf. cont. / (c)
4. passive (by people) / pres. simp. / (d)
5. passive (by a speleologist) / past simp. / (h)
6. past cont. / (h)
7. passive (by the laboratory) / past perf. simp. / (a)
8. pres. simp. / (e)
9. pres. perf. simp. / (g)
10. pres. perf. cont. / (c)

**→ Talking point**

**Golf** – the high mortality rate is partly due to heart attack from old age and partly to lightning.

**→ 6.3.**

1. a) "has probably had – have been using". The results are important now – the text is concerned with the influence of Aristotle up to now.

1. b) "it must be remembered – it is therefore". The remarks (about antiquity) are addressed to the reader today.
2. almost exclusively past tense – concerned with historical information
3. "is living" – on-going, present time, now
   "has been developed" – from then (80 years ago) up to now
   "has enlarged" – the results are important now.
   "were taken" – "historical" dates (passive)

**→ 6.4. Checkpoints**

IN OTHER WORDS ◄·····················

**A letter** is basically a written message, in other words, a means of communication.
**A drug** is basically a way of treating an illness, in other words, a medicine.
**A nose** is basically an organ used for smelling, in other words, a sensor.
**Petrol** is basically a source of energy, in other words, a fuel.

BACK TO BASICS ◄·····················

It transforms mechanical energy **into** electrical energy.
They wanted to turn base metal **into** gold.
→ *see G. Notes 16*

THE WORD WEB ◄·····················

- crystalline *G. Notes 1*
- volcanic
- natural
- refractive
- optical
- valuable
- colourless
- yellowish
- greenish
- reliable
- industrial
- useful

## *Exit test*

1. has recognised
2. was considering
3. is influencing / has influenced
4. had improved

5. have identified
6. is drilling
7. has managed
8. were studying
9. eat / is eaten
10. had been utterly destroyed

## UNIT 7

### *Entry test*

1. lead
2. thus / therefore
3. due to
4. spark (off)
5. outcomes
6. resulted in
7. owing to
8. by-product
9. since
10. thereby

### *Examples in context*

- as – due to the fact that / since
- hence – therefore / thus
- as a result – hence
- thanks to – because of
- stems from – comes from
- outcome – result
- thus – consequently / thereby
- results in – triggers off / leads to
- therefore – consequently
- thereby – as a result of this
- triggers – sparks
- giving rise to – causing

### *Exercises*

**➔ 7.1. – A**

1. comes from / b
2. arises / h
3. hence / since / e
4. owing to / f
5. thanks to / owing to ("since" is possible if it has a temporal and not a causal meaning) / a
6. lead to / g
7. since / d
8. was brought about / c

**➔ 7.2.**

- Where does the financial backing come from?
- What is lightning responsible for?
- What did the rockets carry?
- What do laser beams do?
- What does the laser beam generate?
- When did they trigger a discharge?

#### *Franklin's kite*

***Benjamin Franklin** (1706-1790) was a US statesman (he helped write the "Declaration of Independence") and scientist. He is famous for having proved that atmospheric electricity is the same as the electrostatic charge that can be found in a Leyden jar. In his famous (and very dangerous experiment – 1752), he flew a kite during an electric storm and conducted electricity down a wet string to a Leyden jar.*

### ➜ 7.3.

- since it has the highest ...
- on account of the ageing population ...
- stems from a failure ...
- by-product of the conversion ...
- hence / thus / since there is only ...
- is brought about by the pathological development ...
- trigger certain harmful consequences ...
- thus / hence deformed ...
- resulting in blind spots ...
- outcome is that patients are no longer ...

### ➜ 7.4. Checkpoints

IN OTHER WORDS

**A manager** is a person whose job is to run a firm.
**A dentist** is a person whose job is to treat teeth.
**A biologist** is a person whose job is to study biology.
**An electrician** is a man whose job is to repair electrical equipment.

BACK TO BASICS

1. lie
2. raise
3. lay
4. rises
5. lay
6. raise
7. rises
8. lies

THE WORD WEB

1. overexposed
2. overproduction
3. unchecked
4. overeat
5. underachieve
6. underemployed
7. unmatched
8. overestimate
9. understaffed

***Exit test***

1. owing to
2. therefore
3. spark (off)
4. stemmed
5. spin-off
6. arises
7. outcome
8. triggered (off)
9. bring about
10. effect

## UNIT 8

***Entry test***

1. is transformed
2. would be
3. had not collided
4. means
5. will go off / goes off
6. would take
7. becomes
8. would have been burned
9. will be
10. unless

***Exercises***

### ➜ 8.1. – A

1. a) It explains the rules.
   b) You are talking to someone who is a possible candidate for the prize.
2. a) You are talking about a possible future event – for instance, the issue is being debated in Parliament.
   b) This is just a speculation, but it would logically lead to certain results.

3. a) Speculation. On condition that the hypothesis is satisfied, this future consequence is inevitable.
   b) Oil hasn't been discovered so the standard of living has not changed.

**➔ 8.1. – C**

*(some variation in the answers is possible – for type of conditional, see Key points)*

1. ... there would be a danger of famine.
2. ... you want to become a member of the Antarctic research team.
3. ... the ovaries continue to produce progesterone.
4. ... you would have got the job.
5. ... you would have to learn Russian.
6. ... millions would have died.
7. ... micro-organisms would be destroyed.
8. ... would not have learned to fly.

**➔ 8.2. – question 1**

- If the trajectory of an asteroid or a comet intersects ... it is labelled ...
- It is not, however ... unless it comes ...
- If their trajectory brings ... the gases evaporate ...
- Provided they have sufficient ... these objects may reach ...

**➔ 8.2. – question 2 (examples)**

- If it hadn't been a false alarm, there would have been global tsunamis.
- The Task force wouldn't have been set up if there hadn't been a threat.
- If the asteroid had not landed in the Taiga forest, the damage would have been enormous.
- If the Earth had not received carbon and water from meteorites, life would not have been possible on Earth.

**➔ 8.3.**

1. Unless implant techniques are improved, there will be no progress.
2. Biometrics has a future provided huge data bases are set up.
3. Amplification and regeneration techniques must be improved, otherwise development will be delayed.
4. Progress can be expected on condition that there is a breakthrough in chip miniaturisation.

**➔ 8.4. Checkpoints**

IN OTHER WORDS ◄·····················

**A map** – if you want to know which road to take, then you use a map.
**A fax** – if you want to send a message quickly, then you use a fax.
**A switch** – if you want to turn off the electricity, then you use the switch.
**A parachute** – if you want to jump out of a plane, then you had better use a parachute.

BACK TO BASICS ◄·····················

He has **hardly any** friends. (few)
It rained **hard** all day. (a lot)

→ *if you made a mistake, look at the* ***G. Notes 20*** *for more detail*

THE WORD WEB ◄·····················

1. ... action can be taken.
2. ... made arrangements ...
3. ... damage was done ...
4. ... take a completely different approach.
5. ... little can be done ...
6. ... noise made by the shock wave.
7. ... do something about the shortage ...
8. ... progress has been made ...
9. ... taking measures ...

***Exit test***

1. provided / providing
2. is pumped out
3. would dry up
4. condition
5. would have been
6. range
7. had taken place
8. would spread / had spread / was going to spread
9. unless
10. otherwise

## UNIT 9

### Entry test

1. should not
2. unlikely
3. may
4. ought to
5. likely
6. must have been
7. should
8. will doubtless
9. might
10. a) It is almost certain.
    b) Perhaps it was, perhaps it was not.
    c) This is one of the possible explanations.
    d) It is a fact.

### Examples in context

*(other answers are possible)*

can / (c) ▪ will / (d) ▪ should / (g) ▪ could / (f) ▪ may / (e) ▪ might / (a) ▪ must / (b)

### Exercises

**➜ 9.1. – B**

1. The temperature can range ...
2. This must be the right ...
3. ... we should see ...
4. The techniques might / may enable ...
5. Farmers could use ...

**➜ 9.1. – C**

6. The epidemic must have killed ...
7. He should have saved ...
8. The minister could have resigned ...
9. The pilot may / might / could have misunderstood ...
10. He can't / couldn't have caused ...

**➜ 9.2.**

- unexpected – surprising
- likely – probable
- ought to – will theoretically
- will – it is certain
- may – will perhaps
- can – it is possible
- assume – adopt the hypothesis
- might – it cannot be excluded
- should – it is advisable
- must – it is almost certain
- could – this is a possibility

**➜ 9.3.**

- **(1)** – Tsunamis must be among ...
- They can be caused ...
- The resulting waves can / may attain ...
- ... low-lying islands may / can be utterly submerged.
- ... it is estimated that more ...
- ... 36,000 people may have been killed.
- ... could / may well present ...
- **(8)** – It is assumed that this ...
- ... this must have been caused ...
- Supposing that the mountain ...
- ... will be dumped ...
- ... it is unlikely that the trajectory ...
- ... there should be no real ...
- ... which might occur ...
- ... would doubtless generate ...

**➜ 9.4. Checkpoints**

IN OTHER WORDS ◄··········

**A Landrover** – you can use a Landrover either in town or on mountain tracks.
**Water** – you can use water either to wash with or to drink.
**The money** – you can use the money either to go on a holiday or to buy a computer.
**A computer** – you can use a computer either as a word processor or to consult the Web.

BACK TO BASICS ◄··········

1. all the information (no "-s")
2. the news + is
3. more advice (no "-s")
4. three pieces / bits of equipment

→ *see G. Notes 22*

THE WORD WEB ◄··········

- to give out exam papers – distribute
- to give up smoking – stop
- to take on a difficult job – accept responsibility

- to take out a tooth – remove
- to step up production – increase
- to step in to prevent a conflict – intervene
- to cut up meat – divide into small pieces
- to cut off the electricity – stop the supply

### *Exit test*

1. might / may (have)
2. should
3. must have
4. could / can
5. may / could / might have
6. will
7. assume
8. feasible
9. expected
10. likely

## UNIT 10

### *Entry test*

1. target
2. supplying
3. so as to
4. aim
5. thereby
6. designed / devised
7. by means of
8. enables
9. allowed
10. through

### *Examples in context*

1. What does the human being provide?
2. How does the machine operate?
3. How does the man keep his balance?
4. What do the counterweights do?
5. What is the water pipe for?
6. What do the steel springs do?
7. In what way is the pressure transmitted?
8. What do the valves control?
9. What was responsible for industrial stagnation?

### *Exercises*

**→ 10.1. – A**

1. designed
2. provides
3. responsible for
4. make it possible
5. in order to
6. so that
7. purpose
8. aims

**→ 10.1. – B**

1. / f ▪ 2. / a ▪ 3. / b ▪ 4. / e ▪ 5. / g ▪ 6. / d ▪ 7. / c

**→ 10.2.**

- ... human factor that is responsible for 80% of air accidents...
- ... the primary objectives of the aircraft industry ...
- ... is to devise / design ways of improving these figures...
- ... will be able to provide early warning ...
- ... by means of voice recognition ...
- ... has been able to design / devise software ...
- ... which enables these minute ...
- ... be identified so that the pilot's voice ...
- ... the system makes it possible to detect tiredness ...

**→ 10.3.**

- What has it enabled them to do?
- What was the primary aim?
- Why do they adopt unusual behaviour?
- Why did she shift position?
- What was the objective?
- What made it impossible to gain access?
- What were the counter measures devised to do?
- Why did he walk away?

- Why did he remain hidden?
- What can function as a tool?

### ➔ Talking point

**Chimpanzee A is thinking:**
– "I know where the food is. The others do not. If I take it now the others will seize it from me. On the other hand, if I leave the others will probably leave then I will come back and eat it by myself."

**B is thinking:**
– "That is strange, A is suddenly leaving. I wonder why. Often, when he leaves he then comes back and finds food. Perhaps he will do it this time. I will pretend to leave, hide behind a tree and watch what happens."

### ➔ 10.4. Checkpoints

IN OTHER WORDS

**A turbine** is an object that has been designed to transform pressure into electricity.
**A solar panel** is a device that has been designed to turn photons into electricity.
**A voice recognition program** is software that has been designed to turn speech into text.
**A loudspeaker** is a system that has been designed to transform electric waves into sounds.

BACK TO BASICS
*(other answers are possible)*

- flowers grow
- a child grows up
- to suddenly realise
- to carry out clinical tests
- the last bus
- the latest news
- a personal experience
- a scientific experiment

→ *see G. Notes 24*

THE WORD WEB

- destructive
- reliable
- occurrence
- warning
- improvement
- accuracy
- ability
- reasonable
- eruption
- deformations
- seismographic / seismic
- recordings
- volcanic
- likelihood

### *Exit test*

1. target
2. through / thanks to
3. enable
4. by means of
5. thus / therefore
6. make it possible
7. purpose
8. devise
9. so as to
10. thereby / thus

## UNIT 11

### *Entry test*

1. have been sent
2. was set up
3. were being used
4. It is not widely known
5. have been taken
6. is provided
7. is / are being recruited
8. will be given
9. will have to be mastered
10. should be realised

### *Examples in context*
*(answers are open to interpretation)*

1. / c ▪ 2. / g ▪ 3. / a ▪ 4. / f ▪ 5. / e ▪ 6. / d ▪ 7. / b

### *Exercises*

**→ 11.2. – question 1**

- an electronic nose is being developed
- their molecular structure can be engineered
- the airflow is ensured by a circulation pump
- the detection process is speeded up
- 3 million people are killed each year

**→ 11.2. – question 2**

- is reported by our correspondent
- has been modelled by the research team
- are enclosed by the designers
- can then be identified by pattern recognition software
- can be immediately distinguished by the e-nose
- have to be analysed by biologists

**→ Talking point**

*(your flow chart should include the following stages)*

1. Vaporisation of sample
2. Sample pumped through the sensor container
3. Electrified sensors react chemically to gas.
4. Chemical reaction produces electrical variation.
5. Data is processed and matched to memory bank.
6. Data identified

**→ 11.3.**

1. were kept
2. can be damaged
3. is being done
4. has been designed
5. was developed
6. can be assumed
7. is brought
8. can be easily handled
9. should be removed
10. has been shown
11. can be obtained
12. are now being manufactured

**→ 11.4. Checkpoints**

IN OTHER WORDS ◄··········

A **weekend** is a period during which we have time to relax.
**Ramadan** is the period during which Moslems fast (do not eat).
**Hibernation** is the period during which the metabolic rate of animals drops.
A **semester** is a period during which we work at University.

BACK TO BASICS ◄··········

- Forty-seven
- Ninety three thousand, six hundred **and** seventy three
- 9 to the power minus 6 (nine to the minus six)
- The second of March, two thousand and five / March the second
- Five three double oh six five
- It costs a hundred euros
- Nought point five oh three
- Half past two / two thirty
- A quarter to six / five forty five

→ *see G. Notes 26*

THE WORD WEB ◄··········

1. minimise
2. enriched
3. enlarged
4. fossilised
5. specialised
6. enabled
7. characterised
8. ensure

### *Exit test*

1. ... are being tested.
2. ... the clinical trials have not been completed.
3. ... blood vessels are required ...
4. It is (widely) acknowledged that a key role has been played ...
5. ... was discovered ...
6. ... specific molecules could be used ...
7. ... blood vessel growth has been thoroughly examined.

8. Using injectable polymers ...
9. It has been reported / said ...
10. ... more and more replacement tissue will be needed.

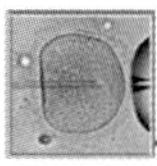

## UNIT 12

### Entry test

1. light sensitive cells
2. a geostationary espionage satellite
3. a petrol (burning) engine
4. a 2 metre (wide) meteorite crater
5. a computer controlled injection system
6. a fast increasing unemployment rate
7. a senior microbiology research technician
8. a 4-day conference
9. a one-legged landmine victim
10. a three child family

### Examples in context

- a light-weight, battery-operated, fully ambulatory physiological monitoring system
- space motion sickness
- 9-volt lithium thionyl chloride batteries
- blood volume pulse
- skin conductance level

### Exercises

**➜ 12.1. – A**

1. Activity which is located in the brain of rats.
2. A column which is made of concrete and weighs 25 tonnes.
3. A period during which incubation takes place and which lasts 3-6 days.
4. A mine which is placed underwater and can be controlled at a distance.
5. Proteins which protect by preventing freezing.

**➜ 12.1. – B**

a) 3, 5, 7, 10
b) 2, 6, 9
c) 1, 4, 8

**➜ 12.1. – C**

*(other answers are possible)*

1. a heat measurement instrument / device
2. an alpha-ray detection device
3. a passenger transport system
4. a space research organisation
5. an information transmission appliance
6. a heart muscle regulator
7. a paper data bank
8. a disease carrying organism

**➜ 12.2.**

1. a vehicle
2. a robot
3. a path
4. pumps
5. a generator
6. alloy
7. a frame
8. a case
9. its (clearance) capacity

**➜ 12.3.**

- assisted fertilisation technologies
- low sperm count
- outside donor sperm
- computer controlled glass pipette
- 65% implantation success rates
- fastest-growing areas
- St Louis infertility centre
- genetically related sperm defect
- long-term effect
- human gene pool

**➜ 12.4. Checkpoints**

IN OTHER WORDS ◄..................

**To diet** means to eat less food so that you lose weight.
**To hurry** means to go faster so that you do not arrive late.
**To examine** means to study closely so that errors can be detected.

**To sum up** means to repeat the main points so that everyone understands.

BACK TO BASICS

1. ... a zoologist working at Ø ... Ø arachnid ecology.
2. The scorpion is a ... Ø ultraviolet light at Ø night.
3. ... Ø high temperatures ... a few hours ... Ø activity.
4. ... Ø sexual activity Ø females ... the male.
5. ... the Middle East, Ø South Africa and the Philippines ... Ø neurotoxins ... the nervous system ... Ø death.

→ *see* ***G. Notes 29***

THE WORD WEB

1. to throw away / c
2. to look through / f
3. to put forward / a
4. to speed up / h
5. to carry on / e
6. to cool down / g
7. to make out / b
8. to put it off / d

→ *multi-word verbs: see* ***G. Notes 30***

### *Exit test*

1. a three man space module
2. a gene sequencing program
3. long-term survival techniques
4. profit-oriented drug research
5. rising carbon dioxide levels
6. an 88 millimetre (diameter) steel tube
7. bone destroying cancer cells
8. a 4-day trial period
9. satellite controlled sensoring techniques
10. a four-legged, six-winged insect

## OHP

### *Part 1*

1. Figure A provides comparative data on the probability of unnatural death in the USA.
2. The causes of death are indicated in the left hand column.
3. As you can see in the bottom left hand corner, the data was first published in 1994.
4. Per capita consumption as a percentage of US consumption can be seen on the horizontal axis.
5. Basically, the poorer countries are, the less they consume.
6. US consumption of meat is roughly ten times as much as in Zambia.
7. To begin with, there was a slow but steady increase and then the curve began to rise sharply.
8. After a sharp increase, the curve levelled off.
9. Immediately after attaining a peak of 250 per thousand, the number of cases fell abruptly.
10. From then on, the disease virtually died out.
11. Each sector corresponds to the statistical distribution of the total radiation risk.
12. Clearly, the risks of natural radiation are far greater.
13. The danger of radiation from radon sources is roughly seven times as high.
14. Since productivity is low, this means that there is a low crop output. Consequently, there is no surplus available which accounts for the lack of capital to invest. Inevitably, this situation leads to technological stagnation.

# Grammar Notes

## 1. Spelling

### t → d / c → s / f → v

A minor change in spelling can occur between nouns and verbs and between singular and plural with words ending in "-t", "-c", "-f".

The shift is from an "unvoiced sound" (no vibration of the vocal chords) to a "voiced" sound.

| t → d | | c → s | | f → v | |
|---|---|---|---|---|---|
| extent | → to extend | device | → to devise | half | → halves |
| intent | → to intend | advice | → to advise | yourself | → yourselves |
| descent | → to descend | choice | → to choose | life | → lives |

### Red – redden

Monosyllabic words finishing with a single consonant preceded by a **single vowel** double the consonant.

➢ *red / re**dd**en* · *big / bi**gg**er* · *hot / ho**tt**er*

N.B. – In the following example the consonant is not doubled as it is preceded by **two vowels**.

➢ *cool / cooler*

The same rule applies for many (but not all) polysyllabic words ending with **one consonant**.

➢ *begin / begi**nn**ing* · *travel / trave**ll**er* · *crystal / crysta**ll**ine*

### American and British English

There are some minor spelling differences between British and American English:

- **"-ise" / "-ize"** are in most cases interchangeable verb endings. The first is common in the UK and the second more widely used in the US.

  ➢ *to organise / organize* · *privatise / privatize* · *theorise / theorize*

- Some words, however, must be spelt **"-ise"**.

  ➢ *to advertise* · *to devise* · *to compromise*

▌In Am. E. there is a tendency to simplify and spell phonetically.

| | **Br. E.** | **Am. E.** |
|---|---|---|
| *-OUR → -OR* | behavi**our** – lab**our** – col**our** | behavi**or** – lab**or** – col**or** |
| *-RE → -ER* | cent**re** – met**re** – theat**re** | cent**er** – met**er** – theat**er** |
| *-AMME → -AM* (and double consonants) | progra**mme*** – trave**ll**er – leve**ll**ed | progra**m** – trave**l**er – leve**l**ed |

* In Br. E., "**program**" is used when referring to computer sciences.

## *2. Pronunciation of π*

π is pronounced /paɪ/ cf. "**my, high, sky**".

## *3. Questions*

▌The question form for **auxiliary verbs** and **modals** is:

| *(Q WORD)* + | *AUXILLIARY MODAL* + | *SUBJECT* + | *VERB FORM ADJ / ADV* |
|---|---|---|---|
| | *Is* | *she* | *there?* |
| | *Must* | *he* | *work?* |
| *(Why)* | *Is* | *he* | *working?* |

▌For verbs which are not auxiliaries, the pattern is:

| *(Q WORD)* + | *DO DOES DID* + | *SUBJECT* + | *INFINITIVE* |
|---|---|---|---|
| | *Do* | *you* | *work?* |
| | *Does* | *he* | *work?* |
| *(Why)* | *Did* | *he* | *work?* |

▌N.B. – When the Q word is the **subject** of the sentence the form is:

| *(Q WORD)* + | *VERB* | |
|---|---|---|
| ***Who*** | *worked?* | *(answer: **John** worked)* |

## *4. Comparative*

- **Short adjectives:** "cold, fast, quick ..."

adj + -er + than

➤ *It is colder* ***than*** *yesterday.*

- Short adjectives ending with **one consonant** preceded by **one vowel:** "hot, big, red ..."

double consonant + -er

➤ *It is ho**tt**er than yesterday.*

- Short adjectives ending in **"-y"**: "easy, tiny ..."

-y → -i

➤ *It is eas**ier** than I thought.*

- **Long adjectives:** "expensive, important ..."

more / less + adj + than

➤ *It is* ***more expensive than*** *I expected.*

- **Parallel comparatives** (the second action is dependent on the first)

(the + comp + S + V) + (the + comp + S + V)

➤ ***The hotter*** *she is,* ***the more*** *she drinks.*
***The hotter*** *she is,* ***the less comfortable*** *she feels.*

## *5. Quite*

This word has two very different meanings:

- **Quite = relatively** when modifying words which are "gradeable" (i.e. which can be associated with "**more**" or "**less**"). Something can be more or less "**warm, good, hot** ..."

  ➤ *It is* ***quite*** *warm today* · *The film was* ***quite*** *good* · *The book was* ***quite*** *interesting ...*

- **Quite = totally** with words which are not "gradeable" (i.e. you cannot use "**more**" or "**less**"; words which express qualities that are "**binary**", "**either / or**"). You are

**either** dead or alive, something is **either** right or wrong, I **either** agree or disagree with you.

➤ *The animal was* ***quite*** *dead* • *You are* ***quite*** *wrong* • *It is* ***quite*** *impossible ...*

## *6. Important*

**Important** is a false friend. In many languages it has two meanings: "**big**" and "**significant**". In English **important** never has the meaning "**big**". It has only the meaning: "**significant, valuable, crucial, having an effect ...**"

Look at the examples:

➤ *It is a small but* ***important*** *town.* (strategically significant)
➤ *The increase in exports was* ***important****.* (not necessarily a big increase, but it had a crucial impact for the country)
➤ *The number of people at the meeting was limited, but it was not* ***important****.* (i.e. it did not matter)

## *7. **Yet** (multiple meanings)*

- Meaning: "**but, by contrast**"

➤ *He was suffering from cancer,* ***yet*** *he never complained.*

- Meaning: "**up to now**" (only used in negative and interrogative phrases)

➤ *I have not* ***yet*** *finished the book.*

- Meaning: "**time in the future**"

➤ *Despite the bad results, the research may* ***yet*** *prove to be valuable.*

## *8. Actually*

This is one of the most common false friends. It does not mean "**now, currently**". It is used to express a difference between reality and what people think. It expresses **contradiction, surprise, and personal opinion**.

➤ *She was convinced that she was clever, but* ***actually****, she was rather stupid.*
➤ *NASA expected 25% of the pilots to volunteer for space training.* ***Actually****, 75% volunteered.*

## *9. Doubtless*

This is not really an equivalent of "**it is certain**". It means, "***I, the speaker*** *have no doubt – considering the knowledge that I have, there is no reason to think otherwise.*"

➤ *He will* ***doubtless*** *come* • *You will* ***doubtless*** *find a solution ...*

### 10. e.g. / i.e. – Latin expressions

A large number of Latin expressions and abbreviations are still widely used in modern English:

- *AD* = after the birth of Christ (Anno Domini) (BC = "Before Christ", is not of Latin origin).
- *a.m. / p.m.* = before / after midday (ante / post meridiem).
- *e.g.* = for example (exempli gratia).
- *i.e.* = that is to say (id est).
- *N.B.* = note (nota bene).
- ***non sequitur*** = it does not logically follow.
- *op.cit.* = in the work that has been quoted (opere citato).
- *PhD* = doctor (philosophiae doctor).
- *post hoc* = after the fact.
- *status quo* = the existing state of affairs.

### 11. Thereby / therefore

The difference between **thereby** and **therefore** is not always obvious.

- Therefore means "consequently".
- Thereby means "as a consequence **of this action**".

In most cases, **thereby** is followed by an "-ing" form.

> *An anticoagulant is added, **thereby** maintai**ning** the blood in a fluid state.*

It can also, however, be followed by other verb forms.

> *A photosensitive molecule can change shape and **thereby set off** a chain of reactions.*

### 12. According to – personal opinions

**According to** is rarely used when speaking about yourself. It is usually reserved for "outside" or "expert" opinion. It is used to indicate what somebody else thinks, but it is not necessarily true (cf. *"John claims that ..."*).

> ***According to*** *Shenfield, the fossils are 27,000 years old.*
> ***According to*** *the news, it will rain tomorrow.*

When speaking of your own opinions you should use phrases like:
"I would say · Personally, I think / believe · It seems to me · In my opinion ..."

> ***Personally****, I think that the state of public transport is scandalous.*
> ***I would say*** *that she is at least 30 years old.*

### 13. Just

There is a slight difference between US and UK usage. The British normally use the present perfect with **just**. The Americans often prefer the past simple.

> *I **have just seen** him.* (Br. E.)
> *I **just** saw him.* (Am. E.)

## 14. Never

In slightly simplified terms we can say that **never** can be used with the present perfect when the subject is living, with the meaning: "**during my life, up to now in my life ...**"

➢ *I **have never been** to Miami.* (so far, up until now, not yet in my life)

If the subject is dead the past tense is used, for inevitably the action is part of "history".

➢ *Napoleon **never went** to Miami.*

Notice, however, that a living subject may wish to refer to a period of his life that is finished ("historical"). In this case, the past tense may be used. Compare:

➢ *I **have never played** Black Jack.* (so far in my life)

*and*

➢ ***When I was in Miami**, I **never played** Black Jack.* (during that period of my life which is now finished)

## 15. The tenses: active and passive forms – a comparative table

| | **Active** | **Passive** |
|---|---|---|
| *Present* | | |
| – *SIMPLE* | I study | It is studied (by ...) |
| – *CONTINUOUS* | I am studying | It is being studied (by ...) |
| *Present perfect* | | |
| – *SIMPLE* | I have studied | It has been studied (by ...) |
| – *CONTINUOUS* | I have been studying | – |
| *Past* | | |
| – *SIMPLE* | I studied | It was studied (by ...) |
| – *CONTINUOUS* | I was studying | It was being studied (by ...) |
| *Past perfect* | | |
| – *SIMPLE* | I had studied | It had been studied (by ...) |
| – *CONTINUOUS* | I had been studying | – |

## 16. To transform / to turn / to change into

The difference between **in** and **into** is that **into** indicates a change of state or a change of place.

➢ *He was reading **in** a chair • She was working **in** the town centre ...*

➢ *The cat jumped **into** the chair • He drove **into** the town centre ...*

Consequently, **into** is used with verbs like "**to change, to turn, to transform, to make**" which indicate a transformation.

➢ *The prince was **turned into** a frog • To **transform** water **into** steam ...*

## 17. To trigger (off) / to spark (off)

The verbs **trigger** and **spark** can be used with or without the particle "**off**". **Off** emphasises the meaning "**initiate, start**". In practice, the difference between the two forms is small and they can be considered as being interchangeable.

➢ *A psychosis can be **triggered (off)** by stress.*
➢ *An electron or a proton can **spark (off)** a cascade of changes.*

## 18. To raise – to rise / to lay – to lie

Compare:

➢ *The government **is raising** the taxes.* ▶ *The taxes are **rising**.*
➢ *He **lays** the book on the table.* ▶ *The book **is lying** on the table.*

▮ Raise and lay are **transitive verbs** (i.e. they are followed by a complement). The meaning is **to put** something or someone in a different position.

• To raise means "to put something in a higher position".
• To lay means "to put something in a flat position".

▮ Rise and lie are **intransitive verbs**.

• To rise means "**to go to** a higher position".
• To lie means "**to be** in a flat position".

▮ Notice the irregular past forms:

| | | | |
|---|---|---|---|
| To raise | → raised / raised | To rise | → rose / risen |
| To lay | → laid / laid | To lie | → lay / lain |

## 19. Past conditions (3rd conditional)

Typically, but not always, past conditions refer to the past.

➢ *If he had been elected, he **would have stopped** corruption.* (i.e. he would have stopped corruption **last year**)

If past conditions have present effects, **would** is used in the main clause.

➢ *If he had been elected, he **would** stop corruption.* (i.e. he would stop present corruption)

## 20. Hard / hardly

Compare the examples:

➢ *He works **hard** / He **hardly** works*

• To work hard means "to work a lot".
• To hardly work means "to do almost no work".

▮ **Hardly** (cf. barely, scarcely) has a negative meaning, and is often followed by **any**.

➢ *I have **hardly any** money left.* (almost none)

- **Hardly** is an adverb. **Hard** can be both an adjective and an adverb.
  - ➢ *Steel is a **hard** metal.* (adj)
  - ➢ *He has tried **hard**.* (adv)

- The adverb **hard** goes **after** the verb.
  - ➢ *It was raining **hard**.*

  **Hardly** usually goes **before** the word it qualifies.
  - ➢ ***Hardly anyone** came to the meeting.*
  - ➢ *He **hardly said** a word.*
  - ➢ *The food contained **hardly any vitamins**.*

## 21. Modals: structure

➢ *She **should** not work so much.*

- Modals never take **"-s"** in the third person singular.
- They do not take **do / does / did** to form the **negative** and **interrogative**.
- They are always followed by the **infinitive without "to"**.
  N.B. – In the modal "**ought to**", the "to" is part of the modal – not of the infinitive.
  - ➢ *He **(should)** come* · *He **(ought to)** come* · *I want him **(to come)** ...*
- The progressive form can be used with modals.
  - ➢ *Where is Helen? She **may be working** at home.*

## Modals: meaning

We mentioned in the *Key points (Unit 9)* that modals often have several distinct meanings. In the table below, additional meanings are listed in the dark box.

**WILL**

*Total certitude about future events, predictions – probability 100%*

➢ *The sun **will** rise at 5.32 tomorrow.* (a fact – there is no possible doubt)

***A form of imperative***

➢ ***Will** you post the letter for me?* (please do it. Are you willing to do it?)

**MUST**

*Almost total certitude – probability 90%*

➢ *It **must** be 5 o'clock.* (I am convinced that it is 5 o'clock)

➢ *She's absent, she **must** be ill.* (it is the only logical explanation)

***Obligation***

➢ *You **must** pay your taxes.* (it is the law. You have to. You are obliged to)

➢ *You **must** lubricate the car.* (it is necessary)

**MAY**

*Probability*

➢ *It **may** rain tomorrow.* (perhaps it will rain, perhaps it won't)

***Permission***

➢ *You **may** not smoke inside the theatre.* (it is forbidden, it is not allowed)

**MIGHT**

*Reduced probability – often followed by "but ..."*

➢ *It **might** rain tomorrow.* (but I would be surprised)

***Permission (very formal – rarely used)***

➢ *Do you think I **might** have some more wine?*

**CAN**

*Ability or capacity – what is intellectually or technically possible, what is feasible.*

➢ *He **can** speak German.* (he has the capacity, the knowledge)

➢ *You **can't** live on Mars.* (it is not feasible)

- ***Can is also used to express permission.***

➢ *You **can** use the library until 7 p.m.* (it is allowed)

➢ *You **can** stop work when you like.* (you have the permission)

- ***Can is used as a polite imperative.***

➢ ***Can** you pass me the salt?* (pass me the salt please)

➢ ***Can** I go home now?* (please, let me go home)

- ***Can is used with the verbs, "see, hear, feel, smell, taste".***

➢ *I **can see** a plane in the distance · I **can hear** a noise*

**COULD**

*Possibility*

➢ *The short circuit **could** cause a break-down.* (there are several possibilities – this is one hypothesis)

- ***Polite requests for permission.***

➢ ***Could** I use your car?* (please may I?)

- ***Polite imperative (more polite than can)***

➢ ***Could** you pass me the salt?* (would you be so kind as to pass me the salt?)

## *22. Countable / uncountable nouns*

▮ Words like "**information, advice, equipment, news, progress, knowledge, research** ..." are **uncountable** nouns. That is to say that normally, there is no plural form; you cannot associate them with the numerals "**one**" or "**two**".

➢ *I have ~~**an** important information.~~*

➢ *I have ~~**3** information**s**.~~*

- In order to itemise these words, use expressions like "**a bit, a piece ...**"
  - ➢ *I have an important **bit / piece** of information / news.*
  - ➢ *They replaced **2 pieces** of equipment.*
- N.B. – "**News**" is singular, although it ends in "**-s**".
  - ➢ *The news **is** bad.*

## 23. Designed / devised + to / for

- **To design** means to make or draw plans for a certain purpose. It refers to the elaboration of a **new concept**, in contrast to its **production**.
  - ➢ *The car was **designed** in Italy and made in Brazil.*
- **To devise** has a similar sort of meaning. However, this word insists on the **complexity** of the process or the **difficulty** that is overcome (cf. to elaborate, work out).
  - ➢ *He **designed** a very simple little country house.*
  - ➢ *He **devised** a clever way of overcoming the problem.*
- **To / for**

  **To** is used before verbs. **For** is used to introduce nouns (including verbal nouns: **"-ing"**).
  - ➢ *Mir was originally designed **to operate** 5 years.*
  - ➢ *A new system was devised **for** underwater **exploration**.*
  - ➢ *The computers were designed **for processing** massive amounts of data.*

## 24. Word pairs

| | | |
|---|---|---|
| TO GROW | To get bigger | *The population **is growing**.* |
| TO GROW UP | To become adult | *She **grew up** in the East End of London.* |
| TO CARRY OUT | To do, perform | *The tests were **carried out** in secret.* |
| TO REALISE (A) | To become aware | *I **realised** that I had made a major mistake* |
| (B) | To fulfil | *It took three years to **realise** the objective.* |
| LAST | The final one | *You have missed the **last** bus.* |
| LATEST | The most recent | *Have you heard the **latest** news?* |
| EXPERIENCE | Personal contact with reality | *He was severely traumatised by his **experience** of war.* |
| EXPERIMENT | A scientific test | *Mice are often used for **experiments** as they breed fast.* |

## 25. "By" and the passive

- With passives it is possible to refer to the actor at the end of the sentence by using **"by"**, however, this is not very common (only about 20% of cases). As the main reason for using the passive is to reduce the importance of the actor, it is logical that he should not be mentioned. The actor may be suppressed for a variety of reasons:

- because he is unknown:
  ➤ *He was killed during the war* • *Marilyn Monroe may have been murdered ...*
- because he is irrelevant or of secondary importance:
  ➤ *The liquid must be heated* • *The letter was typed and sent immediately ...*
- because the information is obvious, or refers to "people in general":
  ➤ *He was arrested (obviously by the police)* • *War was declared* • *It is widely believed ...*
- because the speaker wishes to avoid responsibility for what is said:
  ➤ *It is said that hypnotism can ...*

▮ Intransitive verbs cannot take the passive form – they have no complement to become subject:

➤ *The sun rises* • *The President died ...*

## *26. Numbers*

▮ In British English, numbers are read in the following way.

➤ *5,632,571 = five million, six hundred* ***and*** *thirty two thousand, five hundred* ***and*** *seventy one* (N.B. – **"and"** is inserted after **hundred**).

▮ **Hundred**, **thousand**, **million**, only take "**-s**" if no number precedes them.

➤ ***Thousands*** *of people came.*

▮ The distinction between **"a"** and **"one"**:

- **"a"** is the neutral form, it is used if there is no opposition to another number.
  ➤ *€ 100* ▸ *It costs a hundred euros*
  ➤ *150* ▸ *A hundred and fifty people came.*
- You say "**one** hundred / thousand" to indicate that the number is in opposition to another number.
  ➤ *I didn't say* ***two*** *hundred. I said* ***one*** *hundred.*
  ➤ *3,153* ▸ ***Three*** *thousand* ***one*** *hundred and fifty three.*

**ZERO**

There are three words for zero in English: **zero** / **oh** / **nought**.

▮ Zero is frequently used by the military or when referring to temperatures.

➤ *Zero degrees Kelvin.*

▌ In decimals, when two zeroes are present, **nought** and **oh** can be used alternately.

➢ *0.503* ▶ *Nought point five oh three.*

#### TIME

➢ *2.00 (or 14.00)* ▶ *It is two o'clock.*

(if it is necessary to make the distinction between morning and night you say **"a.m."** [ante meridiem] and **"p.m."** [post meridiem])

➢ *2.10* ▶ *It is ten past two.*

➢ *2.15* ▶ *It is a quarter past two / two fifteen.*

➢ *2.30* ▶ *It is half past two / two thirty.*

➢ *2.40* ▶ *It is twenty to three / two forty.*

➢ *2.45* ▶ *It is a quarter to three / two forty five.*

#### TELEPHONE NUMBERS

In the UK, telephone numbers are usually said individually.

➢ *722356805* ▶ *Seven double two three five six eight oh five.*

#### DATES

Dates can be written in different ways.

➢ *02.03.2005* ▶ *2nd March 2005 / March 2nd 2005*

(the second of March / March the second, two thousand and five)

## *27. Compound nouns: implicit meanings*

In phrases such as:

"X-ray therapy • a steel box • a 2 inch strip of copper • computer software ..."

the notions "**using** X-rays", "**made** of steel", "**measuring** 2 inches", "**designed for** computers" are implicit and do not need to be expressed.

## *28. Compound nouns: plural modifiers*

As we have seen in the *Key points*, the modifying noun in a compound noun is nearly always singular.

➢ *a five dollar note*

However, there are exceptions.

▌ Words which normally do not have a singular form with the same meaning.

➢ *a sports car • a newspaper • a physics book • a goods train • a communications network ...*

▌ Latin plurals are frequently used.

➢ *a data bank • media studies ...* (singular: datum, medium)

## 29. Articles: "the" / "a"

- **The definite article "the"** is used when words are **determined**. That is to say, they are identifiable – you can answer the question "who?" or "which?" – **"a"** is used for nouns which are not determined.

 ➤ *I saw **a man** on a bike. **The man** was wearing **a hat**. **The hat** was brown.*

 On the first occasion the noun (man / hat) is not determined. On the second it is (which man? – the man I saw).

 Words which are considered to be **unique** are accompanied by **"the"**.

 ➤ ***the** sun • the sky • the moon • the government • the president ... (of our country, etc.)*

 **"the"** is used in scientific and formal language when referring to the totality of the class.

 ➤ ***The** dog is a four legged carnivore.* (all dogs – the species "dog")

 N.B. – An alternative way of saying the same thing would be to use the plural form.

 ➤ *Dogs are four-legged carnivores.*

- **The indefinite article "a"** is used for professions.

 ➤ *He is **a** microbiologist • She is **a** doctor ...*

 You cannot use **"a"** with uncountable nouns. See *G. Notes 22*.

 ➤ *She needs advice.*

- **Zero article – Ø**

 No article is used for abstract singular words.

 ➤ *His only subjects of conversation are **love**, **beauty** and **philosophy**.*

 No article is used for materials and other uncountable nouns (unless they are determined).

 ➤ *Gold, iron and copper are metals / **The** gold **that he used** was 18 carat*

 No article is used for continents, cities or countries.

 ➤ *He went to Africa and visited Botswana, Swaziland and Zambia.*

 N.B. – If the name is qualified, **"the"** is if course used.

 ➤ ***the** United States • **the** Suez Canal • **the** Middle East ...*

## 30. Multi-word verbs – examples

One of the striking features of English is the way in which verb meanings can be modified by adding particles (adverbs or prepositions – also called prepositional and phrasal verbs).

Below you will find a list of multi-word verbs which are common in scientific English. At this stage, you should try to familiarise yourself with these structures so you can recognise them.

### TO BREAK

- *The machine* ***broke down****.* (to stop functioning)
- *The government* ***broke off*** *negotiations* (to interrupt)
- *A cholera epidemic* ***broke out****.* (to start)

### TO CARRY

- *Despite the rain, they* ***carried on*** *working.* (to continue)
- *They were unable to* ***carry out*** *their intentions.* (to finish, complete)

### TO CHECK

- *John* ***checked into (≠ out of)*** *the hotel at 12 o'clock.* (to register arrival)
- *Don't forget to* ***check through*** *the results.* (to verify from beginning to end)
- *I am not sure of the figures; could you* ***check up****?* (to make a complete verification)

### TO CUT

- *The department must* ***cut down*** *on expenses.* (to reduce)
- *She* ***cut up*** *the meat with a knife.* (to divide into small pieces)
- *The electricity supply was* ***cut off*** *after the snow storm.* (to disconnect)
- *They had to* ***cut off*** *his leg because of the gangrene.* (to amputate)
- *The tungsten disk* ***cut through*** *the plastic coating.* (to penetrate)

### TO GIVE

- *He* ***gave in*** *his exam papers.* (to return)
- *She* ***gave back*** *all the money.* (to repay, return)
- *You should try to* ***give up*** *smoking.* (to stop)

### TO GO

- *They decided* ***to go ahead with*** *the project.* (to proceed)
- *I can't* ***go on*** *working like this.* (to continue)
- *Could you* ***go through*** *this paper for me?* (to read and check)

### TO TURN

- *Don't forget to* ***turn off*** *the electricity.* (to disconnect)
- *She* ***turned on*** *the hot water.* (to connect)
- *She* ***turned down*** *the offer of an internship in the US.* (to refuse)

### N.B. – "UP"

Notice that the particle **"up"** can have at least three completely different meanings:

- *The temperature* ***goes up****. The planet is* ***warming up****.* (to increase)
- *The baby* ***drank up*** *the milk. To* ***cut up*** *the meat. To* ***blow up*** *a building.* (to finish, completely, to destroy totally)
- *To* ***set up*** *an experiment.* (to create)

## *31. Changes in address*

Web addresses change frequently because the sites are replaced or because the pages are rewritten. It is for this reason that when complex addresses are written we have entered the specific pages in **bold**.

➤ http://www.birthpsychology.com**/lifebefore/fetalsense.html**

If you find that an address does not function, it means that the site has been rewritten. You will probably be able to reach the same information if you type the home page and try searching from there.

➤ http://www.birthpsychology.com/

## *32. Examples in context*

To obtain more interesting examples during a Web search, try using complex search strings including words linked to your own field of interest.

For example, instead of just entering "**rate**", you could enter

< *rate avalanche* > or < *rate biopsy murder* >

Below is an example on the home page of the **Google** research engine:

## *33. Graph search*

When searching for graphs you will find it helpful to select Images on the tool bar and use strings like < *graph data* > or < *graph statistics* >.

# *Lexis*

If you are using this book you probably already have a knowledge of at least 1,000-1,200 words in English. The following supplementary vocabulary consists of high frequency words found in both specialised and general scientific texts.

In order to help you to assimilate the words, the Lexis has been divided into 10 sections corresponding to important areas of scientific discourse. It is organised in the following way :

- Words are listed in only one section, even though they may be associated with two or more categories.
- Multiple meanings are indicated by 1. ... 2. ... etc.
- Nouns, verbs, adjectives and adverbs which have the same root and commonly used suffixes are listed together.
- The different definitions correspond to the order of the examples.
- When antonyms are given they refer to the **last** example given.
- Groups of words that frequently occur together (collocations) are printed in heavy type.
- Boxed notes are included for points of particular interest ("False friends", etc.)
- A general index is to be found at the end of the book.

The Lexis is not a dictionary, it is a learning tool. It has been simplified as much as possible and unnecessary grammatical information has been excluded. Its aim is to provide you with a clear definition of what it is essential to know and, at the same time, to give you a rich variety of examples of how the word is used in context. Once it has been learnt, it will enable you to deal with approximately 95% of the lexical items in any general scientific text.

### Abbreviations used in the Lexis

| | |
|---|---|
| n | *noun* |
| adj | *adjective* |
| adv | *adverb* |
| v | *verb* |
| prep | *preposition* |
| pro | *pronoun* |

| | |
|---|---|
| conj | *conjunctions* |
| num | *number* |
| Br. E. | *British English* |
| Am. E. | *American English* |
| det | *determiner* |

# The phonetic alphabet

The symbols used correspond to those in the "English Pronouncing Dictionary" (14th edition). Many of the consonant symbols are identical. Less familiar symbols are illustrated with key-words below.

**CONSONANTS**

| | |
|---|---|
| tʃ | **ch**eap, **ch**ild |
| dʒ | **j**am, **j**ump |
| θ | **th**in, **th**ink |
| ð | **th**en, mo**th**er |
| ŋ | si**ng**, thi**ng** |
| ʃ | fi**sh**, **sh**all |
| ʒ | mea**s**ure |
| j | **y**es, **y**ellow |

**VOWELS**

| | |
|---|---|
| iː | s**ee**, m**e** |
| ɪ | h**i**s, w**i**n |
| e | g**e**t, l**e**t |
| æ | b**a**d, c**a**t |
| ɑː | f**a**ther, c**ar** |
| ɒ | n**o**t, h**o**t |
| ɔː | d**oo**r, m**o**re |
| ʊ | p**u**t, co**u**ld |
| uː | t**oo**, wh**o** |
| ʌ | c**u**t, m**u**st |
| ɜː | b**i**rd, w**o**rd |
| ə | doct**o**r, **a**bout (→ *this is the weak vowel. It is never stressed. It is hardly pronounced at all)* |

**DIPHTHONGS**

| | |
|---|---|
| eɪ | s**ay**, m**a**ke |
| əʊ | g**o**, n**o** |
| aɪ | fl**y**, m**y** |
| aʊ | n**ow**, c**ow** |
| ɪə | n**ear**, h**ere** |
| eə | th**ere**, w**ear** |
| ʊə | p**oor**, s**ure** |
| ɔɪ | b**oy**, t**oy** |

- The sign / ˈ / indicates that the syllabe which follows has a **strong stress**.

  *Example: a qualified engineer*

  → / əˈkwɒlɪfaɪd endʒɪˈnɪə /

# 1. MEASUREMENT

**About** /ə'baʊt/
1.adv The car weighs **about** 1 tonne.
**About** 10% of the population caught the disease.
→ ***Approximately ≠ exactly***
2.prep A book **about** astronomy.
What are you **thinking about**?
→ ***On the subject of, related to***

**Accurate** /'ækjərət/
adj Quartz watches are **extremely accurate**.
This technique provides an **accurate** evaluation of the chemical reactions.
adv Altitude can be most **accurately** determined by triangulation.
n To measure with great **accuracy**.
→ ***Exact. Precision ≠ inaccuracy***

**Acute** /ə'kjuːt/
adj An **acute angle** is less than 90°.
There was an **acute** shortage of food.
In cases of **acute** suffering, such as burns, morphine may be used.
→ ***Sharp, very great, severe ≠ mild***

**Almost** /'ɔːlməʊst/
adv It was **almost** time to stop work.
The population has **almost** doubled in the last 25 years.
The neutron has **almost exactly** the same weight as the proton.
→ ***Nearly***

**Amount** /ə'maʊnt/
n A large **amount of money**.
A **growing amount** of radio-active waste.
The total **amount** of sulphur dioxide emissions has been reduced by 50%.
→ ***Quantity***

**Area** /'eəriə/
1.n The **area** is the length multiplied by the width.
The cool air sinks, creating an **area** of high pressure.
→ ***The size of the surface. A zone, sector***
2.n He is a specialist in this **area**.
→ ***A field of study, discipline***

**Assess** /ə'ses/
v To **assess** the effects of solar radiation.
The long-term impact is **difficult to assess**.
n A yearly **assessment** of world population.
A **thorough assessment** of the health risks is required.
→ ***To evaluate. An evaluation***

**Attain** /ə'teɪn/
v An adult zebra **attains** a height of about 1.7 m.
Natural gas can **attain** temperatures in excess of 1,900°C.
India finally **attained** independence in 1947.
→ ***To reach, to succeed in getting something, to achieve***

**Average** /'ævərɪdʒ/
adj The **average** life expectancy for human beings is about 80 years.
The **average** velocity is 10 m per sec.
n Industrial output was **above average** last month.
**On average**, he visits Madrid three times a month.
→ ***Median, mean, normal***

**Away** /ə'weɪ/
adv The next town is 10 kilometres **away**.
She will be **away** this weekend.
The comet is moving **away from** the Earth.
→ ***At a distance. Not at home. In the opposite direction ≠ towards***

**Breadth** /bredθ/
n They measured the length, the height and the **breadth** of the box.
The pancreas has a **breadth** of about 3.8 cm.
→ ***Width, the distance between the sides***

**Broad** /brɔːd/
adj The river becomes **broader** as it approaches the sea.
A **broad** definition.
adv **Broadly** speaking, I agree with you.
→ ***Wide, large, approximate ≠ narrow***

**Chart** /tʃɑːt/
n The daily evolution of the patient's temperature was **plotted on a chart**.
Ptolemy's **chart** of the sky contained more than 1,000 stars.
→ ***A table, graph, diagram, map***

**Check** /tʃek/

1.v To **check the oil level** of a car.
The **results must be checked** before publishing them.
n Workers exposed to radiation must have a monthly **check-up**.
→ ***To verify, inspect. Inspection***
2.v New vaccines will **check** the spread of the disease.
→ ***To stop temporarily, to slow down***

> **Note** — To check is often followed by a particle which changes its meaning.
> → *to* ***check in*** *at the airport*
> *(to register)*
> → *to* ***check out*** *of a hotel*
> *(to leave, to pay the bill)*
> → *to* ***check over*** *someone's work*
> *(to reread, to verify)*
> → *to* ***check up*** *on some calculations*
> *(to verify)*

**Cost** /kɒst/

n Mass production **reduces costs**.
The **cost of living**.
The **cost** of recycling industrial waste is increasing.
v *(cost, cost, cost)* The car **costs** a lot of money.
Developing alternative fuels will **cost** millions of dollars.
→ ***What must be paid, the price. To require money***

**Couple** /ˈkʌpl/

1.n To have a **couple** of drinks.
She noticed a **couple** of mistakes.
→ ***Two together***
2.v To **couple** two circuits together.
Economic growth is closely **coupled** to capital investment.
→ ***To join, to link***

**Cross-section** /krɒsˈsekʃn/

n To examine the **cross-section** of a sample under a microscope.
The resistance of wire is proportional to its length and its **cross-section**.
A **cross-section** of society.
→ ***A view of an interior surface. A typical sample***

**Data** /deɪtə/

n The **data** is **stored** on the hard disk.
To study **data-processing**.
With a binary system, **data can be handled** much more quickly.
→ ***Information, facts***

> **Note** — Data is a Latin word:
> Sing. **"datum"**. Pl. **"data"**.
> **"Datum"** is rarely used. **"Data"** can be either singular or plural.
> → *the data is ... / the data are ...*

**Deep** /diːp/

adj Avalanches are most common when the snow is **deep**.
adv The notion of male superiority is **deeply rooted** in traditional societies.
n What is the **depth** of the river?
→ ***Profound. Distance below the surface***

**Draw** /drɔː/ *(draw, drew, drawn)*

1.v **To draw** a straight line.
Under hypnosis, adults appear to **draw** like children.
n To study a technical **drawing**.
→ ***To mark on paper, to make a picture. Graphic representation***
2.v The air is **drawn** into the lungs via the nose.
It is too early for a **conclusion to be drawn**.
→ ***To move in a direction. To arrive at***

**Even** /ˈiːvn/

1.adj The microscope must stand on an **even surface**.
The temperature must remain **even** throughout the experiment.
adv The population is **evenly distributed**.
→ ***Smooth, regular. Equally***
2.adj 4, 6, 8, are **even numbers**.
→ ***Divisible by 2 ≠ odd***
3.adv **Even** the doctor was ill.
**Even if** you take a taxi, you will still be late.
→ ***Surprisingly, believe it or not***

**Extend** /ɪkˈstend/

v The region **extends** from Hungary to Poland.
The electromagnetic spectrum **extends** to ultraviolet and to X-rays.
→ ***To cover a distance, to reach, to include***

**Extent** /ɪkˈstent/

n **To what extent** does meteorology effect human behaviour?
**To a certain extent**, disease depends on the standard of living.
→ ***Degree, amount***

**Far** /fɑː/

1.adv **How far** is it to the post office?
**So far**, no one has been able to find an answer.
**As far as I am concerned**, the matter is of no importance.
→ ***Distant. Up to now. To that extent***
2.adv It is **far too** hot to work.
Working conditions are now **far better**.
→ ***Much, considerably***
3.adj He lives on the **far side** of the town.
The **Far East**.
→ ***Distant, remote ≠ near***

**Figure** /ˈfɪgə/

1.n Computers can **process figures** rapidly.
The **figures** for imports for last month were significantly better.
→ ***A number, statistics***

2.n The increase in output is shown in **Figure** 2.
→ ***A diagram***

**Graph** /græf/

n The annual variation of temperature is shown on the **graph**.
The **graph** illustrates the increase in road accidents.
To plot the data on a **graph**.
→ ***Diagram with two or more variables***

**Heavy** /ˈhevi/

adj Mercury is a **heavy** metal.
**Heavy** hydrocarbons are semi-solid and have large molecules.

adv The civilian population suffered **heavily** from the bombing.
→ ***Of considerable weight, high density. Severely ≠ lightly***

**Height** /haɪt/

n What is the **height** of the Eiffel tower?
**At the height** of the crisis.

v Car accident risks are **heightened** by alcohol.
→ ***A vertical extension, an altitude. Peak. To increase ≠ to reduce***

**Inaccurate** /ɪnˈækjərət/

adj The estimation was **inaccurate**.

n A certain amount of **inaccuracy** is inevitable.
The **inaccuracy** was due to distortion in the telescope lens.
→ ***Lacking in precision ≠ accuracy***

**Lack** /læk/

n He died through **lack** of food.
A **lack** of qualified engineers.

v To **lack time** to finish the job.
To **lack** the necessary skills.
→ ***Not enough, absence, shortage. To be short of***

**Length** /leŋθ/

n What is the **length** of a football field?
To go to **considerable lengths** to find an answer.

v It will be necessary to **lengthen** the duration of the clinical trials.
→ ***The measurement of the longest side, distance. To make longer ≠ shorten***

**Level** /ˈlevl/

1.n 200 meters above **sea level**.
As the tumour grows, **hormone levels** increase.
→ ***A degree, an amount***

2.v Before building the house, the ground must be **levelled**.
After increasing for five consecutive years, output **levelled off**.
→ ***To make / become horizontal, flat***

**Light** /laɪt/

1.n **Ultra-violet light**.
A biochemical reaction in the eye converts **light** into electrical signals.
→ ***Energy in the form of photons ≠ darkness***

2.adj She was wearing a **light** blue coat.
→ ***Reflecting many photons, bright ≠ dark***

3.adj A gas which is **lighter than air**.
In fusion, two **light** atoms are united into a heavier one.
→ ***Of small weight ≠ heavy***

4.v *(light, lit, lit)* **To light a fire**.
→ ***To make something burn, to ignite***

**Load** /ləʊd/

n The bridge can carry a **load** of 10 tonnes.
The circuit can take a **load** of 15 amperes.

v To **load** a ship.
The road network is **overloaded**.
→ ***The weight, the force that can be carried. To put weight, a cargo, pressure on something***

**Map** /mæp/

n A **road map** of southern Italy.
**The scale of the map** was 1 : 50,000.
Satellite technology means that more accurate **maps** can be made.
→ ***A diagram, chart displaying topographical features***

**Mean** /miːn/

1.v What do you **mean**?
Increased pollution **means** higher temperatures.

n What is the **meaning** of life?
→ ***To signify. Signification***

2.adj The **mean temperature** for July is 33°C.
To calculate the **mean** life of an unstable nucleus.
→ ***Average***

**Means** /miːnz/

*(N.B. – usually considered as singular)*

n The quickest **means** of getting there is by plane.
Amniotic liquid is withdrawn from the uterus **by means of** a thin tube.
→ ***Way, method***

**Measurement** /ˈmeʒəmənt/

n pH indicates the **measurement** of acidity in a solution.
Galvanometers cannot be used for

the **measurement** of alternating current.
→ ***Dimension, size, magnitude***

**Minus** /ˈmainəs/
prep The temperature falls to **minus** 30°C in winter.
Ten **to the power minus** 9 ($10^{-9}$).
→ ***Negative, less than ≠ plus***

**Monitor** /ˈmɒnɪtə/
1.v Satellites are used to **monitor** changes in ocean temperature.
Radiation levels are **monitored** continually.
A network of observation stations will **monitor** solar activity.
→ ***To observe, examine the results, progress***
2.n The shape of the wave form was displayed on the screen of the **monitor**.
→ ***An (electronic) display for showing results***

**Narrow** /ˈnærəʊ/
adj A **narrow road**.
There is a **narrow gap** between the electrodes.
v The river **narrows** as it enters the canyon.
→ ***A small distance across. To make / become smaller, to shrink ≠ widen***

**Odd** /ɒd/
1.adj Something very **odd** happened yesterday.
An **odd phenomenon**.
→ ***Strange, unexpected ≠ common, typical***
2 1, 3, 5, 7, ... are **odd** numbers.
→ ***Not divisible by 2 ≠ even***

**Plot** /plɒt/
v To **plot** the monthly production figures on a graph.
The computer automatically **plots** the curve on the screen.
→ ***To mark the position, to illustrate progress on a graph with dots***

**Power** /ˈpaʊə/
n The satellite instruments run on **solar power**.
An X-ray with a short wavelength has a greater penetrating **power**.
v The pace-maker is **powered** by a lithium-iodine battery.
adj A gas-**powered** engine.
The experiment requires **powerful**, 120 trillion watt lasers.
→ ***A force, capacity. To provide energy. Strong, having power ≠ powerless***

**Primary** /ˈpraɪməri/
adj The **primary aim** is to increase production.
The **primary cause** of anaemia is deficient production of red blood cells.
adv Earthquakes occur **primarily** along the boundaries of geological faults
→ ***Main, foremost, above all***

**Prime** /ˈpraɪm/
adj It is of **prime importance**.
13 is a **prime number**.
→ ***First, major. Divisible only by itself***

**Radius** /ˈreɪdiəs/
n The circle has a **radius** of 20 cm.
→ ***Half the diameter***

**Random** /ˈrændəm/
adj The position of gas molecules is **random**.
Electrons in the outer orbit of the atom move **at random**.
adv A **randomly** selected number.
→ ***Unpredictable, arbitrary***

**Range** /reɪndʒ/
1.v The temperature **ranges** from 5°C to 25°C.
Vibrations are produced which **range** from 8 to 40 cycles per second.
→ ***To fluctuate, to vary between two extremities***
2.n A large **range** of electrical appliances.
A **wide range** of food.
→ ***A choice, diversity***
3.n **Short range** ballistic missiles.
The target is **out of range**.
→ ***A distance, a limit, an extent***

**Rate** /reɪt/
n The **rate of acceleration**.
To increase production **at a steady rate**.
Over the last twenty years, there has been a decrease in the **birth rate**.
→ ***A measure, speed, proportion, value***

**Ratio** /ˈreɪʃiəʊ/
n **The ratio** of female births to male births is 100 : 105.
The **ratio** of old people in the population is increasing.
→ ***A proportion, a numerical relation***

**Reach** /ˈriːtʃ/
v **To reach a conclusion**.
Production figures have **reached** 100,000 TV sets per year.
The gas is compressed until it **reaches** a temperature of 85°C.
→ ***To arrive at, to attain***

**Reading** /ˈrɪːdɪŋ/
n He **checked the reading** on the volt-meter.
The seismograph **readings** are recorded automatically.
→ ***A figure, a level indicated by a measuring instrument***

**Root** /ruːt/
1.n Desert plants have deep **roots**.
***→ Underground part of a tree or plant which absorbs water and nutrients***
2.n The **root of a problem**.
The **square root** of 16 is 4.
***→ Basic source***

**Scale** /skeɪl/
n A **large-scale** simulation.
The Richter scale for earthquakes is a **logarithmic scale**.
The **scale** of the map is 1 : 200,000.
***→ A measuring system. A ratio of numbers comparing measurements***

**Shallow** /ˈʃæləʊ/
adj The Mediterranean is a relatively **shallow** sea.
The temperature is higher in **shallow** water.
***≠ Deep***

**Short** /ʃɔːt/
adj A **short** report was published in "Nature".
The material is **in short supply**.
To be **short of money**.
n There was a **shortage of food** during the war.
v Antibiotics can **shorten** the duration of the disease.
***→ Not long, restricted. Insufficiency. To make short, reduce ≠ to lengthen***

**Single** /ˈsɪŋgl/
adj A **single child**.
In fission, a **single** atom is divided into two parts.
***→ Only one, unique***

**Size** /saɪz/
n What **size** shoes do you wear?
The **size** of a proton is approximately $10^{-12}$ cm.
The resolution of the telescope depends on the **size** of the lens.
***→ Dimension***

**Slight** /slaɪt/
adj There was a **slight increase** in output.
In September, there is usually a **slight drop** in unemployment.
adv The metal melts at **slightly more than** 600°C.
***→ Small, minor. A little, to a certain extent ≠ much***

**Speed** /spiːd/
n To travel at a **high speed**.
Debris in orbit travels at **speeds** approaching 11 km per second.
***→ A rate of movement, a velocity***

**Square** /skweə/
adj Alaska is roughly **square** in shape.
Six **square cm** of skin contains up to 4.5 metres of blood vessels.
***→ With a geometrical shape of 4 equal sides and 4 right angles***

**Stage** /steɪdʒ/
n The experiment can be divided into three **stages**.
**In the early stages**, the temperature of the universe was $10^{10}$ °C.
***→ Section. Moment, period***

**Standard** /ˈstændəd/
n For most people, the **standard of living** is improving.
**Safety standards** are set by the government.
***→ A level, an accepted measure of quality***

**Step** /step/
n The **first step in the process** is called phototransduction.
To **move one step closer** to finding a cure for the disease.
v He **stepped on** the wet cement.
***→ A stage. A movement, a small distance. To walk on***

**Strength** /streŋθ/
n A galvanometer records the **strength** of a current.
Alloys are lighter and have greater mechanical **strength**.
v The frame of the machine must be **strengthened**.
***→ Force, power, resistance. To make stronger ≠ to weaken***

**Survey** /ˈsɜːveɪ/
n A **recent survey** of genetic research.
**To carry out a survey** of public opinion.
v Unmanned space probes have **surveyed** all the planets except Pluto.
***→ Examination, overview. To inspect, study***

**Thick** /θɪk/
adj The book is 5 cm **thick**.
Radio-active waste must be surrounded by **thick** protective walls.
v Progestogen makes the cervical mucus **thicken** and stops the sperm.
***→ A (large) dimension between surfaces. To make / become thick ≠ thin***

**Thin** /θɪn/
adj He was a tall, **thin** man.
The surface was covered by a **thin layer** of gold.
***→ Short distance between surfaces ≠ fat, thick***

**Vicinity** /vəˈsɪnəti/

n Einstein predicted that light would bend **in the vicinity** of the Sun.
The cost will be **in the vicinity** of 20,000 euros.
→ ***Near, close, in the neighbourhood***

**Weigh** /weɪ/

v The car **weighs** 900 kg.
Evaporation can be measured by **weighing** the sample after heating.
n The **weight** of the baby depends on the mother's diet.
→ ***To measure in kg, etc. Heaviness, mass***

**Wide** /waɪd/

adj The Amazon is the **widest** river in the world.
adv A **widely distributed** newspaper.
v To **widen** the road.
n The **width** of the chip is 1 micron.
→ ***Dimension across. To make bigger, to enlarge. Transversal dimension***

**Widespread** /ˈwaɪdspred/

adj A **widespread fear** of unemployment.
A **widespread belief** in astrology.
→ ***Covering a large area, extensive, common***

# 2. FREQUENCY, SPACE & SHAPE

**Above** /ə'bʌv/

prep The plane was flying **above** the clouds.
The level of contamination is **above** 600 becquerels.
**Above all**, he likes football.
***→ Higher, more than ≠ below***

**Ahead** /ə'hed/

adv Despite protests about the new airport, the government has decided to **go ahead**.
The US is 5 years **ahead of** Japan in space research.
***→ Forward. In advance, in front ≠ behind***

**Alone** /ə'ləʊn/

adv He preferred to work **alone**.
Female birds usually incubate their eggs **alone**.
adv More than 1 million blood samples are tested daily in the U.S.A. **alone**.
***→ Unassisted. Excluding others***

**Among(st)** /ə'mʌŋ/

prep Genetic selection comes from competition **among** different members of a species.
**Among** adult patients, few with Parkinson's disease ever get better.
He found the letter **amongst** the papers on his desk.
***→ Between. In the middle of***

**Arrow** /'ærəʊ/

n To find the car park, just follow the **arrows**.
In the graph, the peak temperature is indicated by an **arrow**.
***→ Sign indicating direction***

**Axis** /'æksis/

n The Earth turns on its **axis** once every 24 hours.
On the graph, time is indicated on **the horizontal axis**.
***→ A centre line (imaginary) around which something turns, a line of reference***

**Back** /bæk/

1.n To sit in the **back** of the car.
She was carrying the child on her **back**.
***≠ Front***

2.adv **To come back** home in the evening.
The firm was obliged to **pay back** the money.
***→ To return (to the starting point)***

3.v **To back** a car into a garage.
***≠ To go forwards***

4.v The government **backed** the project.
n To get **financial backing** from the government.
***→ To give support, help. Aid***

**Behind** /bɪ'haɪnd/

1.prep A policeman stood **behind** the President.
What are the brain mechanisms **behind** this behaviour?
***→ At the back of. Underlying, supporting***

2 To be **behind schedule**.
***→ Late***

**Below** /bɪ'ləʊ/

prep There are huge stocks of mineral resources **below** the Antarctic ice.
The production figures are **below** last year's.
The temperature fell to 15°C **below zero**.
***→ Under, lower than ≠ above***

**Beneath** /bɪ'ni:θ/

prep **Beneath the surface** of the sea.
Cancerous cells were found **beneath** the membrane.
***→ Under***

**Between** /bɪ'twi:n/

1.prep The shop closes **between** 12.00 a.m. and 2 p.m.
A regular flight **between** Geneva and New York.
***→ The period or space separating two times, places***

2 What is the link **between** colour and emotions?
There is a reaction **between** the cells and their environment.
***→ Connecting, relating two things***

**Beyond** /bɪ'jɒnd/

prep To prove something **beyond doubt**.
**Beyond a period** of 5 days, weather forecasts are unreliable.
The task is **beyond** the capabilities of most computers.
***→ Further than, past the limits of***

**Blank** /blæŋk/

adj Write your name in the **blank space** at the top of the paper.
The computer crashed and the screen went **blank**.
→ ***Unfilled. Empty***

**Border** /ˈbɔːdə/

n The troops **crossed** the **border** at midnight.
The country is **on the border** of a major crisis.
→ ***Frontier, boundary, edge***

**Bottom** /ˈbɒtəm/

n Submarine robots will explore the **bottom** of the sea.
**At the bottom** of the page.
→ ***The lowest part ≠ top***

**Close** /kləʊs/

1.adj The bank is **close to** the station.
The panda is **close to** extinction.
**A close examination** of the heart showed signs of infection.
→ ***Near, in the vicinity of. Thorough, detailed ≠ superficial***

2.v /kləʊz/ (*N.B. – notice the difference in pronunciation of the adjective and the verb)*
**To close** the windows at night.

adj A **closed circuit** T.V.
→ ***To shut ≠ to open***

**Cluster** /ˈklʌstə/

n A village consists of a **cluster** of houses.
German astronomers have discovered a new **cluster of stars**.
→ ***A group, collection***

**Core** /kɔː/

n **The core of an atom** is the nucleus.
Iron makes up the major part of the **Earth's core**.
They analysed an **ice core** from the Antarctic.
→ ***The central part. A sample obtained by deep drilling***

**Corner** /ˈkɔːnə/

n There is a shop **on the corner** of the street.
He signed his name in the **bottom right hand corner** of the letter.
The sum of the angles at four **corners** of a rectangle is 360°.
→ ***The point at which two lines meet***

**Crowd** /kraʊd/

n A large **crowd** of people watched the football match.

adj The increase in traffic means that airspace is becoming dangerously **crowded**.
The 19th century industrial towns were **overcrowded**, unhealthy and dangerous.
→ ***A multitude. When too many people gather together***

**Curve** /kɜːv/

n A **curve** in the road.
The **curve** on the graph indicates the rise in temperature.

v Light is **curved** by gravitational attraction.
→ ***A bend, a crescent-like deviation. To deviate from a straight line***

**Daily** /ˈdeɪli/

adj A **daily newspaper**.
**Daily** behaviour patterns are linked to circadian rhythms.
→ ***Every day***

**Dot** /dɒt/

n Pixels consist of very small illuminated **dots** on a screen.
The Hindus were the first to use a circle or a **dot** as a symbol for zero.

adj The projection for the next 5 years is shown on the graph by a **dotted line**.
→ ***A small point, a spot***

**Edge** /edʒ/

n A tree was standing on the **edge** of the river.
A cube has got twelve **edges**.
Bacteria was growing on the **edge** of the sample.
→ ***A boundary of a surface. The meeting line of two surfaces***

**Era** /ˈɪərə/

n The **modern era**.
Modern amphibians did not appear until the **Mesozoic era**.
→ ***Period, span of time, epoch***

**Feature** /ˈfiːtʃə/

n There are **several features** which make this car unique.
**A remarkable feature** of the brain is its capacity to function when damaged.

v The development project **featured** two new research laboratories.
→ ***An aspect, a characteristic. To possess an attribute***

**Field** /fiːld/

1.n There were three horses in the **field** in front of the house.
A **gravitational field**.
To carry out **field-work** on Antarctic ecosystems.
→ ***An area of land, a zone. In the natural environment***

2.n He is an expert in this **field**.
→ ***An area of activity, a discipline***

**Flat** /flæt/

1.adj The Earth is not **flat**.
You need a **flat** surface to draw.

v The town was **flattened** by bombs.
***→ Smooth, level. To make level***

2.n He lives in a **flat** in the city centre.
***→ An apartment***

**Frame** /freɪm/

n The **frame** of the window is made of metal.
**A frame of reference**.
***→ The surrounding structure of something***

**Framework** /ˈfreɪmwɜːk/

n The steel **framework** of a building.
To work **within the framework** of a project.
***→ (Complex) supporting frame or structure***

**Ground** /graʊnd/

n The **ground** was covered with snow.
Satellite telescopes are controlled from the **ground**.
***→ The surface of the Earth***

**Grounds** /graʊndz/

n There are good **grounds** for thinking that the results are not valid.
***→ Reasons***

**Hole** /həʊl/

n There was a **hole** in his shoe.
**Black holes** are caused by intense gravitational forces.
***→ An empty space, a gap, an orifice***

**Hollow** /ˈhɒləʊ/

adj A **hollow** tree.
Animals' bones are **hollow**.
The steel sphere was **hollow** inside.
***→ With an empty space inside***
***≠ solid***

**Inner** /ˈɪnə/

adj The **inner diameter** of a tube.
He lives in the **inner city**.
Airsickness is triggered by a disturbance of the **inner ear**.
***→ Inside ≠ outer***

**Layer** /ˈleɪə/

n Sedimentary rocks lie in **layers**.
The **ozone layer** is in danger.
The surface was covered by a thin **layer** of gold.
***→ Horizontal division. Thin covering, coating***

**Locate** /ləʊˈkeɪt/

v **To locate** an error in the circuit design.
The primary tumours must be **located** and destroyed.
***→ To detect, to discover the position of something***

**Non-stop** /ˌnɑnˈstɑp/

adj The first **non-stop** transatlantic flight was made in 1927.

adv He worked **non-stop** until the sun rose.
***→ Without interruption, continually***

**Occur** /əˈkɜː/

1.v An accident **occurred** last night.
Eclipses of the sun seldom **occur**.
A higher degree of aggressiveness **occurs** among animals in captivity.

n Several **occurrences** of malaria have been reported in the UK.
***→ To take place. Something which happens. A case***

2.v It did not **occur to me** to ask his name.
***→ To have an idea, to think of something***

**Once** /wʌns/

1.adv I have only **once** been to Venice.
***→ A single time***

2 Chloroform was **once** commonly used as an anaesthetic.
***→ In the past, previously***

3 He saw the mistake **at once**.
***→ Immediately***

4.conj **Once** it has penetrated the cell wall, the drug begins to have an effect.
***→ As soon as***

**Outer** /ˈaʊtə/

adj He lives in **outer** London.
To explore **outer space**.
The **outer** membranes of the cell react to the stimulation.
***→ Located outside, on the periphery***
***≠ inner***

**Outline** /ˈaʊtlaɪn/

n As you fly into New York, you can see the **outline** of the Empire State Building.
The seven stars of Ursa Major have an easily identified **outline**.
**To write an outline** of a research project.
***→ Silhouette. Main points, summary***

**Partly** /ˈpɑːtli/

adv The problem has been **partly** solved.
The government is **partly responsible**.
The experiment failed **partly** because the X-ray source was too weak.
***→ In part, to a certain extent, not completely ≠ totally***

**Pattern** /ˈpætn/

n Economic development usually follows the same **pattern**.
There have been **recurring patterns** of malaria epidemics.
We need a better description of the **patterns** of neural connections.
***→ An arrangement or sequence of things that is not random***

**Peak** /piːk/

n The **peak** of the mountain is covered with snow.
The **peak** output of electricity occurs between 7-8 p.m.
There are cyclic **peaks** in the sun's activity.

v The dollar **peaked** after the export figures had improved.
→ ***Highest point, tip, apex. To reach the highest point***

**Plan** /plæn/

1.v **To plan** for the future.
The manager **plans** to modernise the plant.

n There is a **plan** to widen the motorway.
→ ***To make a project, to intend. A project, a scheme***

2.n To make a **plan** of the building.
→ ***A drawing, map, graphic representation***

**Pulse** /pʌls/

n Hypoxia causes the **pulse rate** to increase.
An electronic **pulse** generator.
→ ***Rhythmic peaks of blood pressure from heart beats. A cyclic signal***

**Recur** /rɪˈkɜː/

v If the symptoms **recur**, you should consult a doctor at once.

n As a rule, the **recurrence** of infectious disease is cyclic.

adj Malaria is characterised by **recurrent** attacks of fever.
→ ***To happen again. Repetition. Periodic***

**Remote** /rɪˈməʊt/

adj He lives in a **remote** village in the mountains.
**Remote** underground sensors are used to record seismic waves.
The satellite was monitored by a **remote-controlled** telescope.
→ ***Distant, far away. From a distance***

**Replace** /rɪˈpleis/

v The battery must be **replaced** every 2 months.
Natural gas is progressively **replacing** oil as a fuel.

n Hormone **replacement** therapy is now widely used.
→ ***To change, to take the place. Substitution***

**Ring** /rɪŋ/

n Most married people wear a **gold ring** on their fingers.
To **draw a ring** round the correct answer.
→ ***Something circular, a band, a circle***

**Scatter** /ˈskætə/

v The population lives in tiny villages, **scattered** across the valley.
Radio waves are **scattered** by ionisation.

n A **scatter** of dots on a graph.
→ ***Dispersed, lying in disorder ≠ a cluster***

**Schedule** /ˈʃedjuːl/

n Every week the **work schedule** changes.
The train arrived **on schedule**.
To **work to schedule**.

v The Museum was **scheduled** to open at the end of the year.
→ ***a plan, timetable, scheme. To organise, to plan***

**Scheme** /skiːm/

n The government proposed a new **tax scheme**.
A better public transport **scheme** is required.
A new **scheme** has been proposed to reduce desertification.
→ ***Plan, arrangement***

**Scope** /skəʊp/

n The question is **beyond the scope** of this article.
Over the years, the **scope** of biology has shifted significantly.
Improved telescopes will **considerably widen the scope** of astronomy.
→ ***Field of reference, range***

**Seldom** /ˈseldəm/

adv It **seldom** rains in August.
Earthquakes are **seldom** recorded in the UK.
→ ***Not often, rarely ≠ frequently***

**Series** /sɪəriːz/ *(N.B. – singular)*

n A **series** of accidents occurred.
The ethanol must be concentrated to 95% by a **series** of distillations.
Telescopes are built with a **series** of concentric mirrors.
→ ***Recurring events, a succession***

**Shape** /ʃeɪp/

n France is hexagonal in **shape**.
The **shape** of the wave can be displayed on the oscilloscope.

v Computer technology is **shaping** the future of the world.
→ ***The form, the outline. To give form to, to influence***

**Side** /saɪd/

n Trees were growing along the **side** of the road.
They are **two sides to an argument**.

adj A square is a **4-sided** figure.
→ ***Lateral boundary. Aspect***

**Note** – A **4-sided** figure
A large number of compound adjectives are formed by adding **"-ed"** to nouns:
→ *a large-**sized** car*
→ *a right-**angled** triangle*
→ *a 6-**wheeled** lorry*

**Slope** /sləʊp/
n The steeper the **slope** is, the more erosion occurs.
adj Chalets have **sloping** roofs to prevent snow accumulating.
***→ A hillside. A gradient, inclined surface***

**Space** /speɪs/
n More **space** is needed for the new equipment.
You should leave a **space** at the end of each paragraph.
Sputnik I was the first vehicle to travel in **outer space**.
***→ Gap, unoccupied area***

**Spot** /spɑt/
1.n The albatross has a black **spot** on its head.
There is a **spot** of ink on the paper.
The North Pole is not the coldest **spot** in the Arctic.
***→ A round mark. A particular place***
2.v To **spot** an aeroplane **in the distance**.
To **spot an error**.
***→ To see something small, to detect***

**Steady** /stedi/
adj A **slow but steady decline** in production.
There is a **steady flow** of electrons towards the positive pole.
adv The temperature **increased steadily**.
***→ Regular ≠ fluctuating, sporadic***

**Straight** /streɪt/
1.adj A **straight** road.
**To draw a straight line**.
***→ Direct, without deviation ≠ Curved***
2.adv **To go straight back** home after work.
He didn't answer **straight away**.
***→ Directly, immediately***

**Strip** /strɪp/
1.n She marked her place in the book with a **strip** of paper.
Electrical contact was made by a thin copper **strip**.
***→ Something which is long and narrow in shape***
2.v Before demolition, the factory was **stripped** of all the machinery.
**To strip** insulation off an electrical wire.
***→ To take off / away (rapidly, completely)***

**Swing** /swɪŋ/ *(swing, swung, swung)*
v A pendulum **swings** from left to right.
The hand of the voltmeter **swings** to the right when there is a discharge.
n A **swing** in the voting pattern.
***→ To oscillate, move from side to side. A movement***

**Through** /θruː/
1.prep Gas flows **through** the pipe.
Sound waves travel faster **through** water than **through** air.
adv To **read through** an article.
***→ To go from one end to the other***
2.prep They died **through** lack of water.
***→ Because of, due to***

**Throughout** /θruːˈaʊt/
prep **Throughout the war**, there was a shortage of sugar.
The temperature must be kept at −5°C **throughout** the experiment.
Bacteria are found **throughout the world**.
***→ During, for the whole time. Everywhere***

**Tip** /tɪp/
n The **tip** of an iceberg.
You can see the **tip** of the mountain in the distance.
The **tip** of the drill is made of tungsten.
***→ The end point, apex***

**Top** /tɒp/
n The **top** of the table is covered with dust.
He took the **top** off the box.
adj The **top** layer of water is warmer.
***→ The highest surface, point ≠ bottom***

**Track** /træk/
1.n The railway **track**.
You can see the **track** of the car wheels in the snow.
***→ A path, way. The trace made by something***
2.v **To track** the movement of the particles on the screen.
Radio isotopes can be used for **tracking** microbes.
***→ To follow the tracks, to monitor the trajectory***

**Twice** /twaɪs/
adv Unemployment is **twice as high** for women.
So far, the atomic bomb has been dropped **twice** for military purposes.
***→ Two times ≠ once***

**Underneath** /ˌʌndəˈniːθ/
prep **Underneath** the surface of the Earth.
Older fossils lie **underneath** the Palaeozoic rocks.
***→ Below, under ≠ above***

**Wave** /weɪv/

n Oscilloscopes display the shape of a **wave**.
The **wave length** of the colour red is 620-760 nm.
There was a **wave of protest** throughout the country.
→ ***Oscillation, cyclic movement***

**Within** /wɪˈðɪn/

prep You must pay your taxes **within** 14 days.
Malignant cells **within** the tumour must be destroyed.
→ ***Inside***

**Yearly** /ˈjɪəli/

adj Amnesty International publishes a **yearly** report.
The meteorological records provide the **yearly** pattern of rainfall.
→ ***Annual***

# 3. COMPARISON & RELATION

**Add** /æd/
v **To add** two numbers together.
The strength of the signals is increased by **adding** them together.
If an electron is **added** to a neutral atom it acquires a negative charge.
→ ***To put together. To make a total ≠ to subtract***

**Agree** /əˈgriː/
v The manager **agreed** to give him a job.
Neurologists **agree** that schizophrenia has different causes.
n A diplomatic **agreement between** France and Spain.
→ ***To accept, to have the same opinion. An arrangement, a pact***

**Alike** /əˈlaɪk/
adj No two people are exactly **alike**.
The segments of early arthropods were **much alike**.
adv Both samples were treated **alike**.
→ ***Similar. In the same way***

**Available** /əˈveɪləbl/
adj The apparatus will not be **available** till next week.
I will send you the components as soon as they are **available**.
→ ***Ready to be used, accessible ≠ unavailable***

**Belong** /bɪˈlɒŋ/
v Less than 5% of the land **belongs to** small farmers.
Mercury **belongs to** group IIb of the periodic table.
→ ***To be owned by. To be a part of***

**Bind** /baɪnd/ *(bind, bound, bound)*
v As a result of nuclear interactions, protons and neutrons **bind** to form nuclei.
The successful sperm initially **binds** to the outer layer of the ovum.
→ ***To combine, to cohere***

**Bond** /bɒnd/
n A **bond** is formed when two atoms share an electron.
v Polymers are formed by **bonding** monomer molecules.
→ ***A strong link. To make a strong connection***

**Both** /bəʊθ/
adj He shut **both** of his eyes.
Biochemistry is a branch of **both** chemistry and biology.
**Both** the hippocampus and the cortex were damaged.
→ ***The two together ≠ neither***

**(In) charge of** /ɪn tʃɑːdʒəv/
n Who is **in charge of** the export department?
To be **in charge of** industrial relations.
The person **in charge of** the laboratory is absent.
→ ***To be responsible for***

**Choice** /tʃɔɪs/
n The **choice** of materials that was available was limited.
The final **choice** of equipment will depend on the cost.
**A multiple-choice question**.
→ ***A selection. What is chosen***

**Choose** /tʃuːz/ *(choose, chose, chosen)*
v To **choose** the best location for building a nuclear reactor.
There were only 4 possibilities **to choose from**.
→ ***To select***

**Compete** /kəmˈpiːt/
v Animals have to **compete** for food in order to survive.
adj Members of the **competing** teams stayed in the Olympic village.
→ ***To struggle to be first. Opposing***

**Decrease** /dɪˈkriːs/
v The population has **decreased** by 5%.
As the pressure is reduced, the temperature **decreases**.
n A **decrease** in the annual rainfall.
adj **Decreasing profits**.
→ ***To become less. A reduction ≠ increasing***

**Depend on** /dɪˈpendɒn/
v She **depends on** the bus to get to work.
Good results **depend on** accurate data collection.
The boiling point of hydrocarbons **depends on** the molecular structure.
→ ***To count on, to rely on, to be determined by***

**Disagree** /dɪsə'griː/

v The experts **disagreed about** the causes of the crash.
Biologists often **disagree** on the meaning of the word "progress".

n A **major disagreement** between members of the government.
→ ***Have an opposing, conflicting opinion, difference of opinion***

**Drop** /drɒp/

1.n A **drop** of blood fell on the floor.
→ ***A globule of liquid***

2.n A **drop** in the population.

v Oil prices **dropped sharply** last year.
→ ***A decrease, to go down ≠ to rise***

3.v The second atomic bomb was **dropped** on Nagasaki.
→ ***To let something fall***

**Duty** /'djuːti/

n To do your **duty**.
A doctor's **duty** is to save lives.
Enzymes perform diverse **duties** as catalysts.
→ ***(Moral) obligation, responsibility, task***

**Enhance** /ɪn'hɑːns/

v Speed can be **greatly enhanced** by using optic fibres.
Drugs can be used for **enhancing** sporting performance.
**Computer-enhanced** learning.
→ ***To make better, improve***

**Enlarge** /ɪn'lɑːdʒ/

v The University intends to **enlarge** the biology research facilities.

n In myocarditis, weakened muscles lead to an **enlargement** of the heart.

adj A microscope provides an **enlarged** image of the sample.
The **enlarged** brain of Homo Sapiens was a prerequisite for language.
→ ***To make bigger, extend. An expansion. Increased ≠ reduced***

> **Note** — The prefix **"en-"** is used to form verbs with the meaning of "*to make*".
> → *to* ***enable*** *him to work*
> → *to* ***ensure*** *success*
> → *to* ***enrich*** *his family*

**Equal** /'iːkwəl/

adj Women should have **equal pay for equal work**.
The number of electrons is **equal** to the number of protons.

v The firm has already **equalled** last year's production.
→ ***The same as, to be exactly similar. To reach the same results***

**Exceed** /ɪk'siːd/

v He was stopped by the police for **exceeding** the speed limit.
It is impossible **to exceed** the speed of light.
Annual meat production **exceeds** 2.7 m. tonnes.
→ ***To be greater than, to go beyond***

**Exceedingly** /ɪk'siːdɪŋli/

adv The walls of capillaries are **exceedingly** thin.
Eclipses of the Sun are **exceedingly rare.**
→ ***Extremely, exceptionally***

**Expand** /ɪk'spænd/

v Gases **expand** when heated.
The electronics industry is **expanding rapidly**.

adj The "Big Bang" implies an **expanding universe**.
→ ***To become greater in volume ≠ to contract, shrink***

**Fall** /fɔːl/ *(fall, fell, fallen)*

v In winter the temperature **falls**.

n **A fall** in production
→ ***To go down. A decrease ≠ a rise***

**Fit** /fɪt/

1.v Do the shoes **fit** you?
The theory does not **fit**.
→ ***To be the right size, adapted***

2.v To **fit** a car with an alarm system.
→ ***To equip***

3.adj The house is not **fit** to live in.
→ ***Good enough, of suitable quality***

**Follow** /'fɒləʊ/

v The dog **followed** the man back home.
If 2X = 4Y, then it **follows** that X = 2Y.

adj The **following** points are important.
→ ***To go after. To be a logical consequence. To come next***

**Foremost** /'fɔːməʊst/

adj He was one of the **foremost** astronomers of his time.
Italy is among **the world's foremost** car manufacturers.
→ ***Leading, top ≠ minor***

**Gap** /gæp/

n The **generation gap**.
There is a huge **technological gap** between rich and poor countries.
An electric spark occurs across the **gap between** the electrodes.
→ ***An empty space or time***

**Gather** /'gæðə/

v **To gather** information.
**Data gathering** techniques.
More than 300 specialists **gathered** in Toronto for the meeting.
→ ***To collect, to come together ≠ to scatter***

**Improve** /ɪm'pruːv/

v Computers are used to **improve** the quality of images.
They are **improving** techniques for diagnosing the disease.

adj This is an **improved model**.

n There has been an **improvement** in the unemployment figures.
***→ To make better, to enhance. Amelioration ≠ worsening***

**Increase** /ɪn'kriːs/

n There was a **gradual increase** in the number of red blood cells.

v There is pressure **to increase** safety levels.

adv It is **increasingly difficult** to find a job.

adj An **increasing number** of people are dying of cancer.
***→ Expansion, rise. To raise. More and more ≠ decreasing***

**Join** /dʒɔɪn/

v The Missouri **joins** the Mississippi near St Louis.
Each vertebra is **joined** to the next one by ligaments.

n The tubes are connected by a **flexible rubber joint**.
***→ To be / become connected, linked***

**Key** /kiː/

1.n To open a door with a **key**.
***→ Metal instrument for opening a lock***

2.adj The C.E.A. has played a **key role** in developing underwater robots.
One of the **key problems** in pollution is how to dispose of chemical waste.
***→ Major, critical***

**Last** /lɑːst/

v The journey to Turin **lasted** 5 hours.
The period of revolution of Mercury **lasts** 88 Earth days.
Hydrocarbon resources will not **last for ever**.
***→ To continue in time***

**Lead** /liːd/ (*lead, led, led*)

1.v **"All roads lead to Rome"**.
The increase in robotics may **lead to** unemployment.
When the ice melts, it **leads to** a decrease in surface pressure.
***→ To go in the direction, to result in***

2.n /led/
**Lead** is a heavy metal used for making batteries.
The Romans emperors went mad because they ate from plates made of **lead**.
***→ A soft heavy metal; chemical symbol : Pb***

**Note** – The verb **"to lead"** and the noun for the metal **"lead"** are not related and they are pronounced differently.
***→ to lead*** /liːd/ *(cf. need, speed)*
***→ the lead*** /led/ *(cf. bed, head)*

**Leading** /'liːdɪŋ/

adj Pericles was a **leading** figure in Athenian politics of the 5th century BC.
Oppenheimer played a **leading role** in the development of the atomic bomb.
***→ Major, important ≠ secondary***

**Left** /left/

n In England, cars drive **on the left**.

adj About 10% of people write with their **left hand**.
**Left-wing** politics.
***→ On the same side as the heart ≠ right***

**Lessen** /'lesn/

v Reducing speed **lessens the danger** of road accidents.
The hole in the top of the parachute **lessens** the initial shock of deceleration
***→ To reduce, to moderate ≠ to increase***

**Likewise** /'laɪkwaɪz/

adv Microbes, and **likewise** viruses, are unaffected by the treatment.
The went home on foot. James did **likewise**.
***→ In the same way, similarly***

**Link** /lɪŋk/

n There is a **link between** weight and heart disease.

v The road **links** the two towns.
Polymers are formed by **linking** monomer molecules.
***→ A connection. To join ≠ disconnecting***

**Low** /ləʊ/

adj The lorry could not get under the **low** bridge.
Hydrocarbons with small molecules have **low boiling points**.

v Following the oil crisis, the speed limit in the UK was **lowered**.
***→ Not high. To reduce ≠ to heighten, raise***

**Match** /mætʃ/

v The two colours do not **match**.
The chemical composition of meteorites **matches** that of the sun.
In statistics, samples must be carefully **matched**.
***→ To be suitable to each other, to correspond, to be compared***

**Miss** /mɪs/

v To **miss the train**.

adj Some pages of the book are **missing**. It was thought that *"Australopithecus africanus"* was the **missing link**.

***→ Not to catch. Not to be there, to be absent***

**Net** /net/

n He took the fish out of the aquarium with a **net**. In tennis, a **net** separates the two players. A fine **net** was used to filter out the living organisms.

***→ A sort of filter, usually made of string or wire; typically used for catching fish***

**Network** /ˈnetwɜːk/

n France has an extensive **railway network**. IBM has a world-wide sales **network**.

***→ Complex interconnected communication system***

**Per** /pɜː/

prep Seventy **per** cent. A newton accelerates 1 kilogram at 1 metre **per** second.

***→ For each***

**Pursue** /pəˈsjuː/

v To **pursue an ideal**. Several teams are **actively pursuing** this line of research. Many birds **pursue** prey by swimming under water.

n Lions travel about 8 km a day **in pursuit of** food.

***→ To follow (in order to catch). Search***

**Raise** /reɪz/

v To **raise** your hand. The World Bank aims **to raise** the standard of living in the Third World. The **issue was not raised** during the meeting.

***→ To move upwards, to increase. To mention, to discuss***

**Reduce** /rɪˈdjuːs/

v **To reduce the amount** of fuel used. Chemotherapy **has considerably reduced** the mortality rate. It is vital **to reduce** unemployment figures.

***→ To make smaller ≠ to raise***

**Relate** /rɪˈleɪt/

v Production is **related** to demand. Salary is usually **related** to education.

n There is a statistical **relationship between** sex and suicide.

***→ To be connected, linked. A link***

> **Note** — The suffix **"ship"** is used to form abstract nouns. It means *"the fact of – the state of being."*
> *→ the* ***friendship*** *between two people*
> *→ a* ***partnership*** *between Italy and France*

**Relevance** /ˈreləvəns/

n Darwin immediately saw the **relevance** of Malthus's work.

adj To make a realistic decision, first of all we need the **relevant data**. Unemployment rates are clearly very **relevant** to crime figures.

***→ Importance. Appropriate, pertinent ≠ irrelevant***

**Remain** /rɪˈmeɪn/

v At 6 p.m. only two people **remained** in the office. The details of the evolutionary process **remain** a mystery.

adj Two men escaped; the **remaining** members of the crew were killed.

***→ To continue to be, to be left***

**Right** /raɪt/

1.adj Most people write with their **right** hand.

***≠ Left***

2.adj This is the **right** answer. Provided weather conditions are **right**, the satellite will be launched tomorrow.

***→ Correct, suitable ≠ wrong***

**Rise** /raɪz/ *(rise, rose, risen)*

v Hot air **rises**. When gas is compressed the **temperature rises**.

n A **rise** in production figures.

***→ To move upwards. An increase ≠ a fall***

**Share** /ʃeə/

v **To share** the money between two people. The research budget must be **shared** between the different laboratories.

n Airbus is increasing its **share of the** aviation **market**.

***→ To divide, to distribute. Part belonging to someone***

**Span** /spæn/

n The average **life-span** of a giraffe is about 26 years. The Boeing B-52, built in 1950, had a **wing span** of 56 m.

v The bridge **spans** the river. The Bronze Age **spans** the period from about 2,000 to 700 BC.

***→ A duration, a distance. To go from one side, extremity to the other***

**Spread** /spred/ *(spread, spread, spread)*
v The **news spread** across the continent.
Aircraft technology **spread rapidly** to other countries.
The microbes are **spread** through the body via the blood system.
***→ To travel, to extend. To disperse***

**Struggle** /ˈstrʌgl/
n Marx introduced the concept of the **class struggle**.
According to Darwin, the **struggle** for life improves the species.
v **To struggle** to improve production.
***→ Competition. To make efforts to succeed***

**Subtract** /səbˈtrækt/
v The cost of maintenance must be **subtracted** from the total profits.
Y must be **subtracted** from both sides of the equation.
***→ To take away, to remove ≠ to add***

**Suit** /suːt/
1.n It is advisable to **wear a suit** for the appointment.
Astronauts must wear **space suits**.
***→ Clothes (formal), jacket and trousers are made of the same material***
2.v This colour does not **suit** you.
A job on a newspaper would **suit** her.
Psychoanalysis is not **well-suited** for the treatment of psychotic disorders.
adj Rats are **suitable** for gene manipulation as they reproduce fast.
***→ To be appropriate. To be right for a specific purpose ≠ unsuitable***

**Supply** /səˈplaɪ/
v The power station **supplies** electricity to industry.
n A **supply** of drinking water.
Unless food **supplies** arrive quickly, there will be a famine.
***→ To provide what is needed. Stock, reserve***

**Tend** /tend/
v Dark objects **tend to** absorb solar heat.
As people grow older, they **tend to** absorb less calcium.
***→ Usually to do this, to have a tendency to do something***

**Tendency** /ˈtendənsi/
n Female monkeys show a **greater tendency** to protect their young.
There is **a growing tendency** to marry several times.
***→ A predisposition, inclination, fashion***

**Trend** /trend/
n The **latest trend** in computer design.
Currently there is a **trend towards** using more plastic in car design.
***→ A movement, a fashion, a tendency***

**Twin** /twɪn/
n Monozygotic **twins** have the same genetic heritage.
adj The question is how to address the **twin** problems of poverty and health.
A **twin-engined** plane.
***→ Brothers / sisters born at the same time. Identical ≠ single***

**Unlike** /ʌnˈlaɪk/
prep **Unlike** plants, animals must search for food.
Digital films, **unlike** conventional photographs, can be viewed immediately.
***→ Dissimilar, in contrast to ≠ in the same way as***

**Upper** /ˈʌpə/
adj The **upper** part of the Amazon is still largely unexplored.
The **upper** surface of a wing.
***→ Higher part, top, superior ≠ lower***

**Worsen** /ˈwɜːsn/
v The economic situation is **worsening**.
After the war, the housing shortage **worsened**.
***→ To get worse ≠ to improve***

# 4. Modification

**Barely** /ˈbeəli/

adv The child was **barely** able to walk.
The particles were **barely** visible to the naked eye.
The wing span of the smallest bird **barely exceeds** 7 cm.
→ ***Only just, hardly***

**Basic** /ˈbeɪsɪk/

adj The **basic problem** is that we cannot identify the virus.
The **basic principles** of radioisotopes are clear.
adv **Basically**, there are three types of telescopes.
→ ***Fundamental. Essentially***

**Brief** /bri:f/

adj There was a **brief interruption**.
To give a **brief explanation** of the situation.
adv He **briefly summarised** the project.
→ ***Short. Rapidly ≠ in detail***

**Bright** /braɪt/

adj A **bright light**.
The light from Quasars is **brighter** than a whole galaxy.
→ ***Highly luminescent, shining ≠ dark***

**Busy** /ˈbɪzi/

adj At 6 p.m. the city centre is very **busy**.
He is **busy** repair**ing** the TV set.
adv Food technologists are **busily** develop**ing** low-fat products.
→ ***Involving a lot of activity. Occupied***

**Care** /keə/

n To **take care of** the baby.
Glass must be **handled with care**.
adj You have broken the window. You should be more **careful**.
adv Pedigree animals are **carefully** selected for breeding.
→ ***To look after, to act with precaution, attention ≠ careless***

**Note** — Many adjectives are formed by adding the suffix **"-ful"** to the noun. Frequently, but not always, adjectives with opposite meanings can be formed by adding **"-less"**.
→ *careful / careless* · *hopeful / hopeless*
→ *useful / useless* · *powerful / powerless*
→ *beautiful / **Ø*** · *skilful / **Ø***
→ ***Ø** / valueless* · ***Ø** / endless*

**Cheap** /tʃi:p/

adj To buy a **cheap**, second-hand car.
Genetically engineered crops will make food **cheaper**.
As they are **cheaper**, polymers are used as conductors instead of gold.
→ ***Not costing much money ≠ expensive***

**Chief** /tʃi:f/

adj The **chief reason** for the strike was the working conditions.
The **chief advantage** of platinum resistance thermometers is their accuracy.
adv Road accidents are **chiefly** caused by alcohol.
→ ***Main, most important. Above all***

**Common** /ˈkɒmən/

adj Depression is **one of the most common** emotional problems.
Mercury (II) sulphide is a **common** antiseptic.
adv Kappa Crucis is a galactic cluster **commonly known** as the "jewel box".
→ ***Ordinary, widespread. Frequently ≠ rarely***

**Convenient** /kənˈvi:nɪənt/

adj The time of the meeting is not **convenient**.
Electricity is far more **convenient** as a power supply.
adv The system allows the readings to be checked quickly and **conveniently**.
→ ***Suitable. Easily***

**Crude** /kru:d/

adj Cro-Magnon man made **crude** tools.
To import **crude oil**.
The X-ray data only gives a **crude** picture of the structure.
→ ***Primitive, unprocessed ≠ refined***

**Current** /ˈkʌrənt/

adj What is the **current** theory about Black Holes?
adv The process is **currently** approved in all European countries.
Radioactive contamination is higher than **currently accepted levels**.
→ ***At the present time ≠ past, obsolete***

**Damp** /dæmp/

adj The climate on the West coast is relatively **damp**.
Poisonous plants often grow in **damp areas**.

n Lumbago is usually caused by prolonged exposure to cold or **dampness**.
***→ Humid, wet. Humidity ≠ dryness***

**Dramatic** /drəˈmætɪk/

adj There has been a **dramatic improvement** in production.
A **dramatic breakthrough** in low temperature physics.
***→ Exciting, spectacular, sudden***

> **Note — Dramatic** is a false friend. In many languages it often has the meaning "bad".
> This is not so in English. It only has the meaning "spectacular". e.g.
> → a ***dramatic*** success

**Drawback** /ˈdrɔːbæk/

n The high costs are a **major drawback** to the project.
**One of the drawbacks** of incineration is that it causes pollution.
The decimal system has **several drawbacks**.
***→ A weakness, defect ≠ advantage***

**Dry** /draɪ/

adj It was a **dry** summer.
Video equipment must be **kept dry.**

v **Dry** your hands after washing them.
***→ Without rain, humidity. To evacuate water ≠ to wet***

**Ease** /iːz/

v The by-pass helped to **ease** the traffic flow.

n The equipment can be transported **with ease**.
An important feature of the new model is **ease of maintenance**.

adj It is **far easier** to remain silent.
***→ To reduce trouble. Facility. Simple ≠ difficult***

**Efficiency** /ɪˈfɪʃnsi/

n Lubrication will increase **efficiency**.

adj Electric motors are **highly efficient**.

adv It freezes more **efficiently** than other cryogenic systems.
***→ Productivity. Wasting little energy ≠ inefficiently***

**Empty** /ˈempti/

adj A glass can be half full or half **empty**.

v When the water tanks are **emptied**, the submarine rises to the surface.
***→ With nothing in it. To evacuate ≠ to fill***

**Entire** /ɪnˈtaɪə/

adj To spend the **entire** evening working.

adv The work is **entirely** satisfactory.
I am not **entirely convinced** that you are right.
***→ Whole. Totally, utterly ≠ partly***

**Eventually** /ɪˈventʃuəli/

adv **Eventually**, life on Earth will die out.
After 1,000 years, the radio-active isotopes will **eventually** reach the biosphere.
***→ In the end, at last, in due course ≠ immediately***

> **Note — Eventually** is a false friend.
> It means: "after waiting a long time"
> It **does not** have the meaning of "possibly, maybe"

**Fair** /feə/

1.adj Unequal pay for men and women is not **fair**.
Amnesty International defends each man's right to a **fair** trial.
***→ Just, equitable ≠ unfair***

2.adv Mutations occur **fairly** frequently.
A **fairly** expensive machine.
***→ Relatively ≠ exceedingly***

**Fat** /fæt/

adj In industrialised countries many adolescents are far too **fat**.
Mammals and birds in the Arctic are insulated by **layers of fat**.

adj Arteriosclerosis is caused by an accumulation of **fatty deposits** in the arteries.
***→ To be corpulent, overweight. Naturally occurring oily substances found in animals, esters of glycerol***

**Free** /friː/

adj According to Rousseau, every man is born **free**.
Electrons are **free** to flow at random.
**Tax-free** alcohol can be bought at the airport.
***→ Able to act as one wants. Not restricted. Without (tax)***

**Fresh** /freʃ/

adj A **fresh-water** lake.
They wish to adopt a **fresh approach**.

adv **Freshly** cut wood contains up to 50% water.
***→ Not salt, new. Recently***

**Great** /greɪt/

adj Scientists are showing **great** interest in ultra-violet astronomy.
Echography can give us **a great deal** of information about the fetus.

adv Agriculture will **benefit greatly** from genetically engineered organisms.
***→ A lot of, much. Considerably ≠ little***

**Harm** /hɑːm/

v CFCs **harm** the ozone layer.
Human noise pollution can **harm** ocean animals such as whales.

n Solonium can **cause harm** to wildlife.

adj **Harmful** toxins have killed 15% of the yellow-eyed penguins.
***→ To damage. Dangerous ≠ harmless***

**Hazard** /ˈhæzəd/

n The **natural hazards** of climate cannot be avoided.
Radon gas can pose a serious **health hazard**.

adj The legislation controlling **hazardous** chemicals is too weak.
***→ Risk. Harmful ≠ safe***

**Huge** /hjuːdʒ/

adj A **huge amount** of money.
Modern agricultural techniques lead to a **huge increase** in crop yields.
Volcanoes release **huge quantities** of energy.
***→ Very big, enormous ≠ tiny, minute***

**Irrelevant** /ɪˈreləvənt/

adj What she said was **quite irrelevant**.
His studies were **irrelevant** to the job requirements.
***→ Not pertinent, unrelated ≠ relevant***

**Loud** /laʊd/

adj The explosion made a **loud noise**.
To speak in a **loud voice**.
***→ Relatively many decibels ≠ quiet, low***

**Loudspeaker** /laʊdˈspiːkə/

n The **loudspeaker** is connected to the amplifier.
The flight was announced over the airport **loudspeaker**.
***→ Appliance for converting electrical signals into sound waves***

**Main** /meɪn/

adj Protein is the **main** component of living matter.
The **main cause** of the breakdown.

adv The interest in transgenic animals is **mainly due to** commercial interests.
***→ Principal, most important. Above all***

**Major** /ˈmeɪdʒə/

adj A **major problem**.
The **major constituents** of seawater are chloride, sodium and magnesium.
***→ Important, principal ≠ minor***

**Mild** /maɪld/

adj The UK has a **mild climate**.
To suffer from a **mild** attack of pneumonia.
***→ Moderate ≠ severe***

**Minor** /ˈmaɪnə/

adj Tourism plays a **minor role** in the economy of the region.
It was a relatively **minor** form of the disease.
***→ Of secondary importance ≠ major***

**Minute** /maɪˈnjuːt/

adj In Tibet, only a **minute** fraction of the population can read.
**Minute amounts** of mercury can be found in Earth rock.
**Minute** organisms, like bacteria, can be studied under the microscope.
***→ Very small, tiny ≠ huge***

> Note the difference in pronunciation:
> → ***minute :*** *(60 seconds)* /ˈmɪnɪt/ *stress on 1st syllable*
> → ***minute :*** *(very small)* /maɪˈnjuːt/ *stress on 2nd syllable*

**Naked** /ˈneɪkɪd/

adv In ancient Greece men ran **naked** at the Olympic games.
The Andromeda galaxy is visible to **the naked eye**.
***→ Without clothes. Without assistance***

**Outdated** /ˌaʊtˈdeɪtɪd/

adj An **outdated** communication system.
The policy was based on **outdated concepts**.
***→ Old-fashioned, obsolete ≠ modern***

**Outstanding** /aʊtˈstændɪŋ/

adj Airbus has been an **outstanding success**.
Insects provide an **outstanding** example of social solidarity.
Some autistic patients have an **outstanding ability** to calculate.
***→ Exceptional, out of the ordinary***

**Overall** /ˌəuvərˈɔːl/

adj There has been an **overall increase** in the standard of living.
Antibiotics have contributed to the **overall reduction** in the death rate.

adv **Overall,** copper is the most widely used conductor.
***→ Global. Generally speaking***

**Plain** /pleɪn/

adj She was wearing a **plain** yellow dress.

adv **Plainly**, she was worried.
***→ Simple, without decoration. Clearly***

**Plenty** /ˈplenti/

n There is **plenty of time** to finish.
Domestic animals need **plenty** of exercise.

Treatment usually involves rest, aspirin and **plenty** of fluids.
→ ***More than enough, a lot, a great deal***

**Proper** /ˈprɒpə/
adj At last, he has got a **proper** job.
The laboratory lacks the **proper** equipment.
adv If the prism is **properly** cut, the light will be polarised.
→ ***Acceptable, suitable. Correctly***

**Quite** /kwaɪt/
1.adv Summer is coming, it is getting **quite warm**.
Cases of colon cancer are increasing **quite** rapidly.
→ ***Relatively, fairly ≠ extremely***
2.adv It has become **quite clear** that smoking causes cancer.
It is **quite impossible** to do molecular biology without the aid of a computer.
→ ***Completely, utterly***

**Rather** /ˈrɑːðə/
1.adv It is **rather cold** today.
The explanation is **rather complicated**.
→ ***Relatively***
2 Intermediate technology aims to improve **rather than** destroy traditional cultures.
Their diet consists of eggs **rather than** meat.
→ ***Instead of, in preference to***

**Raw** /rɔː/
adj Wild carnivorous animals eat **raw meat**.
To import **raw materials**.
The **raw data** must be analysed.
→ ***Uncooked. In a natural state. Untreated ≠ processed***

**Readily** /ˈredɪli/
adv Plants can form viable hybrids **much more readily** than animals.
The vaccine is not yet **readily** available.
→ ***Easily, effortlessly***

**Reliable** /rɪˈlaɪəbl/
adj Quartz watches are very **reliable**.
The office needs a **reliable** secretary.
v On the whole, you can **rely on** the TGV to be on time.
To **rely on** a friend for help.
→ ***Which always works. To depend on***

**Rough** /rʌf/
1.adj A **rough surface** increases friction.
The surface was too **rough** to allow the molecules to bond.
→ ***Irregular, uneven ≠ smooth***
2.adj A **rough estimation**.
adv The larger asteroids are **roughly** spherical.
→ ***Approximate ≠ exact***

**Safe** /seɪf/
adj Modern aircraft are much **safer**.
The food must be clean and **safe to eat**.
**Safe storage** of nuclear waste.
n When speed is reduced, **road safety** increases.
→ ***Without risk. Security ≠ danger***

**Sensitive** /ˈsensɪtɪv/
adj Children are extremely **sensitive** to pain.
The human organism is very **sensitive** to foreign bodies.
More **sensitive** seismic apparatuses are now available.
→ ***Quick to react or feel. Reacting with precision***

> **Note** — Sensitive / sensible
> **Sensible** is a frequently misused false friend.
> In English **sensible** means "reasonable".
> → *it was a **sensible** idea*
> **Sensitive** means *"quick to react"*.
> → *a cat's ears are very **sensitive** to sound*

**Several** /ˈsevrəl/
det **Several** people telephoned last night.
There are **several different reasons** for cancelling the project.
Over the past few years, **several** countries have built synchrotrons.
→ ***A certain number – more than a few, less than a lot***

**Sharp** /ʃɑːp/
adj A **sharp** knife.
A **sharp increase** in prices.
There is no **sharp distinction** between hot and cold.
adv As a result of the crisis, production decreased **sharply**.
→ ***Which cuts well, acute. Clear. Abruptly ≠ gradually***

**Smooth** /smuːð/
adj A **smooth** surface causes little friction.
Geckos can climb up perfectly **smooth** walls.
→ ***With an even surface, regular ≠ rough***

**Soft** /sɒft/
adj Gold is a **soft** metal.
Organisms with **soft** bodies are not preserved as fossils.
v Thermosplastic compounds **soften** when heated.
→ ***Not hard ≠ to harden***

**Sole** /səʊl/

adj He was the **sole** survivor of the air crash.

adv The responsibility lies **solely** with the manager.
Vitamin D can be produced **solely** in the presence of the sun.
→ ***Unique. Only***

**Spare** /speə/

1.adj I have got little **spare time**.
Mountaineers should always carry **spare food** and first-aid equipment.
It was difficult to obtain **spare parts** for the machines.
All cars have got a **spare wheel**.
→ ***In addition to what is required. Replacement***

**Steep** /sti:p/

adj The sides of the canyon are extremely **steep**.
There has been a **steep** decline in agricultural production.
→ ***Abrupt, rising / falling sharply, acute ≠ gradual***

**Thorough** /ˈθʌrə/

adj He made a **thorough examination** of all the components.
The police carried out a **thorough enquiry**.

adv *Escherichia coli* is the most **thoroughly studied** of all organisms.
→ ***Complete, detailed. Carefully ≠ superficially***

**Tiny** /ˈtaɪni/

adj **Tiny** particles, even electrons, can now be detected.
A **tiny** tube with a diameter of 50 nanometres is used.
Sea water contains **tiny quantities** of gold.
→ ***Very small, minute ≠ huge, enormous***

**Tremendous** /trəˈmendəs/

adj U.N.O. has had a **tremendous influence**.
DVDs hold **a tremendous amount** of information.

adv The popularity of cycling has **increased tremendously**.
→ ***Huge. Enormously***

**Use** /ju:z/

v He **uses** a plastic bag to carry his books.

n What is the **use** of working so hard?

adj Certain snakes are **useful** because they feed on rats and mice.
→ ***To employ. Advantage. Which helps ≠ useless***

**Utter** /ˈʌtə/

adj The explosion was followed by **utter** confusion.
The meeting was an **utter** waste of time.

adv Nagasaki was **utterly** destroyed.
→ ***Total. Completely ≠ partly***

**Valuable** /væljuəbl/

adj A **valuable** painting.
Aerial survey has become **extremely valuable** in mapmaking.
Penicillin has been particularly **valuable** in the treatment of syphilis.
→ ***Worth a lot of money, profitable, useful ≠ worthless***

**Virtual** /ˈvɜ:tʃuəl/

adj The **virtual image** of a lens.
He is the **virtual** manager of the business.

adv **Virtually** 90% of the population voted.
The project is **virtually finished**.
→ ***Not real, potential. Almost, practically***

**Weak** /wi:k/

adj Many dinosaurs had relatively small eyes and **weak** vision.
A system is required to amplify the **weak** electric current.

adv Some lunar rocks are **weakly** magnetic.

v The vibrations **weakened** the metal.
→ ***Deficient, not strong ≠ strengthen***

**Wealth** /welθ/

n **Mineral wealth** is heavily concentrated in southern Poland.
Scanners provide a **wealth of information** concerning diseases.

adj Picasso became not only famous, but also extremely **wealthy**.
→ ***Prosperity. A large amount. Rich ≠ poor***

**Wet** /wet/

adj The highest accident rates are on **wet** roads.
Senegal has a **wet season** from July to October.

v If you **wet** the electrode, conductivity will be increased.
→ ***Damp. To humidify ≠ to dry***

**Whole** /həʊl/

adj The **whole town** was destroyed by the volcano.
Food was in short supply during the **whole period**.

n **On the whole**, the death rate increases as you go south.
→ ***Complete. Generally speaking***

**World-wide** /ˈwɜ:ldwaɪd/

adj A **world-wide** distribution network.

adv Coca Cola is sold **world-wide**.
→ ***International, all over the world***

**Worth** /wɜːθ/

adj How much is the car **worth ?**
Seismology has become a business **worth** billions of dollars.
The book is not **worth reading**.
→ ***To have (financial) value, merit***

**Worthwhile** /wɜːθ'waɪl/

adj It is a **worthwhile** research project.
The process is relatively efficient and economically **worthwhile**.
→ ***Valuable, useful ≠ worthless***

**Wrong** /rɒŋ/

adj To arrive at a **wrong** conclusion.
There is something **wrong** with the motor.
Would it be morally **wrong** to transplant organs from anencephalic children?
→ ***Not correct ≠ right***

# 5. Link words & logic

**According to** /ə'kɔːdɪŋ/
prep **According to** the radio, it will rain tomorrow.
**According to** Dr Mitchell, the patient is out of danger.
Prices vary **according to** demand.
→ ***As said by, as reported by. Depending on***

**Actual** /'æktʃuəl/
adj The **actual cost** of nuclear power is higher than expected.
There is no **actual proof** to demonstrate that it is true.
adv He looks poor, but **actually** he is very rich.
Absolute zero can be approached, but cannot **actually** be reached.
→ ***Real, existing as a fact. In fact***

**Although** /ɔːl'ðəʊ/
conj **Although** magnesium is a metal, it burns.
**Although** the sea temperature is only 2°C, it can be used as an energy source.
→ ***In spite of the fact***

**Apart** /ə'pɑːt/
1.adv The two towns are 30 km **apart**.
The farther the molecules are **apart**, the weaker the bond.
→ ***Distant from each other, separate***
2 **Apart from** the chairman, nobody spoke.
**Apart from** being expensive, the car also consumes too much fuel.
→ ***With the exception of, besides***

**Besides** /bɪ'saɪdz/
prep **Besides** providing fish for the population, the Nile fertilises the land.
**Besides** growing new skin, some salamanders can regenerate whole legs.
adv Gold is an excellent conductor of electricity, **besides**, it does not oxidise.
→ ***In addition to. Moreover***

**Bracket** /'brækɪt/
n The translation of the word is written **between brackets**.
Square **brackets**.
→ ***Typographical signs which include, parenthesis. e.g. { ... }***

**Clear** /klɪə/
1.adj A **clear distinction** should be made between the two problems.
Ethyl alcohol is a **clear**, colourless liquid.
adv **Clearly**, environmental pollution must be drastically reduced.
→ ***Easy to see. Transparent. Obviously***
2.v After the experiment, he **cleared away** the apparatus.
n The **clearance** of trees in the forest reduces biodiversity.
**Clearing** the rainforests leads to erosion.
→ ***To remove, to get rid of unwanted things***

**Comprise** /kəm'praɪz/
v The U.K. **comprises** England, Scotland, Wales and Northern Ireland.
The committee **comprises** people of different nationalities.
A nucleus is **comprised of** protons and neutrons.
→ ***To be composed of***

**Consequently** /'kɒnsɪkwəntli/
adv Viruses have become resistant to drugs, **consequently** malaria is spreading.
Atmospheric ionisation, and **consequently** electrical conductivity, are low.
→ ***Therefore, as a result***

**Converse** /kɒnvɜːs/
n The **converse** of protectionism is free trade.
Medically speaking, the body affects the mind, but the **converse** is likewise true.
adv During the day, plants produce oxygen, **conversely**, at night, they produce $CO_2$.
→ ***The opposite, by contrast***

**Deduce** /dɪ'djuːs/
v Newton **deduced** that the orbit of a planet would be an ellipse.
It is possible to **deduce** the DNA sequence from the position of the molecules.
→ ***To draw logical conclusions***

**Despite** /dɪˈspaɪt/
prep **Despite** the danger, he ran into the burning house.
Gases diffuse slowly **despite** high molecular speeds.
**Despite** all the efforts, scientists have failed to discover any antigens.
→ ***Regardless of, even with***

**Doubt** /daʊt/
n There is some **doubt about the matter**.
He **expressed** his **doubts** about the value of the project.
adj The existence of a single cause for leukaemia **seems doubtful**.
adv Pharmacology was **doubtless** well developed in Babylonian civilisation.
→ ***Lack of certainty. Improbable. Certainly***

**Due** /djuː/
1.adj The train is **due at** 11 a.m.
→ ***Expected, scheduled***
2 Energy loss in transformers is **due to** resistance.
The high cost is **due to the fact** that the materials are rare.
→ ***Because of, a result of***

**e.g.** /iː dʒiː/
abbr Renewable energy sources, **e.g.** solar, wind and bio-fuels.
Certain European countries, **e.g.** France and the UK, possess atomic weapons.
→ ***For example, such as***

**Either** /ˈaɪðə/
conj You can buy **either** a diesel **or** a petrol car.
The male is killed by the female **either** before copulation **or** after.
You can answer **either** by fax **or** by e-mail.
→ ***The one or the other ≠ neither***

**Else** /els/
adv You can transmit images, or **anything else** that can be digitally encoded.
**No one else** has any access to the data base.
Temperature can be expressed in Fahrenheit, **or else** in Celsius.
→ ***Besides, instead of, otherwise***

**Elsewhere** /elsˈweə/
adv He left San Francisco and went to live **elsewhere**.
Salt was used as money in Ethiopia and **elsewhere** in Africa.
Doctors in Canada and **elsewhere** are attempting to transplant brain cells.
→ ***In a different place***

**Note – Elsewhere** has the same meaning as **somewhere** else.
→ *to look for a job* ***elsewhere / somewhere else***
**Else** is used in conjunction with many other adverbs and pronouns.
→ ***Everybody else*** *agrees*
→ *It does not work. Try* ***something else***
→ *Does* ***anyone*** *else want some coffee?*
→ *Call the police.* ***What else*** *can you do?*

**Entail** /ɪnˈteɪl/
v Playing the piano well **entails** years of hard work.
The development scheme **entails** increasing the telephone network.
This job **entails** both analytic and environmental chemistry.
→ ***To involve, to require, to make necessary***

**Former** /ˈfɔːmə/
adj In the 1950s, the **former** USSR conducted rocket tests with animals.
adv The Aral lake was **formerly** the fourth largest lake in the world.
n Barcelona / Turin: **the former** is in Spain.
→ ***Before, ex, previously. The first one of two mentioned ≠ latter***

**Furthermore** /ˈfɜːðəˈmɔː/
adv It is cold, **furthermore** it is raining.
Silicon chips are cheap, small, and **furthermore,** very reliable.
The process runs at low temperature; **furthermore** fuel supplies are limitless.
→ ***And also, moreover***

**Hard** /hɑːd/
adj Steel is a **hard** metal.
It is **hard** to say.
adv To **work hard**.
v It takes a few hours for the cement to **harden**.
With age, the blood vessels **harden**.
→ ***Opposite of soft. Difficult. With effort. To become hard ≠ to soften***

**Hardly** /ˈhɑːdli/
adv To have **hardly any** money.
*Australopithecus afarensis* had a brain **hardly any** larger than a chimpanzee.
Apart from carbon, elements **hardly ever** form chains of more than 8 atoms.
→ ***Almost none. Very little. Rarely***

**Hence** /hens/
adv Certain stars are much brighter and **hence** much larger.
A tumour grows exceedingly fast, **hence** it must be destroyed at once.
→ ***Consequently, therefore***

**However** /haʊˈevə/
adv Gold can be extracted from sea water, **however**, it is not commercially economical.
The situation is not good, **however**, it is not hopeless.
→ ***But, although, on the other hand***

**i.e.** /aɪiː/
abbr Natural hazards; **i.e.** floods, hurricanes and famines, are frequently man-made.
The same units are used for expressing heat and energy; **i.e.** joules.
→ ***That is to say, namely***

**Imply** /ɪmˈplaɪ/
v The window is open; this **implies** that someone is at home.
The **results imply** that these microbes are immune to antibiotics.
The lack of oxygen **implies** that there is no life on the planet.
→ ***To indicate, to suggest, a logical conclusion***

**Include** /ɪnˈkluːd/
v Taxes are **included** in the price.
The figures do not **include** potential reserves in Antarctica.
prep Everyone, **including** the engineers, went on strike.
→ ***To be a part of. To be comprised in. As well as ≠ except***

**Induce** /ɪnˈdjuːs/
v Nothing could **induce** her to accept a job in the US.
Androgens are male hormones that **induce** secondary sex characteristics.
It is claimed that acupuncture is superior to Western, **drug-induced** analgesia.
→ ***To persuade, to cause, to lead to***

**Instead** /ɪnˈsted/
adv He did not go to the cinema, he went to the theatre **instead**.
prep **Instead of** using copper, silver was used.
→ ***In place of another thing***

**Involve** /ɪnˈvɒlv/
v He was **involved** in a serious road accident.
The **job involves** working abroad.
The technique **involves** inserting protein genes into the cells.
→ ***To entail, to include***

**Latter** /ˈlætə/
adj Bilbao/Turin: **the latter** town is in Italy.
n Gold and silver are both precious metals, however **the latter** is less expensive.
→ ***The last one mentioned (of two) ≠ former***

**Let** /let/ *(let, let, let)*
v **Let** me explain what I am trying to say.
In cases of prolonged comas, doctors should **let** the patient die.
**Let** x = 2 and y = 3.
→ ***To permit, to allow. The hypothesis is ...***

**Meantime/meanwhile** /ˈmiːntaɪm/
adv The job starts in April. **In the meantime**, he is taking a holiday.
The virus has not yet been identified, **meanwhile**, the epidemic is spreading.
→ ***During the time, in the interval***

**Merely** /ˈmɪəli/
adv He was **merely** 16 years old when he wrote the book.
Male deaths are 1.35% compared to **merely** 0.99% for girls.
adj A **mere** 5% of the population has acceptable living conditions.
→ ***Just, no more than, only***

**Moreover** /mɔːˈrəʊvə/
adv The price is high, **moreover** the house is old.
Pulsars are very dense, **moreover** they spin rapidly.
Aluminium is lighter and **moreover**, it is relatively cheap.
→ ***In addition to what has been said, besides***

**Namely** /ˈneɪmli/
adv The worst recent earthquake, **namely** Tangshan in China, killed 750,000 people.
The first satellite, **namely** Sputnik I, was launched in 1960.
→ ***That is to say, specifically***

**Neither** /ˈnaɪðə/
conj She eats **neither** meat **nor** fish.
**Neither** helium **nor** krypton form chemical compounds.
→ ***Not one or the other ≠ either***

**Nevertheless** /ˌnevəðəˈles/
adv I cannot come, **nevertheless** thank you for inviting me.
Air crashes are fairly rare, **nevertheless** they get widespread publicity.
→ ***In spite of that, however***

**Obvious** /ˈɒbviəs/
adj The cause of the accident was **obvious**.
It is now **obvious** that world climate is changing.
adv **Obviously**, security measures must be taken to prevent contamination.
→ ***Easy to see. Clearly***

**Otherwise** /ˈʌðəwaɪz/

adv You should phone the bank immediately, **otherwise** it will be too late.
The transistors must be cooled by liquid nitrogen, **otherwise** they will overheat.
→ ***If not, or else***

**Owing to** /əʊɪŋ/

prep The rugby match was cancelled **owing to** snow.
**Owing to** the strike, the firm was closed.
Aluminium is used **owing to the fact** that it is a light metal.
→ ***Because of, due to, on account of***

**Previous** /ˈpriːvɪəs/

adj He has no **previous experience**.
Compared to **previous** projects, the new plan will take far less time.
adv The drug had not been used **previously**.
→ ***Before that, earlier. Prior to***
***≠ subsequently***

**Prior** /ˈpraɪə/

prep **Prior to** the 1st World War, few people had cars.
Cells are removed and then engineered **prior to** their reimplantation.
adj The inspector arrived **without prior warning**.
→ ***Before, previous***

**Provide** /prəˈvaɪd/

v The Middle East **provides** most of Europe's oil.
The laboratory could not **provide** enough vaccine.
The control group was **provided** with food at regular intervals.
→ ***To supply, to make available***

**Provided / providing** /prəˈvaɪdɪŋ/

conj **Provided** it is kept cool, it will not evaporate.
The generator works non-stop **providing** it is not allowed to overheat.
→ ***If, on condition that***

**Regard** /rɪˈgɑːd/

v Some people **regard** science as being responsible for modern war.
Can graffiti **be regarded as** an art form?
A **highly-regarded** book.
→ ***To consider, to assess***

**Regardless** /rɪˈgɑːdləs/

prep Workers have the right to equal pay for equal work, **regardless** of sex.
Asteroids, **regardless of** size, rotate on their axes every 5 to 20 hours.
→ ***Without taking account of, in spite of***

**Rule** /ruːl/

n The **rules** of football were first drawn up in 1863.
Aboriginal society is organised around highly sophisticated social **rules**.
**As a rule**, improved diet leads to a decline in diseases.
→ ***Law, principle. Normally***

**Scarcely** /ˈskeəsli/

adv I have **scarcely any** time.
Such tiny variations are **scarcely** measurable.
The importance of Newton can **scarcely** be exaggerated.
→ ***Hardly, barely, with difficulty***

**Set** /set/

1.n A **set of tools**.
A **television set**.
A **set** of numbers.
A complex **set** of factors.
→ ***A collection of things that go together***
2.v *(set, set, set)*. **To set** the counter at zero.
A committee has been **set up** to co-ordinate medical research.
→ ***To put, to start***

> **Note – To set** is a multi-word verb. The meaning depends on the particle which follows.
> → ***to set off*** *to work (to start a journey)*
> → ***to set off*** *a bomb (to start, trigger an explosion / reaction)*
> → ***to set out*** *the samples (to show display)*
> → ***to set up*** *an experiment (to organise, put into place)*

**Since** /sɪns/

conj **Since** Catherine did not want to go, he went alone.
No hypothesis can be elaborated **since** the data is unreliable.
→ ***Because, as***

> **Note – Since** has two completely different meanings.
> **Temporal** : "from the time"
> → *I have lived here **since** 1985*
> ***Causal:*** *"because"*
> → ***Since*** *it's cold, I will stay at home*

**(In) Spite of** /spaɪt/

prep The firm made profits **in spite of** the competition.

He quitted the job **in spite of** the good pay.
**In spite of** all the evidence, we still have no actual proof.
→ ***Although there was, regardless of***

**Subsequent** /ˈsʌbsɪkwənt/
adj The meeting had to be cancelled because of **subsequent** difficulties.
adv The initial scheme was **subsequently** abandoned.
→ ***After that, later ≠ previously***

**Such** /sʌtʃ/
det I have never seen **such** wastage.
Extremely powerful equipment, **such as** lasers, is required.
Synthetic polymers, **such as** PVC, are cheap.
→ ***Of this sort, similar to***

**Note — Such** is used before a noun.
**So** is used before an adjective.
→ *It was **such a** hot **day***
→ *It was **so hot***

**Thanks to** /θæŋks/
prep Meningitis can now be cured **thanks to** penicillin.
**Thanks to** a grant, he managed to finish his research.
→ ***Because of***

**Thereby** /ˌðeəˈbaɪ/
adv The gas is compressed, **thereby** increasing the temperature.
The cell was damaged, **thereby** preventing nutrients from being absorbed.
→ ***Thus, hence, because of this***

**Therefore** /ˈðeəfɔː/
adv "I think, **therefore** I am" (Descartes).
The data is not accurate, **therefore** the results are not reliable.
→ ***Consequently, hence***

**Though** /ðəʊ/
1.conj **Though** it was cold, they went on working.
**Though** it is not universal in mammals, maternal instinct is very common.
The drug was administered **even though** it was potentially dangerous.
→ ***Despite the fact, although***

**Thus** /ðʌs/
adv The new machine is more efficient, **thus** costs will be reduced.
The orbital speed is low, **thus** the satellite gradually loses altitude.
→ ***Therefore, consequently***

**Unless** /ənˈles/
conj You cannot go to South America **unless** you have got a passport.
Fusion will not occur **unless** the temperature is raised to a million degrees.
**Unless** industrial output is reduced, an ecological crisis is inevitable.
→ ***Except if***

**Until** /ənˈtɪl/
prep He worked **until** 7 p.m.
conj Don't switch off the computer **until** you have removed the disk.
→ ***Up to the time. Prior to, before***

**Via** /ˈvaɪə/
prep He flew to Lima **via** Madrid.
I got the news **via** a friend.
Viruses are spread through the body **via** the blood system.
→ ***By way of, through***

**Whereas** /weərˈæz/
conj Sarah lives in the town, **whereas** Kim lives in the country.
Life expectancy for women is 83, **whereas** for men, it is 79.
→ ***By contrast, on the other hand***

**Whether** /ˈweðə/
conj I do not know **whether** I will come or not.
The effects are the same **whether** the radiation is internal or external.
→ ***If or not***

**While** /waɪl/
1.conj **While** searching for trilobites the bone fossils were discovered.
The brain damage occurred **while** he was under anaesthetic.
→ ***During the time***
2.conj **While** clean water is essential for health, it is not sufficient.
Aluminium is a light metal, **while** lead is a heavy one.
→ ***Although. On the other hand***

**Yet** /jet/
1.adv I have not seen the film **yet**.
The USA has **not yet** ratified the treaty.
It is the largest fossil forest **yet** found in the Arctic.
→ ***Up until now, so far***
2.conj It is a cheap **yet** efficient system.
The tails of whales (which contain no bone) are strong **yet** flexible.
The immune system destroys most foreign bodies, **yet** bacteria continue to kill us.
→ ***But, nevertheless, despite that***

# 6. KNOWLEDGE & STATEMENT

**Account** /ə'kaʊnt/

n A **written account** must be made after each incident.
The risk of human error must be **taken into account**.

v Genetic variation in species **accounts for** differences in life-span.
***→ A report, consideration. To explain***

**Acknowledge** /ək'nɒlɪdʒ/

v The government **acknowledged the need for** increased salaries.
It is **generally acknowledged** that Ariane has been a success.

n On receiving the invitation, he sent a **written acknowledgement**.
***→ To answer, to recognise. Acceptance***

> **Note** — Many nouns are formed by adding the suffix **"-ment"**.
> → *a statement-equipment-arrangement-measurement*

**Acronym** /'ækrənɪm/

n "LASER" is an **acronym** for "**L**ight **A**mplification by **S**timulated **E**mission of **R**adiation".
***→ An abbreviation made with the first letter of each word***

**Address** /ə'dres/

v To **address** a **problem**.
UNO should **address the issue** of atmospheric pollution.
The problem of bio-genetic patents has not yet been properly **addressed**.
***→ To face up to, to consider***

**Admit** /əd'mɪt/

1.v To **admit** to making an error.
The government was forced to **admit** that criminal offences were rising.
***→ To acknowledge, to recognise the truth ≠ to deny***

2.v The cornea is a membrane which **admits** light to the inner eye.
***→ To allow entry ≠ to expel***

**Advice** /əd'vaɪs/

n When in doubt, you should **ask for advice**.
Copernicus was asked **to give advice** on calendar reform.
***→ A personal opinion, suggestion, recommendation***

**Advise** /əd'vaɪz/

v The doctor **advised him to** stop smoking.
To avoid intoxication, workers are **advised** to wear masks.
***→ To say what someone should do, to recommend***

**Allege** /ə'ledʒ/

v It was **alleged** that he was killed by the police.
He was obliged to give up his job for **alleged** sexual harassment.

adv He was **allegedly** connected to the Mafia.
***→ To claim, declare something that is not necessarily true***

**Appeal** /ə'pi:l/

n **To launch an appeal** for money to help cancer research.

v The idea of studying abroad **appeals to me**.

adj An **appealing** idea.
***→ A request. To interest. Attractive***

**Approve** /ə'pru:v/

v The female condom was first **approved** for sale in the UK in 1993.
The drug was **approved** for medical use in 1979.

n **Government approval** is necessary before drugs can be marketed.
***→ Agreement. To accept officially ≠ disapproval, condemnation***

**Array** /ə'reɪ/

n An **array of figures** was displayed on the screen.
The disease is characterised by a large **array** of symptoms.
Under the microscope, the filaments form a hexagonal **array**.
***→ A display, a well-ordered arrangement, series***

**Assume** /ə'sju:m/

v **Assuming that** it does not rain tomorrow, I'll play tennis.
**It can be assumed** that the temperature will continue to rise.

n Reincarnation is a **basic assumption** of Buddhism.
***→ To suppose, to presume something to be true. Belief***

**Aware** /ə'weə/

adj He was not **aware** of the danger.
Humans may hear a sound without being **aware** of it.

n There is a **growing awareness** of the consequences of global warming.
***→ Conscious, to realise. Understanding***

**Belief** /bɪ'li:f/

n A religious **belief**.

v Akhenaton was perhaps the first to **believe in** a single God.
**It is believed** that the universe was created 15 billions years ago.
***→ A conviction. To be sure something is true ≠ to doubt***

**Census** /'sensəs/

n The first national **census** of the population in Britain was held in 1801.
A traffic **census** was carried out.
***→ An official counting, survey of the population or of objects***

**Chairman / woman** /'tʃeəmən/

n The **chairman** of a committee.
To be elected **chairman**.
At the end of the meeting, the **chairwoman** called for a vote.
***→ President, head of a committee***

**Claim** /kleɪm/

v The government **claims** that it has reduced inflation.
He **claimed to be** the first to discover the virus.

n After the accident he made a **claim** to the insurance company for a pension.
***→ To declare something is true. A declaration, a request***

**Conceal** /kən'si:l/

v Plastic surgery can **conceal** signs of ageing.
Encryption allows you to **conceal** your password.
***→ To hide, to keep secret***

**Convince** /kən'vɪns/

adj The evidence is not **convincing**.

v Doctors are **convinced** that heart diseases are related to fetal development.
Despite the problems, they are **convinced** that the model will work.
***→ To persuade, to be sure***

**Deny** /dɪ'naɪ/

v The minister **denied** the accusation of fraud.
She **denied** being involved with KGB.
Creationists **deny** the validity of scientific procedure.
***→ To refuse to acknowledge, to contest ≠ to confirm, to accept***

**Describe** /dɪ'skraɪb/

v **To describe** what happened in the accident.
The Dodo was **described** by several 16$^{th}$ century travellers.
Light can be **described** either in terms of waves or in terms of particles.
***→ To say what something is like, to give the details***

**Display** /dɪ'spleɪ/

n A digital **display** on a watch.

v **To display** information on a computer screen.
The fossils were **displayed** in a glass case.
***→ A visual presentation. To show, to exhibit***

**Encounter** /ɪn'kaʊntə/

v **To encounter** economic difficulties.
The suggestion has **encountered** a lot of opposition.
New ideas generally **encounter** a certain amount of hostility.
***→ To meet, to come into contact***

**Event** /ɪ'vent/

n The most **important event** in your life.
**Events** on a sub-atomic level cannot be predicted.
They have analysed the **sequence of events** leading to muscle contraction.
***→ What happens. An action***

**Evidence** /'evɪdəns/

n There is little **evidence to support** the theory.
The theory of evolution is supported by **evidence** from fossils.
Several researchers have **evidence** that the treatment improves rat memory.
***→ Proof. Data which supports a theory***

> **Note — Evidence** is a false friend.
> *It means "proof, scientific data"*
> *It does* ***not*** *mean "it is an obvious fact"*

**Expect** /ɪk'spekt/

v I **expect** that it will rain tomorrow.
The results were not **expected**.
Solar activity is **expected** to increase next year.
***→ To suppose, think that something is probable***

**Face** /feɪs/

v Small firms are **facing** strong **competition**.
The government is **faced with** a difficult **decision**.

They were **faced with the problem** of obtaining pure samples.
→ ***To encounter, to be confronted by***

**Fact** /fækt/
n Fact is stranger than fiction.
There are no **facts** to support this theory.
**As a matter of fact**, she is ill.
→ ***Something that is true, that has actually happened ≠ fiction***

**False** /fɔːls/
adj A **false alarm**.
Ptolemy's conception of the world was based on **a false assumption**.
adv Statistical data is often **falsely** interpreted.
→ ***Not corresponding to the truth. Wrongly ≠ correctly***

**Fear** /fɪə/
n The **fear** of death.
There is a **widespread fear** of the dangers of genetic engineering.
v The government **fears** that unemployment will increase.
→ ***Apprehension, being afraid of***

**Find out** /faɪnd/ *(find, found, found)*
v To **find out** the cause of the engine failure.
Galvani was the first to **find out** that electrical currents have biological effects.
First of all, it was necessary to **find out** how to connect the nerve fibres.
→ ***To discover***

**Finding** /ˈfaɪndiŋ/
n The **findings** of the government inquiry will be published tomorrow.
The hypothesis is backed by the **experimental findings**.
→ ***Results, new data***

**Focus** /fəʊkəs/
v He **focused** the microscope **on** the cell.
To **focus** attention **on** a subject.
n The main **focus** of the seminar.
→ ***To concentrate light, attention. Central point***

**Forbid** /fəˈbid/
*(forbid, forbade, forbidden)*
v **Smoking is forbidden**.
In 1819, a law **forbade** the employment of children under nine.
Because of the epidemic, the export of meat was **forbidden**.
→ ***To ban, to make illegal ≠ to permit***

**Forecast** /ˈfɔːkɑːst/
n **Weather forecasts** are becoming more accurate.
To ensure fuel supplies, **long-term** planning **forecasts** are essential.
v Bankers **forecast** an increase in the exchange rate.
→ ***A prediction. An estimation of a future event***

**Foresee** /fɔːˈsiː/ *(see, saw, seen)*
v It is impossible to **foresee** long-term technological **trends**.
This problem **could have been foreseen**.
adj An **unforeseen** difficulty.
→ ***To predict, to forecast***

**Guess** /ges/
v If you do not know the answer, **guess**.
Scientists can only **guess** why the satellite stopped emitting.
Can you **guess** the number of species becoming extinct each year?
→ ***To estimate, make a hypothesis without knowing the facts***

**Hide** /haɪd/ *(hide, hid, hidden)*
v He **hid** the money under the bed.
A German pharmaceutical company was accused of **hiding** evidence.
Traumatic experiences often remain **hidden** in the unconscious.
→ ***To keep out of sight, to conceal ≠ to expose, to reveal***

**Ignore** /ɪgˈnɔː/
v He **ignored** the doctor's advice.
The friction is so small that **it can be ignored**.
Previous research has **ignored** hereditary factors.
→ ***Not to take into account, to take no notice of ≠ to pay attention***

**Inquire** /ɪnˈkwaɪə/
*(**alternative spelling** of "enquire, enquiry").*
v The police **inquired** about his activities.
He wrote to **inquire** about entry conditions to the university
n There was a **government inquiry into** industrial health hazards.
→ ***To ask for information. Investigation***

**Insight** /ˈɪnsaɪt/
n The teeth of extinct species provide **valuable insights into** the diet.
The study of seismic waves is giving **new insights into** the Earth's structure.
→ ***Understanding, awareness***

**Intend** /ɪnˈtend/
v He **intends** to go to Rome.
The instructions are **intended** to help beginners.
Anti-pollution devices are **intended** to reduce carbon monoxide levels.
→ ***To plan, to aim***

**Introduce** /ˌɪntrəˈdjuːs/

v He **introduced** the new manager to the staff.
Penicillin was not **introduced** until 1942.
Genetic material is **introduced** into the fetus.
***→ To present, to use for the first time, to insert***

**Issue** /ˈɪʃuː/

n This is a **minor issue**.
Industrial pollution is a **major political issue**.
Population growth is one of the **main issues** of modern society.
***→ Subject, topic, question of interest***

**Knowledge** /ˈnɒlɪdʒ/

n Candidates must have **a good knowledge of** English.
Our **knowledge** of the universe increases year by year.
***→ What is known, understanding ≠ ignorance***

**Label** /ˈleɪbl/

n There was a **label** on the bottle marked "Poison".
v In figure 1, the two fixed points that define an ellipse are **labelled** F and F1.
***→ A piece of paper etc., indicating the name. To classify, to mark***

**Law** /lɔː/

n It is **against the law** for children to drive cars.
Newton discovered the **law of gravity**.
Boyle's **law** is only accurate at low temperatures.
***→ A rule. Statement of what always happens***

**Liable** /ˈlaɪəbl/

adj Under stress, people are more **liable to** make mistakes.
Children with gastric infections are **liable to** develop appendicitis.
In the early stages, computer programs are **liable to** contain errors.
***→ Likely to do something, to tend, predisposed.***

**Likely** /ˈlaɪkli/

adv The weather forecast is bad. It is **likely** to rain tomorrow.
Future strategies are **likely** to become increasingly complex.
n There is **little likelihood** that the government will increase the student grant.
***→ Probable, expected. Chance, prospect***

**Motive** /ˈməʊtiv/

n What was the **motive** for the crime?
Profit is the **main motive behind** the current interest in biotechnology.
***→ The reason for doing something. Grounds***

**Notice** /ˈnəʊtɪs/

v He **noticed** that the switch had not been turned off.
It was only two days later that he **noticed** the symptoms.
n There was **a notice on the door** saying the doctor was out.
***→ To observe, to become aware of. A written announcement, message***

**Outlook** /ˈaʊtlʊk/

n **The outlook** for the electronics industry **is good**.
The economic **outlook** for Africa is catastrophic.
***→ The probable future, what is expected***

**Overview** /ˈəʊvəvjuː/

n A **brief overview** of the project.
Before discussing the main points, he gave a short **overview** of the situation.
***→ General summary***

**Point out** /pɔɪnt/

v To **point out** a mistake in the calculations.
The report **points out** that research facilities are under-used.
Sociologists **point out** that homicides increase after executions.
***→ To draw attention, to make someone notice***

**Predict** /prɪdɪkt/

v Astrologists claim to be able to **predict** events on Earth.
Public health authorities **predict** a world-wide crisis.
adj Reactions under stress are not **predictable**.
***→ Forecast. Foreseeable ≠ unpredictable***

**Prerequisite** /ˌpriːˈrekwəzɪt/

n A knowledge of Italian is a **prerequisite** for the job.
Identifying the type of blood cells is a **prerequisite** for transfusion.
The enlargement of the brain area was a **prerequisite** for language.
***→ A prior condition, a requirement***

**Presume** /prɪˈzjuːm/

v To **presume** something is correct.
Angela is absent. I **presume** that she is ill.
We can **presume** that the friction is negligible.
***→ To suppose, to assume***

**Print** /prɪnt/
v The newspaper is **printed** in three different towns simultaneously.
The first book **printed** in Britain was a translation from Arabic.
***→ To write, to make a book mechanically***

**Proof** /pruf:/
n ADN can be used as a **proof** of paternity.
π plays a role in many calculations and **proofs.**
***→ A scientifically acceptable demonstration***

**Prove** /pru:v/
1.v It was Pasteur who **proved** that diseases were spread by microbes.
Euclid **proved** that there are infinitely many prime numbers.
***→ To demonstrate beyond doubt, scientifically***
2.v So far, no drug has **proved to be** totally effective.
***→ To be found to be, to show this in reality***

**Quote** /kwəʊt/
v To **quote** Lord Kelvin, "If you cannot measure it, it is not science".
The most frequently **quoted** variables are temperature and precipitation.
n The **quotation** comes from a 19th century textbook.
***→ To repeat someone else's words***

**Realise** /ˈrɪəlaɪz/
v He **suddenly realised** that he had made a mistake.
In the 1930s, physicists **realised** that nuclear fission was possible.
***→ To understand, to become suddenly aware***
2.v Le Corbusier was not able to **realise** these projects until after the war.
***→ To achieve, fulfil***

**Reckon** /ˈrekən/
v Jane **reckoned** that she would arrive at 7 p.m.
Bankers **reckon** that the inflation rate will be 3%.
n The use of lunar **reckoning** began at least 2,000 years BC.
***→ To work out, to estimate. Calculation***

**Recognise** /ˈrekəgnaɪz/
v She didn't **recognise** me at first.
Lymphocytes can **recognise** foreign molecules in the body.
It took several years before the danger of acid rain was **recognised**.
***→ To identify, to acknowledge***

**Record** /rɪˈkɔ:d/
v All the data is **recorded** on a hard disk.
To **record** the results of an experiment.
n The police **records** were destroyed by the fire.
***→ To store, write down information. Information that has been kept***

> **Note** — Record: the noun and the verb have different stress patterns.
> → *to re'**cord** : stress on the 2nd syllable*
> → *a '**rec**ord : stress on the 1st syllable*

**Request** /rɪˈkwest/
n The hospital made an urgent **request** for blood.
v Visitors are **requested** not to walk on the grass.
He **requested** an interview with the manager.
***→ Demand, appeal. To ask for, to apply for***

**Require** /rɪˈkwaɪə/
v Electronic equipment **requires** little maintenance.
Palaeontologists are **required** to identify new fossils by genus and by species.
n Oxygen is a **basic requirement** for human life.
***→ To need, to demand. A precondition***

**Research** /rɪˈsɜ:tʃ/
n Military **research** is paid for by the government.
Several Spanish **research students** were working in the laboratory.
v The group are **researching** into potential damage to the hydrosphere.
***→ Scientific investigation into new fields***

**Reveal** /rɪˈvi:l/
v Medical examinations **revealed** a significant loss of calcium.
The scanner **revealed** a malignant tumour.
***→To show, to display, to expose ≠ to hide, to conceal***

**Search** /sɜ:tʃ/
v **To search** for gold.
The police **searched** the house.
n After the crash, **a search was carried** out to locate the black box.
***→ To look for carefully, to seek***

**Seek** /si:k/ *(seek, sought, sought)*
v To **seek advice** from a specialist.

The only solution is to **seek** alternative ways of identifying the particles.
A **much sought-after** job.
→ ***To look for, to try to find. Wanted***

**Skill** /skɪl/
n **Computer skills**.
Becoming an airline pilot involves mastering a variety of different **skills**.
adj He is a **skilful** dentist.
adj Industry requires **skilled workers**.
→ ***Expertise, practical knowledge. Competent. Qualified***

**Solve** /sɒlv/
v **To manage to solve** the problem.
Some calculators can **solve differential equations**.
Meissner and his colleagues have partly **solved the problem**.
→ ***To find an answer for***

**Spokesman/woman** /ˈspəʊksmən/
n A **spokesman** for the ministry of defence.
A **government spokeswoman** made a statement to the press.
→ ***Person selected to speak in the name of a group***

**State** /steɪt/
v The Prime Minister **stated** that taxes would be increased.
All distances, **unless otherwise stated**, are measured in meters.
n The government will make an **official statement** tomorrow.
→ ***To say officially, announce. Declaration***

**Study** /ˈstʌdi/
v **To study** electrical engineering.
Erasmus grants are intended to help students **study** abroad.
n **According to a recent study**, sulphur pollution is spreading.
→ ***To spend time learning. Academic investigation. A piece of research***

**Sum up** /sʌm/
v The chairwoman **summed up** at the end of meeting.
It is by no means easy to **sum up** the situation.
→ ***To repeat the main points, to make a synopsis***

**Summary** /ˈsʌməri/
n To write a summary of the year's activities.
→ ***An outline, an abstract, a shortened version***

**Threat** /θret/
n A **threat** of war.
Pieces of debris in orbit are a **threat** to satellites.
v The manager **threatened** to quit the job.
→ ***An indication of future, potential danger. To warn***

**Topic** /ˈtɒpɪk/
n Five different **topics** were dealt with during the meeting.
The only **topic** that interested him was computer technology.
→ ***Subject, issue***

**True** /truː/
adj It was a **true** story.
**It is true to say** that urban growth depends on the transport system.
n There were **some elements of truth** in what he said.
→ ***Exact, corresponding to the facts. To be exact***

**Unlikely** /ʌnˈlaɪkli/
adv He might phone, but it is **unlikely**.
It seems **highly unlikely** that oil prices will increase.
Such molecules are **unlikely** to be found in DNA.
→ ***Improbable, doubtful ≠ likely***

**Update** /ˌʌpˈdeɪt/
v Technical dictionaries are **updated** every two months.
As technology develops, safety regulations must be **updated**.
→ ***To make more modern, to include the latest data***

**View** /vjuː/
n What is your **view** on the question?
Several studies support the **view** that acupuncture is effective.
v Such behaviour **can be viewed** from two different perspectives.
→ ***Opinion, way of seeing. To consider***

**Warn** /wɔːn/
v The doctor **warned** him of the danger.
n The weather forecast gave a **warning** of avalanche risks.
The red **warning light** indicates low oil pressure.
→ ***To inform of potential danger. Indication of a threat***

**Work out** /wɜːk/
v To **work out** a solution to the problem.
They are currently attempting to **work out the causes** of the crash.
The project involves **working out** new security techniques.
→ ***To calculate, to discover by thinking***

# 7. PROCESS & MANIPULATION

**Acquire** /ə'kwaɪə/

v Children usually **acquire** language by the age of two.
According to Lamarck, changes **acquired** during an animal's lifetime are inherited.
Electro-ceramics **acquire** significant conductivity at higher temperatures.
***→ To get, to obtain***

**Advertise** /'ædvətaɪz/

v Rhône-Poulenc is **advertising** for engineers.
n Subliminal **advertising** is illegal.
To place an **advertisement** in the newspaper.
***→ To make a public announcement for sales, etc. Publicity***

> **Note** – Advertise / advertisement
> These words are frequently pronounced incorrectly. In Br. E., the tonic stress is on the first syllable for the verb and on the second syllable for the noun.
> → *to '**ad**vertise*
> → *an ad'**ver**tisement*

**Afford** /ə'fɔːd/

v Few developing countries **can afford to buy** the vaccines.
You **can't afford to waste time**.
As the standard of living increases, people **can afford** to travel more.
***→ To have sufficient money, time, etc., to do something***

**Allow** /ə'laʊ/

v Smoking is not **allowed** in the office.
The life-span of the insects is too short **to allow** for genetic change.
The somatic system **allows** voluntary control over skeletal muscle.
***→ To permit, to make possible ≠ to forbid, prevent***

**Attach** /ə'tætʃ/

v He **attached** the caravan to the car.
The fetus is **attached** to the mother by the umbilical cord.
Macroscopic algae are **attached** to the surface of the rock.
***→ To fix, to fasten, to connect***

**Avoid** /ə'vɔɪd/

v You should **avoid** eat**ing** between meals.
Try to **avoid** driv**ing** through the city centre.
The computer simulation **avoided** the need for further tests.
***→ To take action not to do something, to prevent an action***

**Award** /ə'wɔːd/

v The teachers were **awarded** an increase in salary.
As a result of the car accident, the judge **awarded** 100,000 € damage
De Broglie was **awarded** the Nobel Prize in 1929.
***→ To grant money (or honours)***

**Ban** /bæn/

v Cigarette advertising was **banned** on Malaysian TV in 1982.
The US has not yet **banned** capital punishment.
n There is a UN **ban on** the use of chemical weapons.
***→ To make something illegal. A prohibition***

**Blast** /blaːst/

n The **blast** of the explosion broke the windows.
v **To blast** open the door with dynamite.
***→ A shock wave. To break open with explosives***

**Blow** /bləʊ/ *(blow, blew, blown)*

1.v In the northern hemisphere, cyclonic winds **blow** in an anticlockwise direction.
Glass fibre is made by **blowing** molten glass into tiny filaments.
***→ To create a current, a flow of air***
2.n He was killed by a **blow** on the head.
The accusation of fraud was a **serious blow** to his reputation.
***→ To be hit hard. A shock***

**Break** /breɪk/ *(break, broke, broken)*

1.v **To break** a window.
**To break** the structure of the molecule.
Microbes can be used to **break up** the pollutants in the environment.
***→ To separate into parts, to destroy ≠ to repair, to mend***

2.n This constitutes **a break** with the conventional approach.
→ ***A (radical) change***

**Breakdown** /ˈbreɪkdaʊn/
n A mechanical **breakdown**.
The accident was caused by a **breakdown** in the hydraulic system.
→ ***To stop working, a failure***

**Breakthrough** /ˈbreɪkθruː/
n The invention of transistors was a **major breakthrough** in electronics.
Spectroscopy, first used in 1814, constituted a **breakthrough** for astronomy.
→ ***Victory, decisive step forward***

**Breed** /briːd/ *(breed, bred, bred)*
v Thousands of mice are **bred** for experimental purposes.
Albatrosses return to land only to **breed**.
→ ***To reproduce, to have offspring***

**Bring about** /brɪŋ/ *(bring, brought, brought)*
v The accident was **brought about** by an excess of alcohol.
Viruses will ultimately **bring about** the death of the host cells.
The factory system **brought about** fundamental changes in social structure.
→ ***To cause, to trigger***

**Build** /bɪld/ *(build, built, built)*
v It took 6 months **to build** the bridge.
The data we have is not sufficient **to build** a consistent theory.
→ ***To make, to construct ≠ to destroy***

**Bury** /ˈberi/
v The dog **buried** the bone.
After 1570 BC, the Egyptians began to **bury** the pharaohs.
Radioactive waste will be **buried** deep underground.
→ ***To put, to get rid of underground***

**Cancel** /ˈkænsl/
v The football match was **cancelled** because of heavy rain.
**To cancel** an appointment.
→ ***To stop a meeting, to decide that it will not take place***

**Catch** /kætʃ/ *(catch, caught, caught)*
v To **catch a disease**.
The cat **caught** the mouse.
Most bats **catch** their prey in flight.
→ ***To get an illness. To capture, seize ≠ to release***

**Compel** /kəmˈpel/
v Everyone is **compelled** to go to school.
After WW 2, Britain was **compelled** to abandon her colonies.
In 1633, the Vatican **compelled** Galileo to renounce his theories.
→ ***To oblige, to force***

**Consume** /kənˈsjuːm/
v The car **consumes** 6 litres per 100 km.
Checking computer programs is **a time-consuming job**.
n After midnight the **consumption** of electricity drops steeply.
→ ***To use (energy, time). The amount used***

**Damage** /ˈdæmɪdʒ/
n Lack of oxygen can cause brain **damage**.
The **damage** was caused by an acid leak.
v The car was **badly damaged**.
→ ***Partial destruction. To cause harm ≠ to repair, to mend***

**Destroy** /dɪˈstrɔɪ/
v The Amazonian forests are being rapidly **destroyed**.
The police records were **destroyed** in the fire.
White blood corpuscles **destroy** microbes.
→ ***To terminate the existence, to eliminate ≠ to create***

**Disturb** /dɪˈstɜːb/
v Do not **disturb** him, he is asleep.
adj The news is **disturbing**.
n When there is no **disturbance**, ecosystems appear to be stable.
→ ***To interrupt. Worrying, alarming. Agitation***

**Drill** /drɪl/
1.v **To drill** for oil in the North Sea.
n Black and Decker make electric **drills**.
The **drill** has a tungsten tip.
→ ***To make a hole (rotary movement). A tool for making a hole***
2.n He spent 20 minutes doing **drills** in the language laboratory.
→ ***Repetitive exercise***

**Drive** /draɪv/ *(drive, drove, driven)*
v **To drive** a car carefully.
The generator is **driven** by a turbine.
adj The **driving force** of the weather system is solar radiation.
→ ***To control a car. To provide power***

**Emit** /ɪˈmɪt/
v An internal combustion engine **emits** carbon monoxide.
An electron gun **emits** a beam of electrons.
Lava and ash are **emitted** during a volcanic eruption.
→ ***To give out gas, electrons, etc. ≠ to absorb***

**Enable** /ɪˈneɪbl/

v The grant will **enable** research to continue.
Large computers **enable** scientists to simulate experiments in real time.
The process of ionisation **enables** food to be sterilised.
***→ To make possible ≠ to prevent***

**Enclose** /ɪnˈkləʊz/

v The dogs were **enclosed** behind a wire grid.
The nucleus is **enclosed** by the cell membrane.
***→ To shut in, to surround***

**Ensure** /ɪnˈʃʊə/

v First, **ensure** that the machine has been switched off.
You must **ensure** that the electric appliance has been earthed.
**To ensure** that the oil level is maintained.
***→ To make certain, to verify***

**Fasten** /ˈfɑːsn/

v Please **fasten your safety belts**.
The lock was broken, so he **fastened** the door with a piece of wire.
An electronic sensor was **fastened** to the bird's wing.
***→ To shut, lock, make secure, fix ≠ to release***

**Fill** /fɪl/

v **To fill** the petrol tank.
The underground reservoirs will be **filled** with toxic waste.
**To fill up** the application form.
***→ To make full. To complete***

**Fulfil** /fʊlˈfɪl/

v **To fulfil** one's ambition in life.
There is no chemical reaction unless all the conditions are **fulfilled**.
It is unlikely that the production quota will be **fulfilled**.
***→ To carry out, to satisfy***

**Hand** /hænd/

1.v **To hand** someone some money.
After reading the letter, he **handed** it **back**.
At the age of 65, the chairman **handed over** the job to a younger man.
***→ To give***

2.n **On the one hand** the pay is good, **on the other** the working hours are long.
***→ Although, whereas***

**Handle** /ˈhændl/

v The equipment is fragile. It must be **handled** with care.
He was unable **to handle** the situation.

n To hold a cup by the **handle**.
***→ To manipulate, deal with.***
***Part of an appliance that is designed to be held***

**Hold** /həʊld/ *(hold, held, held)*

v **To hold** a child by the hand.
The petrol tank can **hold** 50 litres.
Last week, a meeting was **held** in Rome.
***→ To take in your hand. To contain. To organise***

**Hurt** /hɜːt/ *(hurt, hurt, hurt)*

v The girl fell and **hurt** her leg.
More than 4,000 people were seriously **hurt** in the accident.
The new law may **hurt** self-employed people.
***→ To injure, to damage, to cause pain***

**Injure** /ˈɪndʒə/

v He was **badly injured** in a car crash.
Electro-magnetic radiation can **injure** mice fetuses.

n There is a real danger of **injury** to the nerve system.
***→ To hurt. To cause physiological damage. Harm***

**Insulate** /ˈɪnsjuleɪt/

v Electric wires are **insulated** with a plastic coating.
**To insulate** a building against heat loss.

n **Thermal insulation** reduces the flow of heat between hot and cold regions.
***→ To cover, to protect against energy wastage. Protection***

**Lay** /leɪ/ *(lay, laid, laid)*

v A gas pipe line was **laid** on the sea bed.
**To lay** stress on the importance of research.
**To lay responsibility** on the government.
***→ To place (horizontally). To put***

**Layout** /ˈleɪaʊt/

n The **layout** of a circuit.
He was not familiar with the building's **layout**.
Special attention must be paid to the **layout** of instruments in the control room.
***→ Design, plan***

**Lie** /laɪ/ *(lie, lay, lain)*

v The book was **lying** on the table.
A Roman temple was found **lying** 20 m beneath the surface.
The planets in the solar system **lie within** the Sun's outer atmosphere.
The **final decision lies with** the government.
***→ To be situated (horizontally). To be the responsibility of***

**Lock** /lɒk/

v He got out of the car, **locked** it and went into the shop.

n He put the key into the **lock** of the door.

→ ***To fasten, to shut with a key. A device for closing a door ≠ to unlock***

**Manage** /ˈmænɪdʒ/

v She **managed** to answer all the questions.
Animals **manage** to survive by hibernating and so reducing metabolic activity.
Engineers have **managed** to produce 0.1 micron chips.

→ ***To do something difficult, to succeed ≠ to fail***

**Master** /mɑːstə/

v Once you have **mastered** the instructions, the program is easy to run.
Fire was **mastered** approximately 1.5 million years ago.

→ ***To understand thoroughly. To gain control***

**Mend** /mend/

v He was unable **to mend** the TV set.
It is often cheaper to replace a component than **to mend** it.

→ ***To repair ≠ to break***

**Need** /niːd/

v Industry **needs** more electronic engineers.
A velocity of 129 km / sec. is **needed** for a rocket to leave the Milky Way.

n A **needs analysis**.
The total **energy needs** for the town are 640 MW.

→ ***To require, what is necessary. A requirement***

**Obtain** /əbˈteɪn/

v He **obtained** the fossils while travelling in China.
He was unable to **obtain permission** to travel abroad.
Results **obtained** so far indicate that a fish diet may reduce cardiac arrest.

→ ***To get, to acquire***

**Operate** /ˈɒpəreɪt/

v How do you **operate** this machine?
Silicone lubricants can **operate** at very high temperatures.
Most antibiotics **operate** by inhibiting cell synthesis.

→ ***To work, to function***

**Overcome** /əʊvəˈkʌm/

*(come, came, come)*

v Fever helps the body **overcome** infectious diseases.
To **overcome** development **problems** in a prototype.
The aim of the project is to **overcome** future fuel shortages.

→ ***To master, to solve***

**Pick** /pɪk/

v **To pick** an apple from the tree.
**To pick** the most suitable candidate
The data **picked up** by the sensor must be converted into an image.

→ ***To take, to select. To detect***

**Prevent** /prɪˈvent/

v Safety measures are taken **to prevent accidents**.
Vaccination will **prevent** the disease from spreading.
Unless something is done **to prevent** it, there will be a famine throughout Africa.

→ ***To stop, to halt, to check***

> **Note — To prevent** is a false friend.
> It means "to stop"
> It does **not mean** "to warn, to inform of future danger"

**Process** /ˈprəʊses/

n Cell renewal is a **continuous process**.
They are **in the process** of renewing the equipment.

v **Data processing** has become essential for meteorology.
The information from the sensory organs is **processed** in the brain.

→ ***A series of connected actions. In the middle of. To handle numbers etc.***

**Produce** /prəˈdjuːs/

v Certain cancerous cells **produce** biochemical substances.
Hydrogen can be **produced** from zinc and sulphuric acid.

n New electronic **products**.
The blood absorbs carbon dioxide and other **waste products** of metabolism.

→ ***To manufacture, to provide. Items, goods, what is produced***

**Pull** /pʊl/

v The tractor **pulled** the car out of the snow.
In case of fire, break the glass and **pull** the lever down.

→ ***To move something towards you ≠ to push***

**Push** /pʊʃ/

v **To push** someone into the river.
**To push** the alarm button.

→ ***To move something away from you ≠ to pull***

**Repair** /rɪˈpeə/

v He **managed to repair** the TV set.
It will take 3 days to get the car **repaired**.

Doctors can now **repair** nerve fibres.
→ ***To make something work, to mend ≠ to damage***

**Save** /seɪv/
1.v **To save time**, she took a taxi.
To **save money**.
Weather forecasts enable airlines to plan their routes and **save fuel**.
→ ***To economise ≠ to waste***
Penicillin has **saved** millions of lives.
To **save data**.
→ ***To protect from death. To record, to store***

**Seize** /si:z/
v The documents were **seized by the police**.
The chimpanzee **seized** the banana and ate it.
You should **seize this opportunity** of working abroad.
→ ***Take something suddenly, quickly***

**Spark (off)** /spɑ:k/
v Massive unemployment **sparked (off)** protest marches.
The genome project has **sparked off** a surge in research.
n The explosion was caused by an **electric spark**.
→ ***To trigger, to cause. A visible (electric) discharge***

**Spill** /spɪl/ *(spill, spilt, spilt)*
v To **spill** acid on the floor.
If the abscess ruptures, the liquid **spills** into the abdominal cavity.
n An **oil spill**.
→ ***To allow liquid to flow into the wrong place. An accidental leak***

**Split** /splɪt/ *(split, split, split)*
v The water molecules are **split** into atoms.
When atoms are **split**, a loss of energy occurs.
n A **split** in a political party.
→ ***To divide into two parts. A division***

**Spoil** /spɔɪl/
v The water **spoiled** his new clothes.
The experiment was **spoiled** by inaccurate measurements.
→ ***To damage, to ruin***

**Spray** /spreɪ/
v **To spray** the corn with insecticide.
n A hair **spray**.
→ ***To project vaporised liquid. A vaporiser***

**Stem** /stem/
1.n The **stem** of the flower is thin and green.
Fibre is produced from the **stems** of the cannabis plant.
→ ***The long, thin, central part of a plant to which the branches are attached***
2.v The problem **stems from** early childhood.
Allergies can be caused by traumas **stemming from** emotional conflicts.
→ ***To come from, to originate in***

**Store** /stɔ:/
v Camels can **store** water in the blood system.
The debris will be **stored** inside the satellite.
n To buy something from a **general store**.
A data **store**.
The spare fuel is kept in a **storage tank**.
→ ***To keep, to stock. A shop. Place where things are kept***

**Stress** /stres/
adj A **stressed syllable**.
n The **stress** of modern life.
As the plane accelerates, **mechanical stress** grows.
v I would like **to stress this point**.
→ ***Accentuated. Pressure, tension. To give importance to***

**Target** /ˈtɑ:gɪt/
n The missile hit the **target**.
The **production target** for next year is 10,000 units.
A beam of high-energy electrons was fired at a **target** of protons.
→ ***Goal. What is aimed at***

**Throw** /θrəʊ/ *(throw, threw, thrown)*
v She **threw** the revolver into the river.
A boomerang can be **thrown** more than 90 m.
The Earth **throws** a circular shadow on the moon.
→ ***To propel with force, to project***

**Thrust** /θrʌst/ *(thrust, thrust, thrust)*
v Angrily, he **thrust** his hands into his pockets.
n Rockets provide the necessary **thrust** for the satellite to escape gravity.
The tail of the flying fish can provide enough **thrust** for a 180 m flight.
→ ***To push with violence. Force for movement***

**Train** /treɪn/
v To **train** a football team.
If nerve fibres are damaged, patients are **trained** to co-ordinate their movements.
adj A **training course** in graphic design.
→ ***To teach a skill. Instruction***

**Treat** /tri:t/
v The problem must be **treated** very **seriously**.

In the US, light aircraft are used for **treating** crops with insecticides.

n He was taken to hospital for **emergency treatment**.

→ ***To consider. To deal with. (Medical) care***

**Trigger (off)** /ˈtrɪgə/

v The alarm system is **triggered** by an optical sensor.

The discovery of semi-conductors **triggered off** a revolution in electronics.

Kissing **triggers off** an acceleration in the rate of the heart-beat.

n To pull the **trigger** of a revolver.

→ ***To cause, to spark off, to start working. A lever which activates***

**Undergo** /ʌndəˈgəʊ/ *(go, went, gone)*

v **To undergo** a heart operation.

First, the prototype must **undergo** trials.

To what extent are species currently **undergoing** genetic change?

→ ***To experience, to be subject to***

**Yield** /jiːld/

v When organisms decompose, they **yield** ammonia.

The deeper rock layers **yielded** new specimens of fossils.

n Genetic engineering can increase crop **yields**.

→ ***To give, to produce. Production***

# 8. EXPERIMENTATION & ACTION

**Ability** /ə'bɪləti/

n People should be paid according to **ability**.
Certain cell membranes have the **ability** to detect magnetic fields.

adj He was **able** to read Greek by the age of seven.
Microbes are **able** to reproduce themselves every 20 minutes.

***→ Capacity, skill. To have the capacity ≠ unable***

**Achieve** /ə'tʃi:v/

v The firm **managed to achieve** an annual growth of 4%.
Higher speeds can be **achieved** by using fibre optics.

n Classifying the elements was a major **achievement** in the history of chemistry.

***→ To succeed in getting, to manage, to attain. Victory ≠ failure***

> **Note — Achieve** can be a false friend.
> It means : to succeed
> It does **not** mean: to finish

**Aim** /eɪm/

v The measures were **aimed at** modernising the industry.
To **aim** an X-ray beam at a target.

n The **aim** of the project is to speed up traffic flow.

***→ To intend to reach, to direct. The purpose***

**Apply** /ə'plaɪ/

1.v To **apply for a job**.

n To fill in an **application** form.

***→ To request, to make a formal demand***

2.v To **apply** a formula.
To **apply** a force of 20 newtons.

n No **application** has yet been found for these drugs.

***→ To use, to administer. Utilisation***

**Attempt** /ə'tempt/

v In the 17th century, doctors **attempted** to transfuse sheep's blood.
Doctors are **attempting** to transplant brain cells.

n She found the answer to the question at the third **attempt**.

***→ To try, to make an effort. The act of trying***

**Attract** /ə'trækt/

v She was **attracted** by the idea of a job in California.
To **attract** prey, some deep-sea fish have luminescent organs.
Unlike magnetic poles **attract each other**.

adj An **attractive** suggestion.

***→ To cause interest, to pull by magnetism. Appealing***

**Beam** /bi:m/

n A laser produces a highly concentrated **beam of light**.
The lenses can be adjusted to produce a **parallel beam**.
An **electron beam** scans the screen.

***→ A ray, a concentrated stream of light, radio waves***

**Bear** /beə/ *(bear, bore, borne)*

1.v She **can't bear** watch**ing** violent films.

***→ To tolerate***

2.v The bridge can **bear** a weight of 30 tonnes.
The government must **bear** the responsibility for inflation.
The prehistoric skeleton **bore the signs** of serious calcium deficiency.

***→ To support, to carry***

**Beat** /bi:t/ *(beat, beat, beaten)*

1.v The child had been **badly beaten**.
Normally the **heart beats** between 60 and 100 times each minute.

n The **beat** of the music.

***→ To hit, strike repeatedly. A pulse***

2.v **To beat the world record**.
Napoleon **beat** the Austrians at the battle of Wagram.

***→ To do better than, to defeat***

**Behave** /bɪ'heɪv/

v The child **behaved** badly.

n To study the **behaviour** of electrons.
The **behaviour** of animals depends on their living conditions.

***→ To act, what someone does. Conduct***

**Bend** /bend/ *(bend, bent, bent)*

n A **bend** in the road.

v **To bend** your arm.
Metal **bends** more easily when heated.

***→ A curve. To deform, to shape into an angle ≠ to straighten***

**Bite** /baɪt/ *(bite, bit, bitten)*
v The dog **bit** the child.
He was **bitten** by a snake.
The anti-inflation measures are beginning to **bite**.
***→ To injure, to attack with the teeth. To have an effect***

**Boil** /bɔɪl/
v At high altitudes, water **boils** at 90°C.
adj Most microbes can be killed by **boiling** water.
Ammonia melts at –77.7°C, while its **boiling point** is –33-35°C.
***→ Temperature at which a liquid becomes vapour ≠ to freeze***

**Boost** /buːst/
v Computer assisted design will help **boost output**.
Genetically selected plants will **boost** food **production**.
n The introduction of computers in the 1960s was a major **boost** to research.
***→ To encourage, to help increase. A stimulus***

**Breathe** /briːð/
v Mammals can't **breathe** underwater.
n **Breathing** is stimulated by the presence of carbon dioxide in the blood.
Oxygen and **breathing equipment** is used in aircraft flying above 10,000 m.
***→ Respiration, taking air into the lungs***

**Burn** /bɜːn/ *(burn, burnt, burnt)*
v The fire was **burning**.
$SO_2$ is produced when coal is **burnt**.
Organic waste can be **burnt**.
***→ To be consumed by flames, to be on fire***

**By-product** /ˈbaɪprɒdʌkt/
n Stress is one of the **by-products** of modern urban life.
Radon gas is a **by-product** of radioactive decay.
Most of the cadmium output is a **by-product** of the zinc industry.
***→ A secondary result of a process. Spin off***

**Carry out** /ˈkæriaʊt/
v Babbage's "Analytical Engine" could **carry out** complicated **calculations**.
**The experiment was carried out** in the chemistry laboratory.
The geological survey could not be **carried out** through lack of money.
***→ To do, to perform***

**Collapse** /kəˈlæps/
v The building **collapsed** after the earthquake.
She **collapsed** from loss of blood.
adj A black hole is a **collapsed** neutron star.
***→ To fall down, disintegrate under pressure***

**Collide** /kəˈlaɪd/
v The two cars **collided** in the main street.
Many asteroids are on orbits that could **collide** with the Earth.
The accelerated ions **collide** with atoms of the gas.
***→ To crash into, to impact ≠ to miss, to avoid***

**Component** /kəmˈpəʊnənt/
n Diodes and transistors are **electronic components**.
**To assemble the components** of a machine.
Proteins constitute the **main components** of living matter.
***→ A part, element of a whole system***

**Conduct** /kənˈdʌkt/
1.v **To conduct a survey**.
This experiment was **conducted** in a vacuum.
***→ To perform, to carry out***
2.v Copper is both malleable and **conducts electricity** well.
***→ To transmit energy***

**Construct** /kənˈstrʌkt/
v The oldest bridge in Australia was **constructed** by prisoners in 1823.
The termite nests are **constructed** from soil cemented by saliva.
***→ To build, to make***

**Contain** /kənˈteɪn/
v The water tank **contains** 500 litres.
Blood **contains** white and red corpuscles.
n The toxic waste was stocked in steel **containers**.
***→ To hold, to stock something. A reservoir, tank***

**Content** /ˈkɒntent/
n She emptied the **contents** of the box onto the table.
If the oxygen **content** of the blood is reduced, brain damage will occur.
***→ What is inside, what is contained***

**Cool** /kuːl/
adj To drink a **cool** glass of water.
A **water-cooled** engine.
There was a leak in the **cooling system**.
v **To cool** a hot gas.
***→ Agreeably cold. To reduce the temperature ≠ to heat, to warm***

**Cope** /kəʊp/
v He could not **cope with** so much work.

Air hostesses are trained **to cope with an emergency**.
Immuno-suppressive disorders result in an inability to **cope with** infections.
→ ***To deal with, to manage***

**Crack** /kræk/
n There was a **crack** in the window.
v The storage tanks **cracked** under the heat.
The ice expands causing the rock to **crack**.
→ ***A fracture line on the surface. To break (partially), to split***

**Crush** /krʌʃ/
v She **crushed** her finger in the door.
Amputation may be required if the leg has been severely **crushed**.
The weight of the glacier **crushes** the rock below.
→ ***To damage, to harm by applying pressure***

**Cure** /kjʊə/
v It was a mild illness. The doctor soon **cured** her.
Penicillin is used to **cure** pneumonia.
n Although no **cure** has yet been discovered, the disease can be controlled.
→ ***To make better. A treatment***

**Deal** /diːl/ *(deal, dealt, dealt)*
1.v This book **deals with** recent developments in low temperature physics.
→ ***Is about***
2.v Extra medical staff will be needed **to deal with** the epidemic.
I haven't got enough time **to deal with the problem**.
→ ***To cope with, to take necessary action***
3.n To make an important business **deal**.
Roosevelt introduced the **New Deal**
→ ***Arrangement, contract for selling, distribution, etc.***
4.n He has **a great deal of money**.
This requires a **great deal of time**.
→ ***Quantity, amount***

**Design** /dɪˈzaɪn/
v **The car was designed** in Italy and built in Germany.
New proteins **can be designed** by arranging the sequence of amino-acids.
n The circuit **design** was defective.
→ ***To make, conceive of a plan for an appliance, etc. A plan, diagram***

**Device** /dɪˈvaɪs/
n Lasers are optical **devices**.
A **fuel-saving device**.
An amplifier is a **device** for increasing the intensity of an electrical input.
→ ***An appliance, a piece of equipment designed to do something***

**Devise** /dɪˈvaɪz/
v To **devise** a system to reduce costs.
The process was **devised** to recycle industrial waste.
→ ***To invent, to think of a system, a process***

**Dig** /dɪg/ *(dig, dug, dug)*
v To **dig** a hole in the ground.
It took 8 years to **dig** the Panama canal.
→ ***To make a hole in the ground***

**Dispose** /dɪˈspəʊz/
1.v Most domestic waste is **disposed** of by incineration.
A scheme to **dispose** of radio-active waste.
n The nuclear industry is faced with a major problem of **waste disposal**.
→ ***To deal with, get rid of. Dumping, destruction***
2.n Company directors have a car **at their disposal**.
→ ***For personal use, to be used as required***

**Dissolve** /dɪˈzɒlv/
v Sugar **dissolves** in coffee.
The drug is **dissolved** in the blood.
Most metals can be **dissolved** in acid.
→ ***When a solid mixes and is incorporated in a liquid***

**Earn** /ɜːn/
v He works in Madrid and **earns** 5,000 € a year.
When he was young, Einstein **earned a living** as a maths tutor.
His success was **well-earned**.
→ ***To be paid, to get money, etc. in exchange for work or goods***

**Engine** /ˈendʒɪn/
n The **steam engine** was invented by James Watt.
Rolls Royce make **aero-engines**.
→ ***A machine converting fuel into mechanical energy***

**Engineer** /ˌendʒɪˈnɪə/
n He is a mechanical **engineer**.
Computer **engineers** can get excellent salaries.
To study **civil engineering**.
→ ***A highly qualified person working in technology. A branch of applied science***

**Exhaust** /ɪgˈzɔːst/
1.n Catalytic **exhaust pipes** reduce pollution.

**Exhaust gases** from motor vehicles are the main cause of nitrogen oxide pollution.
→ ***Waste gas. Gas that has been burnt***

2.v At the end of the day he **felt exhausted**.
The food supplies will soon be **exhausted**.
There seems to be no solution. We have **exhausted all the possibilities**.
→ ***Very tired, with no energy left. Completely finished***

**Experience** /ɪk'spɪərɪəns/

n He talked about his **experiences** in Tibet.
Candidates should have at least two years' **experience** in industry.

v During the trials, they **experienced** serious difficulties.
→ ***What has been lived, practical knowledge. To be confronted by***

**Experiment** /ɪk'sperɪmənt/

n He **carried out an experiment** in the laboratory.

adj Mice are commonly used for **experimental purposes**.
→ ***A (scientific) test***

**Facility** /fə'sɪləti/

n Computer **facilities** are available to all students.
The laboratory is suffering from a lack of **research facilities**.
→ ***Equipment, buildings provided for a specific purpose***

**Fail** /feɪl/

v He **failed** to pass his driving test.
If the male cell **fails** to unite with the female cell, fertilisation cannot take place.

n The plane crashed because of engine **failure**.
Asphyxia is a result of the **failure** of the respiratory system.
→ ***To be unsuccessful. Breakdown ≠ success***

**Fault** /fɔ:lt/

n The fire was caused by a **fault** in the electric circuit.
**Faults** in metals can be detected by X-rays.
**Major faults** have been located where the tectonic plates are in movement.
→ ***Error, structural abnormality***

**Feasible** /'fi:zəbl/

adj Living on the planet Venus is not **feasible**.
The project was **technically feasible** but too expensive to be realistic.

n To carry out a **feasibility study**.
→ ***Possible, viable. Technically realistic***

**Feed** /fi:d/ *(feed, fed, fed)*

v To **feed** the baby with milk.
Third world agricultural production cannot **feed** the population.
→ ***To supply with food, etc.***

**Feedback** /'fi:dbæk/

n The prototype was tested and the **feedback** used to improve the design.
In a beta test, **feedback** from users helps eliminate programming errors.
→ ***Information reintroduced into a system to improve performance***

**Fire** /'faɪə/

n Humans began to use **fire** more than 400,000 years ago.
The building **caught fire**.
The whole factory was **on fire**.

v **To fire** a revolver.
→ ***Combustion, in flames, to burn. To ignite, to detonate***

**Float** /fləʊt/

v Most woods **float** in water.
Albatrosses sleep while **floating** on the ocean.
→ ***To remain, be suspended on the surface of a liquid, gas ≠ to sink***

**Freeze** /fri:z/ *(freeze, froze, frozen)*

v Water **freezes** at 0°C.
In Siberia, the ground is **frozen** 10 months per year.
**Frozen** carbon dioxide is used as a refrigerant.
→ ***To solidify because of low temperature ≠ to melt***

**Goal** /gəʊl/

n The **long-term goal** is to reduce pollution rates by 50%.
Both research teams are attempting to **achieve** the same **goal**.
The **primary goal** is to reduce infant mortality.
→ ***Purpose, aim, desired result***

**Heat** /hi:t/

n The **heat** of the sun is transmitted by radiation.
Bioluminescent animals produce little **heat**.

v The liquid was **heated up** to 150°C.
→ ***A measurement of temperature. To increase temperature ≠ to cool***

**Implement** /'ɪmplɪmənt/

1.n Production was boosted by improvements in farming **implements**.
Archaeologists employ pneumatic hammers, drills, and similar **implements**.
→ ***Tool, instrument***

2.v After the accident, NASA **implemented** stricter safety regulations.
***→ To apply, to put into use***

**Inability** /ˌɪnəˈbɪləti/

n One of the symptoms of depression is the **inability** to concentrate.
Lesions in the cortex can lead to an **inability** to control the muscles.
***→ Incapacity ≠ ability***

**Inhabit** /ɪnˈhæbɪt/

v Snakes, like the Anaconda, **inhabit** the rivers of Amazonia.
n The number of **inhabitants** in small villages is decreasing.
In 215 AD, Caracalla massacred all the male **inhabitants** of Alexandria.
***→ To live, to dwell. The population***

**Insert** /ɪnˈsɜːt/

v Before **inserting** the cassette you should switch on the machine.
Purified protein was **inserted** into the muscle by injection.
Genetic modifications can be made by **inserting** DNA into the fetus.
***→ To put something inside something else ≠ to withdraw, to extract***

**Kind** /kaɪnd/

n **What kind of** car has she got?
**Different kinds of** fossils are found at different geological layers.
**Certain kinds of** diseases, e.g. stomach ulcers, are typical of developed countries.
***→ Sort, type***

> **Note — Kind** has two other common meanings in general English.
> → *a **kind** man – helpful, nice*
> → *it is **kind of** difficult – rather, a little, a bit (Am. E. – spoken language)*

**Launch** /lɔːntʃ/

v To **launch** a new ship.
Sputnik 1 was **launched** in 1961.
The company has **launched** a new advertising campaign.
***→ To send a ship / missile into the water / air. To start***

**Maintain** /meɪnˈteɪn/

v A thermostat is used to **maintain** a constant temperature.
The oxygen supply to the brain must be **maintained**.
Body temperature is **maintained** at 37.4°C by evaporation.
***→ To keep, to conserve in the same condition***

**Melt** /melt/

v When the snow **melts**, the level of the river rises.
A substance can be identified by its **melting point**.
***→ To change from a solid to a liquid state ≠ to freeze***

> **Note — Molten** / ˈməʊltən / *(N.B. – This is an irregular past participle of **"melt"**, used especially to describe high temperature liquefaction.)*
> → *a volcanic eruption of **molten rock** or magma*
> → *alloys can be prepared from **molten materials***

**Obey** /əˈbeɪ/

v You should **obey** the instructions.
Helmholtz proved that electric circuits **obey** the law of conservation of energy.
adj Compared to cats, dogs are **obedient** animals.
***→ To respect the law, to conform. Well disciplined ≠ disobedient***

**Outcome** /ˈaʊtkʌm/

n Future policy depends on the **outcome** of the election.
Beneficial **outcomes** of genetic mutations are reinforced by natural selection.
One of the **outcomes** of increased education has been a shift in marriage patterns.
***→ Result, consequence***

**Pain** /peɪn/

n If the **pain** is too great, the doctor will prescribe morphine.
The gas causes temporary blindness and great **pain**.
adj Osteoarthritis is a relatively mild disease, nevertheless, **it can be painful**.
***→ Physical suffering***

**Pressure** /ˈpreʃə/

n **Atmospheric pressure** depends on the altitude.
With age, arteries lose their flexibility and there is a rise in **blood pressure**.
Ecologists are **putting pressure** on the government.
***→ The exertion of force, influence***

**Probe** /prəʊb/

n **Probes** inserted into the brain are used to locate cerebral activity.
Tumours, inside the body can be destroyed by small cryogenic **probes**.
v The European Space Agency used "Giotto" to **probe** outer space.
***→ Device (to be inserted) for examining (at a distance). To investigate***

**Purpose** /ˈpɜːpəs/

n The **main purpose** of the meeting was to find a short-term solution.
According to Darwin, the **purpose** of sexuality is to create organic diversity.
A **general-purpose** volt-meter.
To do something **on purpose**.
→ ***Aim, function. With intent ≠ by accident***

**Recover** /rɪˈkʌvə/

1.v Nowadays 90% of children **recover** from Hodgkin's disease.
It took 5 years to **recover** from the economic crisis.
→ ***To get better, to overcome***

2.v Most of the meteorites **recovered** on Earth are asteroid fragments.
→ ***To find again, to recuperate***

**Resolve** /rɪˈzɒlv/

v There are several ways of **resolving the problem**.
The conflict in the Middle East will not be **resolved** for years.
**To resolve** a vector into its component parts.
→ ***To find a solution. To separate into constituent parts***

**Sample** /ˈsɑːmpl/

n Different **samples** of the bacteria were analysed.
The **sample** was analysed by carbon 14 dating techniques.

v The blood is **sampled** to check for contamination.
→ ***Small part representing the whole. Typical example. To test a part***

**Sustain** /səˈsteɪn/

v For a satisfactory bond to be obtained, the pressure must be **sustained** for 6 hours.
Pilots lose consciousness under a **sustained force** of 4 to 6 g.

adj **Sustainable development** aims to protect the needs of future generations.
→ ***To maintain, to continue. Which lasts***

**Switch** /swɪtʃ/

v **To switch** from manual to automatic control.
When the electric current is **switched off**, muscular contraction stops.

n The motor driving the compressor is controlled by a **thermostatic switch**.
→ ***To change positions. To interrupt. A circuit-breaker***

**Task** /tɑːsk/

n He managed **to finish the task** on time.
It was not **an easy task**.
The **task** of identifying the virus will take months.
→ ***A (difficult) job***

**Trial** /ˈtraɪəl/

1.n The plane crashed during **trials**.
Drugs cannot be commercialised until **clinical trials** have been completed.
To learn **by trial and error**.
→ ***A test***

2.n At the end of the **trial** he was sentenced to 3 years prison.
→ ***A legal examination***

**Warm** /wɔːm/

v **To warm** your hands in front of a fire.

adj In April, the weather begins to get **warmer**.
Mammals are **warm-blooded** animals.
→ ***To make, be appropriately hot ≠ cool***

**Waste** /weɪst/

1.n The US exports large quantities of **toxic waste** to the Third World.
There is a ban against dumping **nuclear waste** in the sea.
→ ***Unwanted, rejected material***

2.n It is **a waste of time** and money.

v Centralised planning often **wastes** resources.
→ ***Consuming carelessly, without real purpose ≠ to save***

**Willing** /ˈwɪlɪŋ/

adj Not every one is **willing to** work on Saturday.
Are customers **willing to** pay more for better goods?
→ ***Prepared, ready ≠ unwilling***

# 9. MOVEMENT & CHANGE

**Abroad** /ə'brɔːd/
adv To **travel abroad** you need a valid passport.
An increasing number of students spend a year **studying abroad**.
19th century Japan was a closed society. Citizens were forbidden to **travel abroad**.
→ ***A foreign country***

**Actuate** /'æktʃueit/
v The switch can be **actuated** by remote control.
The position of the wings is **actuated** by hydraulic pumps.
→ ***To operate, to control***

**Adjust** /ə'dʒʌst/
v To **adjust** a microscope.
To **adjust** a hypothesis in the light of new facts.
n Minor **adjustments** can be made by hand.
→ ***To change slightly, to make more suitable. Modification***

**Alter** /'ɔːltə/
v The frequency must not be **altered**.
To **alter** the design of the experiment.
The protein's stability can be **altered** by the introduction of amino acids.
→ ***To change, to modify***

> **Note — Alter** is a false friend. In many languages it means to change for the worse. In English it simply means "to change".
> → *the law was **altered** to protect children*

**Anticlockwise** /ˌæntɪ'klɒkwaɪz/
adv To switch off the radio, turn the button **anticlockwise**.
adj Sea currents in the South Atlantic flow in an **anticlockwise direction**.
→ ***The opposite direction to the hands of a clock ≠ clockwise***

**Arise** /ə'raɪz/ *(arise, arose, arisen)*
v An unexpected **problem has arisen**.
Three main **issues arose** during the meeting.
Many new species of animals have **arisen** over the last 100,000 years.
→ ***To appear, to come to notice, to begin to exist***

**Arrange** /ə'reɪndʒ/
v To **arrange a meeting**.
The list was **arranged in alphabetical order**.
Graphite consists of weakly bonded atoms **arranged** in hexagons.
→ ***To put in order, to organise***

**Backwards** /'bækwədz/
adv To swim, push your arms in front of you and then pull them **backwards**.
By working **backwards**, they were able to build up the chain of events.
→ ***In the direction from front to back ≠ forwards***

> **Note** — The suffix **"-wards"** indicates direction. It is used to form numerous adverbs.
> → *to move **downwards / upwards / southwards***
> In Am. E. and in adjectives it is often written without an "-s".
> → *a **forward** movement*

**Bleed** /bliːd/ *(bleed, bled, bled)*
v The child's nose was **bleeding**.
In case of an arterial rupture, the victim may **bleed to death** within minutes.
→ ***To lose blood***

**Blood** /blʌd/
n In 1628, Harvey discovered the **circulation of the blood**.
Under stress, adrenaline is released into the **blood**.
Reptiles are **cold-blooded animals**.
→ ***A red fluid in the body circulated by the heart***

**Burst** /bɜːst/ *(burst, burst, burst)*
v Water pipes **burst** when they freeze.
n A **burst** of activity.
→ ***To break suddenly under pressure. An explosion, outbreak***

**Bypass** /'baɪpɑːs/
n To avoid driving through the town centre, he took the **by-pass**.
v This pipe enables cold gas to **bypass** the cooling circuit.
→ ***Road around a town, alternative route. To go round, avoid***

**Clockwise** /ˈklɒkwaɪz/
adv When you play cards you deal them **clockwise**.
adj Anticyclones are produced by a **clockwise** movement of the wind.
***→ In the direction of the hands of a clock ≠ anticlockwise, counterclockwise***

**Convey** /kənˈveɪ/
v Liquid is **conveyed** along the pipe.
Electricity must be **conveyed** from the power station to the user.
The information is **conveyed along** the nerve fibres.
***→ To carry. To take from one place to another***

**Death** /deθ/
n Is there life after **death**?
**Death** was caused by strychnine poisoning.
**The death rate** of the Australian Aborigines is among the highest in the world.
***→ To die, to stop living***

**Decay** /dɪˈkeɪ/
v In hot, humid forests, wood **decays** fast.
n The **decay** of teeth is caused by oral bacteria.
***→ To decompose, to deteriorate***

**Defect** /ˈdiːfekt/
n The plane crashed because of a **defect** in the hydraulic system.
The electron microscope revealed **microscopic defects** in the metal.
adj The generator broke down because of a **defective** cooling pump.
***→ A failure, weakness. Not working ≠ in working order***

**Delay** /dɪˈleɪ/
n There was a 30 minutes **delay** at the airport because of fog.
v The decision was **delayed** until after the election.
Side-effects of penicillin include **delayed** hypersensitivity and fever.
***→ To retard, to slow down***

**Deliver** /dɪˈlɪvə/
v The post is **delivered** at 10 a.m. every morning.
The steam is **delivered** by a copper pipe.
n We are very busy. There will be a delay in **delivery time**.
***→ To distribute, to convey. Transport and distribution ≠ collection***

**Disrupt** /dɪsˈrʌpt/
v If the price of petrol rises, it will **disrupt** the entire economy.
Antibiotics **disrupt** the cell structure of the bacteria.
n Under the influence of marijuana, there is a **disruption** of cognitive processes.
***→ To disturb, to cause confusion***

**Drift** /drɪft/
v The clouds **drift** slowly across the sky.
Living organisms **drifted** on the ocean's surface, spreading to other continents.
n Plate tectonics can explain **continental drift**.
***→ To move slowly, without aim. Slow movement, deviation***

**Dump** /dʌmp/
v The toxic material had been **dumped** in an open field.
Large quantities of chemical waste were **dumped** in the North Sea.
n In the long run, toxic **waste dumps** will pollute underground water.
***→ To dispose of, to throw away. A place where waste material is left***

> **Note — Dumping** is also used in economics with the meaning: *"selling (unwanted) goods at a low price"*.

**Escape** /ɪˈskeɪp/
v Gas **escaped** from the leaking pipe.
A detail which **escaped** notice.
n The pollution was caused by an **escape** of toxic waste.
***→ To find a way out. To avoid. A leak, spill***

**Evolve** /ɪˈvɒlv/
v Our present alphabet has **evolved** from cuneiform and hieroglyphic symbols.
Bacteria have **evolved** defences against certain antibiotics.
Artificial intelligence has developed programs that can **evolve** or "learn".
***→ To make progress, to develop***

**Flash** /flæʃ/
n The sky was illuminated by a **flash of lightning**.
v When the engine begins to overheat, a red warning light starts to **flash**.
***→ A sudden bright light. A rapid, (intermittent) illumination***

**Flight** /flaɪt/
n The plane crashed during the first **test flight**.
The jet engine made **supersonic flight** possible.
The airflow over the wing provides the lift that sustains the aircraft **in flight**.
***→ Movement through the air, flying***

**Flow** /fləʊ/
v Oil **flows** through a pipe.

Light activates the nerves and causes an electric current **to flow**.
n Traffic control is concerned with improving the **flow** of vehicles.
***→ To circulate, a movement, a stream of liquid, gas, etc.***

**Foreign** /ˈfɒrən/
adj To speak a **foreign language**.
Erasmus grants enable European students to study in **foreign countries**.
T-lymphocytes detect and destroy **foreign** organisms in the body.
***→ From abroad, a different country. Different, unfamiliar***

**Forward(s)** /ˈfɔːwədz/
adv The train began to **move** slowly **forwards**.
Slowly but surely the project is **going forward**.
***→ Towards the front, advancing ≠ backwards***

**Gain** /geɪn/
v To **gain time**.
An internship allows you to **gain experience**.
n There was a slight **gain in efficiency** due to the new equipment.
***→ To win, to obtain. An increase ≠ a loss***

**Grow** /grəʊ/ *(grow, grew, grown)*
v Certain bacteria can **grow** in the absence of air.
Over the past two decades, air transport has **grown** rapidly.
adj There is **growing concern** about the over-use of antibiotics.
n The **growth** of the electronics industry.
***→ To develop. Increasing. Expansion ≠ decline***

**Head** /hed/
v **To head** the government.
The Third World is **heading towards** catastrophe.
n The **head of a department**.
Average consumption **per head**.
***→ To lead. To go in that direction. A director. A person***

**Income** /ɪŋkʌm/
n Most people have to pay **income tax**.
His future **income** will depend on his diploma.
***→ Salary, money that is earned***

**Incoming** /ˈɪnˌkʌmɪŋ/
adj The volcano raised a dust cloud which reduced **incoming solar radiation**.
The cortex analyses **incoming** information from the sense receptors in the body.
***→ Entering, approaching ≠ outgoing***

**Input** /ˈɪnpʊt/
n The transformer requires a 24 V **input.**
The quality of the image depends on the **input signal**.
Discs supply **data input** for a computer.
***→ What is fed into an appliance ≠ output***

**Intake** /ˈɪnteɪk/
n You must check the child's weekly **intake** of calcium.
A reduction in oxygen **intake** causes the heart to pump faster.
***→ Consumption. What is taken in ≠ output***

**Inward(s)** /ˈɪnwədz/
adv Gravity exerts a pressure **inwards**, making the neutron star collapse.
adj The gas pressure in the balloon equals the **inward** pressure of the atmosphere.
***→ In the direction of the centre, the interior ≠ outward***

**Journey** /ˈdʒɜːni/
n The **journey** to Manchester took longer than expected.
After a five-hour **journey**, he went straight to the hotel.
***→ Trip, voyage. Time taken for travelling***

**Land** /lænd/
v Columbus **landed** in the Bahamas in 1492.
Owing to fog, the plane was not able to **land**.
***→ To disembark. When a plane, ship reaches its destination***

**Leak** /liːk/
n The explosion was caused by a gas **leak**.
adj A **leaking** pipe.
v Radio-active gases **leaked** from the cooling system.
***→ A hole or crack allowing gas or liquid to get out. To escape***

**Lift** /lɪft/
1.v The box was too heavy **to lift**.
The land masses were **lifted** by tectonic pressures.
At last, the government has **lifted** import restrictions.
n Air pressure on the wings provides **lift** for a plane.
***→ To pick up, to raise. Upward pressure***
2.n There is a **lift** in the hotel.
***→ An (electrical) platform for changing levels in a building***

**Lose** /lu:z/ *(lose, lost, lost)*

v He **lost** his money on the way to the cinema.
The company is **losing** export orders because of the strike.
***→ To be unable to find, to cease to have ≠ to find, to gain***

**Loss** /lɒs/

n Energy **loss** in transformers is due to resistance.
As people get older, the brain suffers from a continual **loss** of neurones.
***→ Wastage. To not have any more ≠ gain***

**Move** /mu:v/

v He **moved** the table to the other side of the room.
Because of his job, he **moved** from Rome to Turin.
In order **to move**, a complex coordination of muscle and brain is required.
***→ To change position, place***

**Offshore** /ˈɒfʃɔ:/

adj An **offshore island**.
To drill for **offshore oil**.
***→ Away from the land. In the sea ≠ inshore***

**Ongoing** /ˈɒngəʊɪŋ/

adj **Ongoing studies** suggest that industrial development of the Antarctic is feasible.
There is an **ongoing project** of modernisation.
***→ Current, in progress at the moment***

**Onset** /ˈɒnset/

n The road must be finished before the **onset** of the rainy season.
The new drugs delay the **onset** of secondary infections.
At the **onset** of pubescence, fundamental physiological changes occur.
***→ The beginning, the start ≠ the end***

**Onward(s)** /ˈɒnwədz/

adv Uranium was split in 1939. **From then onwards**, progress was rapid.
**From 1888 onwards**, Van Gogh's mental health deteriorated.
***→ After that moment***

**Output** /ˈautput/

n **Industrial output** increased last year.
The generator has an **output** of 220 volts.
The **output** of the computer can be either via screen or printer.
***→ Production ≠ input***

**Path** /pɑ:θ/

n A narrow **path** leads up to the house.
The **path** of the comet.
The **nerve paths** were damaged during the operation.
***→ Track, way, trajectory***

**Pregnant** /ˈpregnənt/

adj **Pregnant women** are liable to transmit the disease to the fetus.
Anti-coagulants should not normally be prescribed to **pregnant women**.
***→ Expecting a baby***

**Proceed** /prəˈsi:d/

v Despite criticism, they **proceeded** with the experiment.
After mending the car, he **proceeded** on his journey.
The growth of cancer cells **is proceeding** at an alarming rate.
***→ To continue, to go forward ≠ to stop***

**Propel** /prəˈpel/

v The heart receives blood from the veins and **propels** it through the arteries.
adj A **jet-propelled plane**.
n Hydrogen is used as a **propellant** for projectiles and rockets.
***→ To drive, to push forward. Fuel***

**Pump** /pʌmp/

n The car overheated because of a failure of the **water pump**.
v The heart **pumps** at a rate of approximately 72 beats per second.
***→ A device which causes liquid to flow under pressure***

**Release** /rɪˈli:s/

v At the age of 72, Mandela was **released** from prison.
The birds were **released** from the cage.
Studies **released** by the government show that industrial injury is increasing.
***→ Set free, to liberate. To make public***

**Remove** /rɪˈmu:v/

v When you have finished, please **remove** the key from the lock.
Do not **remove** the back of the TV set if it is switched on.
The surgeon **removed** the tumour.
n Biopsy involves the **removal** of living tissue for examination.
***→ To take away / out. Extraction ≠ replacement, insertion***

**Rid** /rɪd/

adj **To get rid of** something you do not want.
Insecticides are used to **get rid of** parasites.

The gene helps the body **get rid of** carcinogens.
→ ***To dispose of. To eliminate***

**Run** /rʌn/ *(run, ran, run)*

1.v At the age of 28, he was **running** a small computer company.
They **ran** a 5-day test.
→ ***To organise, to manage***

2.v The motor is **running** too fast.
The chains of DNA molecules **run** in opposite directions.
The trains **run on time**.
→ ***To function, to go***

3.n **In the long run**, the storage tanks will corrode.
→ ***In due course, in time***

**Note — To run** is another verb whose meaning is frequently modified by particles.
→ ***to run into*** *a tree (to collide)*
→ ***to run into*** *difficulties (to encounter)*
→ ***to run over*** *a dog (to kill – with a car)*
→ ***to run out of*** *money (to have no money left)*

**Settle** /ˈsetl/

v Insoluble particles in the liquid gradually **settle** on the bottom of the container.
Recent research data will doubtless **settle** the question.
The first colonists **settled** along the East coast of America.

n The government's attempt to reach a diplomatic **settlement** failed.
→ ***To stop moving, to sink. To resolve. To colonise. An agreement***

**Shift** /ʃift/

n A **shift** in the direction of the wind.
**A shift in priorities**.

v Since the end of the Cold War, the pattern of air transport has **shifted**.
→ ***A small movement. To change, to alter***

**Shrink** /ʃrɪŋk/ *(shrink, shrank, shrunk)*

v Some textiles **shrink** if you put them in water.
Global warming is causing the polar ice cap to **shrink**.
The number of workers in the car industry is **shrinking**.
→ ***To contract, to become smaller ≠ to expand***

**Slide** /slaɪd/ *(slide, slid, slid)*

v **To slide** across the ice.
As the muscles contract, the filaments **slide** past each other.

adj A **sliding** door.
→ ***To go smoothly over a surface with minimal friction***

**Spin** /spɪn/ *(spin, spun, spun)*

v The wheel **spins** on its axis.
A gyroscope remains stable because it **spins** at high speed.

n A boson is an elementary particle that has a **spin** equal to zero.
→ ***To rotate, to turn fast on its axis***

**Spin-off** /ˈspɪnɒf/

n The development of "Velcro" is an example of **spin-off** from space research.
The tourist industry would benefit from positive **spin-off** from a new airport.
→ ***Incidental, collateral benefits. Side-effects***

**Spring** /sprɪŋ/ *(spring, sprang, sprung)*

1.v Suddenly, the cat **sprang** out of the window.
In the 1990s, thousands of computer service companies **sprang up**.
→ ***To jump, move suddenly. To originate, to start***

2.n **Spring**, summer and autumn.
→ ***The first season of the new year***

3.n When the pressure is released the **metallic spring** forces the contacts apart.
→ ***A helical coil which is elastic and can be compressed***

**Stretch** /stretʃ/

v Elastic **stretches**.
The rubber skin of the meteorological balloon **stretches** as the helium expands.
The pressure of the heart beat is absorbed as the arteries **stretch**.
→ ***To undergo an elastic deformation, to expand ≠ to contract***

**Strike** /straɪk/ *(strike, struck, struck)*

1.v He was **struck** on the head by a falling rock.
The gas molecules **strike** the suspended particles at random.

adj **A striking improvement**.
→ ***To hit. Remarkable***

2.n The factory workers **went on strike**.
→ ***To refuse to work***

**Surge** /sɜːdʒ/

n There has been a **sudden surge** of interest in Buddhism.
Lightning caused a power **surge** and the breakdown of the electricity grid.

v The river flooded and water **surged** through the town.
→ ***Sudden increase, burst. To flow quickly***

**Surround** /səˈraʊnd/

v The garden is **surrounded** by a low wall.

The Forum, which was the heart of Rome, is **surrounded** by the Seven Hills.
The atmosphere **surrounding** the planet is maintained by a gravitational field.
→ ***To make a perimeter, to enclose, to encircle***

**Threshold** /ˈθreʃhəʊld/

n The whole economic system is **on the threshold** of collapse.
The **pain threshold** depends on psychological factors.
If the level of hormones falls below a **critical threshold** all activity ceases.
→ ***An edge, limit. Significant borderline***

**Toward(s)** /təˈwɔːdz/

prep To drive **towards** the town.
**Towards the end of the century**.
In the computer industry, there is a **trend towards** more miniaturisation.
→ ***In the direction of ≠ away from***

**Transplant** /trænsˈplɑːnt/

n Dr Barnard carried out the first human **heart transplant** in 1967.
v To avoid damage to the tissue, corneas must be **transplanted** within 48 hours.
→ ***To transfer an organ from one person to another***

**Travel** /ˈtrævl/

v **To travel by** train.
**To travel** at the speed of light.
The shock waves **travel** away from the epicentre.
→ ***To make a journey. To move***

> **Note – To travel** is the general verb indicating movement.
> → *to travel by plane. To travel at 160 kph*

> **Travel** is almost never used as a noun. **Journey** is the general noun used for travelling.
> → *a car journey*
> More specific terms for travelling include:
> → *a* ***voyage*** *– a sea journey*
> → *a* ***flight*** *– an air journey*

**Turn** /tɜːn/

1.v **To turn** the key in the lock.
**To turn** the handle of the door.
35% of the population thinks the Sun **turns** round the Earth.
→ ***To make something go round an axis***

2.v Acid **turns** litmus paper red.
**To turn** uranium **into** plutonium.
→ ***To transform***

3.v **To turn on / off** the electricity.
→ ***To switch on / off***

**Wear** /weə/ *(wear, wore, worn)*

1.v The manager was **wearing** a grey suit and a light blue shirt.
→ ***To be dressed, to have clothes on***

2.v The surface of the metal is hardened so that it will **wear** better.
Mitosis is the process by which organisms grow and replace **worn-out** tissue.
→ ***Resist erosion, friction. Deteriorated by use***

**Withdraw** /wɪðˈdrɔː/
*(withdraw, drew, drawn)*

v **To withdraw money** from the bank.
After the accident, the pharmaceutical firm **withdrew** the drug.
A sample of amniotic fluid was **withdrawn** from the uterus.
→ ***To remove. To extract ≠ to deposit, to insert***

# 10. MATTER & OBJECTS

**Alloy** /ˈælɔɪ/

n Steel is an **alloy** composed of iron and carbon.
Platinium-irridium **alloy** is used to define the standard of mass.
→ ***A metal made by combining two metals***

**Appliance** /əˈplaɪəns/

n Most mechanical **appliances** must be lubricated.
Integrated circuits have reduced the price of electronic **appliances**.
→ ***Apparatus, instrument***

**Ash** /æʃ/

n The **cigarette ash** fell on the floor.
After the cremation the **ashes** were scattered at sea.
→ ***Greyish powder left after incineration***

**Bat** /bæt/

n **Bats** navigate by echo-location.
**Bats** are typically cave-dwelling animals.
→ ***Small, mouse-like, nocturnal mammals that fly***

**Belt** /belt/

n To be a black **belt** in judo.
You should fasten your **safety belt** when you get into the car.
The dynamo was driven by a **belt** from the motor.
→ ***A circular band of plastic, rubber, etc. Used to support trousers, to transmit power***

**Blind** /blaɪnd/

adj A **blind man** stands on the corner of the street.
Approximately 7% of men and 1% of women are born **colour-blind**.

n Cataract and glaucoma are a common cause of **blindness**.
→ ***Without sight. To be unable to see***

**Body** /ˈbɑdi/

n The **body** of a dead man was found in the river.
There are more than 360 acupuncture points in the **human body**.
A falling **body** accelerates because of the force of gravitation.
→ ***The physical structure of a human being, an animal or an object***

**Bone** /bəʊn/

n The human skeleton consists of 206 **bones**.
Calcium is needed for the **bones** to develop.
Normally, only organisms with hard parts, such as **bones**, form fossils.
→ ***Hard, structural internal elements of body, part of the skeleton***

**Brain** /breɪn/

n The human **brain** weighs roughly 450 g.
The hippocampus is the part of the **brain** concerned with memory.
Doctors have transplanted **brain cells** in an attempt to treat Parkinson's disease.
→ ***Organ controlling the central nervous system***

**Breast** /brest/

n She held the baby to her **breast**.
**Breast cancer** is the most common cancer for women.
→ ***Mammary gland***

**Cell** /sel/

n A **cell** has a single nucleus.
He examined the **blood cells** under the microscope.
An anode is the positive electrode of an electrolytic **cell**.
→ ***The smallest working division***

**Channel** /ˈtʃænl/

n She watched a TV programme on **Channel 3**.
A 6-**channel** input.

v Not enough money is being **channelled into** cancer research.
→ ***A communication path. To direct***

**Chemical** /ˈkemɪkl/

n It is forbidden to sell certain **chemicals** to the public.

adj Dehydration can be caused by **chemical reaction**.
→ ***A substance produced by chemistry, related to chemistry***

**Chemistry** /ˈkemɪstri/

n To study **inorganic chemistry**.
→ ***The science of composition, structure and reaction of substances***

**Chip** /tʃɪp/

1.n A **chip** of stone hit him in the eye and blinded him.
***→ A fragment, a small piece of something***

2.n To replace a **chip** in an electronic circuit.
The miniaturisation of electronic circuits has been largely due to the **silicon chip**.
***→ A small, silicon crystal containing a circuit***

**Cliff** /klɪf/

n From the top of the **cliff** you could see the ships in the distance.
High **cliffs** rise on each side of the canyon.
The temples of Abu Simbel were cut into the **cliffs** in the Nile valley.
***→ Precipices, vertical rock face found in gorges or by the sea***

**Coal** /kəʊl/

n To put **coal** on the fire.
There will be a shortage of non-renewable fuels such as **coal**, oil and gas.
**Coal-fuelled power plants** are responsible for sulphur dioxide pollution.
***→ A black, carbon, fossilised mineral used for heating***

**Coast** /kəʊst/

n The Atlantic **coast**.
When wet winds reach the **coast**, the air is forced to rise, causing rainfall.
***→ Frontier between the land and the sea***

**Coat** /kəʊt/

n It was cold. She was wearing a thick brown **coat**.

v An electric wire is **coated** with a plastic insulator.

n Cadmium, deposited by electrolysis, provides a chemically resistant **coating**.
***→ Clothes worn on the outside. To cover. Exterior layer***

**Compound** /ˈkɒmpaʊnd/

adj **Compound** microscopes have at least two lenses.
Insects have **compound** eyes.
**Compound** chemicals are difficult to separate.
***→ A combination of several elements, parts, etc.***

**Concrete** /ˈkɒnkriːt/

n A **concrete** storage tank.
The foundations were made of **reinforced concrete**.
***→ A building material made of stone, sand, cement and water***

**Copper** /ˈkɒpə/

n **Copper** is a good conductor of electricity.
Electric wires are usually made of **copper**.
***→ Red metal. Chemical symbol: Cu***

**Crew** /kruː/

n The submarine has a **crew** of 50 men.
A **crew** of TV reporters was taken hostage.
***→ A team, group working on a ship, etc.***

**Crop** /krɒp/

n The tobacco **crop** must be sprayed with insecticide.
The Irish famine (1845-1849) was caused by a failure of the potato **crop**.
***→ Plants grown by farmers***

**Customer** /ˈkʌstəmə/

n He has been a **regular customer** at the shop for 5 years.
The company lost **customers** because of the poor after-sales service.
***→ A person who buys***

**Dam** /dæm/

n The Aswan **dam** supplies electricity and water for irrigation.

v In Zeeland, the rivers have been **dammed** to prevent flooding from the North Sea.
***→ A barrier, a wall to stop the flow of a river***

**Disease** /dɪˈziːz/

n To suffer from **an infectious disease**.
The **disease spread** fast.
The death rate from alcohol-linked **diseases** is increasing.
***→ An illness, sickness, infection***

**Dust** /dʌst/

n The old book was covered with a thick **layer of dust**.
**Dust** from volcanic eruptions blocks incoming solar radiation.
Electronic chips must be made in **dust-free** conditions.
***→ Small particles of matter suspended in air***

**Dwarf** /dwɔːf/

n Snow White and the seven **dwarfs**.
Very small, dense stars (0.01% the diameter of the sun) are called **white dwarfs**.
***→ An abnormally small person, thing ≠ giant***

**Dwell** /dwel/

v Troglodytes are people who **dwell** in caves.
Desert-**dwelling** animals feed at night.
***→ To live, to inhabit***

**Earth** /ˈɜːθ/
1.n Life on **Earth** will not go on for ever.
***→ The third planet from the sun***
2.n The **earth** was of poor quality and contaminated by nitrates.
v Electric appliances should be **earthed**.
***→ The ground, the soil. To connect an electrical circuit to the ground***

**Earthquake** /ɜːθkweɪk/
n The Richter scale for measuring **earthquakes** is logarithmic.
In **earthquake** zones, buildings must be designed to withstand shock waves.
***→ Seismic disruption***

**Emergency** /ɪˈmɜːdʒənsi/
n In case of **emergency**, call the police.
Airport facilities must include **emergency** and fire-fighting equipment.
***→ Crisis, urgent situation***

**Flood** /flʌd/
n In the rainy season, the Amazon is subject to severe **floods**.
The yearly **flooding** of the Nile makes the soil more fertile.
v The universe is **flooded** with Neutrinos.
***→ An overflow, a surplus of water, etc. To inundate***

**Fuel** /fjuəːl/
n Coal, gas and oil are non-renewable **fuels**.
**Fossil fuel resources** are limited.
A **fuel tank**.
v **To re-fuel** a plane.
***→ A substance which burns producing energy. To provide an energy source***

**Funds** /fʌndz/
n The government supplies **funds** for basic research.
The project ran out of **funds**.
v A great deal of engineering research is **funded** by industry.
***→ Money, a grant made available for a specific purpose***

**Giant** /ˈdʒaɪənt/
adj Commerce is increasingly controlled by **giant**, multinational corporations.
n **Red giants** are very bright, large stars.
***→ Enormous, very big. A monstrously big person, thing ≠ dwarf***

**Gold** /gəʊld/
n The Klondike **gold rush** (1890) attracted more than 30,000 miners to the area.
New polymers are replacing **gold** as electrical conductors.
***→ A soft yellow precious metal. Chemical symbol: Au***

**Goods** /gʊdz/ *(N.B. – plural)*
n **Goods** weighing less than 40 kg should be sent by air.
These **goods** must be handled with care.
A **goods train**.
***→ Things, objects which can be bought or sold***

**Grant** /grɑːnt/
n The Erasmus programme gives **grants** to help students study abroad.
The ministry of industry allocated a **research grant**.
v To **grant financial aid**.
***→ Financial help, funds. To provide financial backing***

**Grid** /grɪd/
n The hole in the road was covered by a metal **grid**.
An electron beam sweeps across a screen consisting of a **grid** of dots called pixels.
Electricity is distributed through the **national grid**.
***→ A framework of parallel bars, lines. The electricity distribution network***

**Hardware** /ˈhɑːdweə/
n **Computer hardware** is getting smaller and smaller.
**Hardware** includes printers, modems and other peripherals.
***→ The machinery of a computer ≠ software***

**Health** /helθ/
n Smoking can **seriously damage your health**.
To a large extent, **health** depends on diet.
adj The cancerous cells are surrounded by **healthy** tissues.
***→ Medical condition, without disease ≠ ill***

**Note — Health / healthy**
Adjectives are often formed from nouns by adding the suffix **"-y"**.
→ *wind – a **windy** day*
→ *dust – a **dusty** book*
→ *ice – an **icy** road*
→ *noise – a **noisy** machine*

**Heart** /hɑːt/
n Half an aspirin a day considerably reduces the risk of **heart attack**.
An **open-heart** operation.
The **heart** of the city.
***→ Organ for circulating blood. Central part***

**Iron** /ˈaɪən/

n **Iron** was first discovered 3,000 years ago.
The **iron** in bird brains makes them sensitive to the Earth's magnetic field.
The core of a magnet can be made of **iron**.
→ ***Ferrous metal. Chemical symbol: Fe***

**Lens** /lenz/

n He dropped the camera and broke the **lens**.
To focus the microscope you must adjust the lower **lens**.
The first optical **lenses** were made in the time of Galileo.
→ ***Glass devices designed to make light converge / diverge***

**Lever** /ˈliːvə/

n The rat can be trained to push a **lever** to receive food.
The Egyptians lifted the blocks of stone by means of long wooden **levers**.
→ ***A long bar, rod which exerts pressure through a pivot***

**Liver** /ˈlivə/

n He is suffering from **cirrhosis of the liver**.
The **liver** produces albumin, stores blood sugar and regulates potassium levels.
→ ***A large organ of vertebrates regulating toxic materials in the blood***

**Lorry** /ˈlɒri/

n The goods were **delivered by lorry**.
Cars and **lorries** are transported by train through the Eurotunnel in 35 minutes.
→ ***Motor vehicle which carries goods, objects. Truck***

**Lung** /lʌŋ/

n Smoking causes **lung cancer**.
After it has been oxygenated in the **lungs**, blood is bright red in colour.
→ ***Organ for breathing, where blood is oxygenated***

**Magnet** /ˈmægnət/

n A **magnet** produces a magnetic field.
The core of an **electromagnet** is made of iron.
→ ***An iron object which attracts other objects containing iron***

**Mankind** /mænˈkaɪnd/

n The Nobel Prize is awarded to the person who has most benefited **mankind**.
In African mythology, the origins of **mankind** derive from a cosmic egg.
→ ***Human beings, the human race***

**Needle** /ˈniːdl/

n The doctor inserted a **hypodermic needle** into the vein.
Magnetic north is shown by the **needle** of the compass.
→ ***A thin (metallic) tube, pointer, arrow***

**Nest** /nest/

n There were 5 eggs in the **bird's nest**.
A micrometastasis consists of a small **nest** of cancerous cells.
→ ***A bird's "home". A group, cluster***

**Nitrogen** /ˈnaɪtrədʒən/

n The atmosphere consists of 78% **nitrogen**.
If the oxygen is replaced by **nitrogen**, biological activity decreases.
→ ***Colourless gas. Chemical symbol: N***

**Noise** /nɔɪz/

n The baby is asleep. Don't make a **noise**.
The relative humidity effects the **noise level**.

adj The town centre is **noisy**.
→ ***Acoustic vibrations, sound, measured in decibels***

**Offspring** /ˈɒfsprɪŋ/

*(N.B. – the plural does not takes "-s")*

n Birds feed their **offspring** until they can fly.
The female Aardvark normally has two **offspring**.
→ ***Babies, the young of an animal, human being***

**OHP** /əʊ eɪtʃ piː/

n When he had finished his presentation, he switched off the **OHP**
→ ***A device for projecting images on a screen behind the speaker***

**Oil** /ɔɪl/

n Saudi Arabia produces **oil**.

v Moving parts of the machine should be **oiled**.
→ ***Fuels composed of hydrocarbons. To lubricate***

**Pipe** /paɪp/

n **Water pipes** are usually made of copper.
There was a leak in the **fuel pipe**.
**A pipe-line**.
→ ***A hollow tube for transporting gas, liquids***

**Plant** /plɑːnt/

n A hydraulic **power plant**.
The **nuclear plant** was inspected by security officers.
→ ***An industrial complex, facilities, equipment***

**Prey** /preɪ/
n Insects comprise the main **prey** of bats.
An anaconda is a snake which kills its **prey** by constriction.
→ ***Animals which predators eat***

**Ray** /reɪ/
n **X-rays** ionise gases.
**Ultra-violet rays** are one cause of skin cancer.
The penetration power in air of **α-rays** is only a few centimetres.
→ ***A narrow beam of light, radiation***

**Rent** /rent/
v **To rent** a car for the weekend.
n To pay the monthly **rent**.
She cannot afford the **rent** for a flat in Paris.
→ ***Payment of money for temporary possession, use***

**Rubber** /ˈrʌbə/
n The glass pipes are connected by a flexible **rubber tube**.
**Rubber** is an efficient electric insulator.
→ ***Elastic substance produced from latex***

**Sale** /seɪl/
n The **sales** of electric cars are rising.
From 1919 onwards, the **sale** of alcoholic drinks was illegal.
He works in the **sales department**.
→ ***Selling, exchanging something for money***

**Salt** /sɔːlt/
n **Salt** can be obtained by distilling sea water.
Ammonium nitrate is a **salt** of ammonia.
→ ***Chemical symbol: NaCl***

**Sand** /sænd/
n The **sand** dunes shift, advancing in the direction of the dominant wind.
Cement must be mixed with **sand** and water.
→ ***Fine yellow particles from siliceous rocks***

**Screen** /skriːn/
1.n Pixels are displayed on a rectilinear grid on the **screen**.
The **car's windscreen** was broken by a stone.
→ ***A surface for displaying images, or for protection***
2.v People should be **screened** for cancer every two years.
The Ministry of Defence **screens** all potential candidates.
→ ***To investigate, to check for disease, political opinion, etc.***

**Sensor** /ˈsensə/
n The switch is controlled by an optically-reactive **light sensor**.
The alarm system includes **smoke sensors** for detecting fire.
→ ***A component designed to detect, to react to stimulation***

**Sewage** /ˈsuːɪdʒ/
n Enzymes are widely used for water purification and **sewage** treatment.
Underground pipes convey the **sewage** to recycling plants.
→ ***Industrial and domestic waste water***

**Shadow** /ˈʃædəʊ/
n To sit in the **shadow** of a tree.
Because of diffraction, the edge of a **shadow** is not well defined.
→ ***Dark areas hidden from the light***

**Sheet** /ʃiːt/
n He wrote the letter on a **sheet** of white paper.
The Antarctic **ice sheet** could collapse as the sea level rises.
→ ***Thin layer, stratum***

**Shell** /ʃel/
n He broke the **shell** of the egg.
Each element of the nitrogen group has an **outer shell** of 5 electrons.
After the fire, only the empty **shell** of the building remained.
→ ***Hard covering, protective exterior***

**Shield** /ʃiːld/
n Around the core of the reactor there is a thick concrete **shield**.
v He **shielded** his eyes against the sun.
→ ***A screen, a protective coating. To protect***

**Shore** /ʃɔː/
n The fossils were found on the **shore** of the lake.
**Offshore** reserves of oil and natural gas have been found in Ireland.
→ ***Coast. The edge between sea and land***

**Shuttle** /ˈʃʊtl/
n There is an hourly bus **shuttle service** between the town centre and the airport.
The **space shuttle** will return to Earth in three days' time.
→ ***A vehicle that provides regular transport between two places***

**Sick** /sɪk/
adj An ambulance transports people who are **sick** or injured.
Inhabitants living close to the factory **fell sick** with unknown symptoms.
n The Tsetse fly transmits an often fatal disease called **"sleeping sickness"**.

Altitude **sickness**, known as hypoxia, results from a state of acute oxygen deficiency.
***→ III. A disease ≠ health***

**Sight** /saɪt/
n His **sight** was failing – he needed glasses.
Pavlov demonstrated that dogs automatically produce saliva **at the sight** of food.
The ship has gone over the horizon – it is **out of sight**.
v The Fiji islands were first **sighted** by the Dutch navigator Tasman, in 1643.
adj It was a **far-sighted decision**.
***→ Capacity to see, vision. To see, observe. Perceptive***

**Silver** /ˈsɪlvə/
n The conquistadors brought back **silver** and gold from Bolivia and Peru.
By adding 7.5% copper to **silver**, a hard alloy can be made.
***→ White, precious metal. Chemical symbol: Ag***

**Skin** /skɪn/
n Dermatologists specialise in **skin diseases**.
The most obvious symptom of allergies is a reddening of the **skin**.
An increase in solar activity will lead to more cases of **skin cancer**.
***→ The natural outside covering of an animal. Epidermis***

**Smell** /smel/ *(smell, smelt, smelt)*
v He could **smell** coffee coming from the kitchen.
n The olfactory nerves convey the sensation of **smell** to the central nervous system.
A rhinoceros has an acute **sense of smell**, but his sight is poor.
***→ To detect with the nose. Odour. One of the five senses***

**Snake** /sneɪk/
n The **snake** offered Eve an apple.
The king cobra (5.5 m in length) is the world's longest poisonous **snake**.
***→ Long, legless reptile***

**Software** /ˈsɒftweə/
n He writes **software** for IBM.
There is a law against copying **software**.
***→ Programs, etc. for computers ≠ hardware***

**Soil** /sɔɪl/
n The **soil** was eroded by the heavy rain.
The biosphere consists of the air, **soil**, and water supporting life on Earth.
***→ The upper layer of the Earth where plants grow***

**Sound** /saʊnd/
n She could **hear the sound** of music in the distance.
**The speed of sound** is 331.6 m per second.
Electrons travel **faster than sound**.
***→ What can be heard, measured in decibels***

**Species** /ˈspiːʃiːz/
n The tiger is an **endangered species**.
Darwin wrote "**The Origin of Species**".
***→ Animals and plants of the same kind***

**Staff** /stɑːf/
n The secretarial **staff** went on strike.
The firm employs a **staff** of 1,600.
v **To staff** an office.
The firm was **under-staffed**.
***→ A group of workers. To supply workers***

**Steam** /stiːm/
n If you boil water, you produce **steam**.
Electricity can be produced by a **steam turbine**.
***→ Vaporised water***

**Steel** /stiːl/
n **High quality steel** tools.
Chromium **steel** resists oxidisation.
***→ An alloy made of carbon and iron***

**Stone** /stəʊn/
n He threw a **stone** at the dog.
The **stone age**.
The Aborigines used the same **stone tools** throughout the Pleistocene period.
***→ Hard mineral matter. A small rock***

**Storm** /stɔːm/
n There was a **rain storm**.
Skyscrapers may be struck by lightning several time during a single **storm**.
***→ Bad weather with high winds. A tempest***

**Stream** /striːm/
n The **gulf stream**.
A **stream of electrons** is projected onto the screen.
Radio-active isotopes are introduced into the **blood stream**.
***→ A flow, a current. A movement of liquid or gas***

**String** /strɪŋ/
n He fastened his shoes with a piece of **string**
Airbus has achieved an outstanding **string of successes**.
Radar systems convert analogue signals into a **string** of numbers.
***→ A thin cotton (etc.) cord. A series. A linear sequence of data***

**Surgeon** /ˈsɜːdʒən/

n The tumour was removed by a brain **surgeon**.
The death rate fell from 45% to 12% when **surgeons** began to use antiseptics.
→ ***A highly skilled doctor who operates inside the body by incision***

**Surgery** /ˈsɜːdʒəri/

n Acupuncture is widely used in Chinese **surgery** to reduce pain.
→ ***Carrying out a medical operation***

**Tail** /teɪl/

n She picked up the mouse by the **tail**.
At a speed of Mach 1, shock waves arise from the nose and **tail** of the plane.
→ ***Prolonged coccyx of an animal. The back part of a plane, etc.***

**Tank** /tæŋk/

n The **fuel tank** was nearly empty.
The **water tank** holds 500 litres.
→ ***A (metal) container holding liquids***

**Tool** /tuːl/

n Some animals use primitive **tools**.
**A tool-box**.
Radiotelescopes are one of the main **tools** of modern astronomy.
→ ***Instruments which facilitate work***

**Vacuum** /ˈvækjuəm/

n The space at the top of the barometer is a **Torricellian vacuum**.
A partial **vacuum** is an excellent thermal insulation.
→ ***A space, empty of all gas***

**Weapon** /ˈwepən/

n It is virtually impossible to control the production of **chemical weapons**.
Enzymes can be an effective **weapon** for the treatment of leukaemia.
→ ***A (military) arm***

**Well** /wel/

n In the oasis, water is drawn from the **well** by a camel.
The first **off-shore oil well** was drilled in the Gulf of Mexico in 1946.
→ ***A hole in the ground which is a source of water, oil***

**Wheel** /wiːl/

n To change the **wheel** of the car.
The **wheel** was introduced into America by the Spanish.
A **six-wheeled** lorry.
→ ***A circular object, turning on an axis to facilitate movement***

**Wing** /wɪŋ/

n The pterodactyl had **wings** and could fly.
The air flows more rapidly over the upper surface of the **wing**.
**Left-wing** politics.
→ ***Lateral, supporting surface for flight. Lateral extension***

**Wire** /ˈwaɪə/

n The loss of power in an **electric wire** is due to the resistance.
When a voltage is applied, an electric current flows along the **wire**.
**Electric wires** overheat if the current is too high.
→ ***A thin filament, made of metal, often used for carrying electricity***

**Wrist** /rɪst/

n She was wearing a gold bracelet around her **wrist**.
The metacarpal artery is located in the **wrist**.
→ ***Joint, articulation between the hand and the arm***

# *GRAMMAR AND USAGE NOTES – INDEX*

# LEXIS – INDEX

Impression & brochage sepec - France
Numéro d'impression : 04545160717 - Dépôt légal : décembre 2014
IMPRIM'VERT®